LOVE
Is the
KEY

DARIUS A. PRINCE

PRESS

F.Y.I.

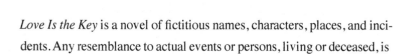

Love Is the Key is a novel of fictitious names, characters, places, and incidents. Any resemblance to actual events or persons, living or deceased, is entirely coincidental and unintentional.

I'm confident that you will find *Love Is the Key* not only to be entertaining, but also honest, unpredictable, poignant, cultural relevant, and thought provoking. The characters learn that the biggest disappointment about life is that many people give up on themselves, afraid to embrace the man or woman they were created to be, so that they find it difficult to be real and true to others.

Email:loveisthekey77@gmail.com
Shop at: LoveIsTheKey77.org

Contents

Got to Go

I just finished washing my car. You know, I gave it that showroom look inside and out. All I needed to do now is stop by the gas station and fill up the tank. Hold up, wait a minute, are my eyes deceiving me? Now, this woman walking down the street is breath-taking or is she just taking my breath away? Yeah, I have tunnel vision. I drove slowly and kept my eyes on her. She was probably walking faster than I was driving. *Lock and load, I have to go and introduce myself to her,* I thought. So, I pulled up next to her, "Excuse me. I normally don't do this, but you caught my attention in a very, very delightful and intriguing way. I felt compelled to introduce myself to you. Hello, my name is Derek. I'm not psychotic or violent. I like to consider myself an ordinary somebody, trying to help somebody who just came from washing his car. So, if a person were to address you how, would they go about addressing you?" I could see that she was flattered and interested by the smile on her face.

"They would address me as Monica. I take it that Derek would be asking Monica if he could give her a ride to where ever she is on her way to." Okay, I realized she was cool and playing along in this fun moment of getting to know one another.

"That's not Derek's style."

"Oh it's not."

"No it's not Derek does not just meet strange women and invite them into his car or to his home."

"Oh, I see."

"Derek would give you his phone number and Monica might give Derek her phone number in exchange if Monica was really interested in getting to know more about Derek. Then they could meet one day for lunch, dinner, or take part in some other sort of fun and enjoyable entertainment."

"That sounds like something Monica might be interested in."

"Derek will give Monica his phone number, and she is more than welcome to call anytime. Derek works until four o'clock."

I looked down at my watch and said, "I don't mean to be rude, but I have to be going."

"Well before you go, you might want to take Monica's phone number. You are better off calling Monica because that's what a gentleman would do."

"Oh, I can respect that because I am a gentleman, and I have some traditional qualities in me, as well."

"Now that I'm not a total stranger, are you going to offer me a ride since we exchanged numbers?"

"No, I still cannot."

"Why?"

"Now you're a semi-stranger."

"You know my name and you have my phone number, doesn't that mean anything?"

"You could have given me a fake name and number."

"I wouldn't do that you seem like a nice honest guy. The way you approached me and how you talked with me was interesting and you did it with confidence and flare."

"Well since you put it that way, I'll give you a ride. Where are you going?"

"I'm going home. I only live a few blocks from here, but I don't want a ride. I'll walk." "What? You just said you want a ride."

"I wanted to see if you had a compassionate and caring heart. Thanks anyway and call me tonight."

I smiled at her, and as I was about to pull off I said, "You're all right." I was halfway home and realized I forgotten to get gas. Man, see what a beautiful summer day and woman can do to you? They throw you all off track; you develop a case of memory lost.

Summer is a season I so enjoy; it has an incredible impact on people. Due to those bright, hot, sunny days, summer influences the attitudes and behaviors of everyone in its path. Although there may be a few individuals who complain about the weather being too hot or humid, I certainly do not complain. Summer, without a doubt, has a way of bringing out the best in some people. After today, summer is surely a season I don't want to see go.

Later that evening I called Monica. A woman answered the phone. The voice sounds like Monica's, but I wasn't sure, so playing it safe I just said, "Hello, may I speak with Monica?"

"Hi Derek, this is me."

"Hello, Monica, what are you doing?"

"I'm sitting outside enjoying this nice and pleasant summer night."

"Yes, it's definitely a beautiful and comfortable night." "How was the rest of your day?"

"It was a busy day, but a good busy if you know what I mean."

"Yes, I do know. Those are the best days, especially when you are at work. So, what are you doing tomorrow evening?"

"I was supposed to go to a play tomorrow evening with one of my girlfriends, but she called to let me know she can't make it. Do you want to accompany me to the play?"

"Monica, you don't have to use that "my friend can't make it" line to get me to attend the play with you. The answer is "yes," I would love to go, and I do enjoy plays. Do you want me to pick you up or do you just want to meet at the theater?"

"You decide, Derek."

"Well I believe the gentlemanly thing and safe thing to do is meet you there."

"What!" shouted Monica, "you think that's the gentlemanly thing to do?"

"I'm only kidding. I would prefer to pick you up. What time would you like me to be there?"

"Well the play starts at eight o'clock."

"So if I say six o'clock you will be ready by seven because I know women are considered fashionably late.""You are batting 0 for 2 tonight, sir. For your information I'm a woman that's always on time. I don't like to be late."

"This is good to hear, Monica. Then I'll pick you up at seven o'clock tomorrow."

The evening of the play, I arrived at Monica's house and rang the bell. A gentleman answered the door, so I played it cool because I did not know what to make of this guy. He was respectable and invited me in, "You must be Derek."

"Yes I am." "I am Monica's brother. Monica will be with you in a few minutes."

Whoa, okay this is her brother, I thought. Then a woman entered the room and said, "Hello, I am Monica's mother."

"Hello ma'am, nice to meet you." Monica entered the room and said, "Hello, Derek. I see you got to meet my brother and mom."

"Yes, I have," said Derek.

"I also have another brother, but he moved out. You will probably get to meet him some day." Monica grabbed Derek's hand and said, "Are you ready?"

"I guess I am since you are pulling me towards the door." While walking towards the door, I looked back and said, "Bye, Monica's mother and brother." We walked to the car. I opened the door for Monica, and we were on our way to the play. The play was *My Fair Lady*; Monica was deeply engrossed in the play. I took this as a sign that she was enjoying the play. The play had lasted two hours. It was still early, and I was feeling a little hungry, "So Monica, are you hungry?"

"I don't feel like a meal, but I could go for some appetizers or a nice salad and soup, Derek."

"I will take you to a place where we could relax, eat, and talk a little."

"That sounds good to me, Derek." We went to this restaurant and sat outside on the deck being that it was a nice summer night. The waitress came over and took our order. We ordered appetizers and a couple of glasses of wine. Monica was sitting on the opposite side of the table from me.

I leaned over and said, "Tell me about you; do you have a boyfriend or have you ever been married?"

"Well Derek, you know I live with my mother and brother at home. I never was out of the house on my own. I spent a lot of my time doing things and going places with my mother. My mother is like my best friend. We spend a lot of time together."

"So, is there something wrong with your mother that you spend so much time with her and for you to still live at home?"

"Well she does depend on me a lot."

"Why didn't you ever get your own apartment?"

"To be honest Derek, I guess I became complacent with mom and just settled. I do worry about my mother and what she would do if I left home."

"Well, what about what could happen to you if you don't start to develop and form your own life?"

"Someday I will have to do this, but for now my mother needs me."

"Hey, don't take this the wrong way, but are you afraid to leave home? Are you being controlled or just insecure? You have to start to develop some direction in your life."

"For your information, I am independent in other ways in my life."

"What do you mean, Monica?"

"What I mean is that I pay the phone bill, the electric bill, help pay the rent, and even sometimes pay for groceries. I'm even thinking about buying a house for my mother and me. I just purchased a car because my mother would complain about how all of us worked and how nobody owned a car."

"You know one day you will have to step out and fly."

"I know that, it's just when I try to move forward with my life, I become concerned with the kind of treatment I might receive from my family. Let me share something with you. I have had no solid foundation or support; everything always has seemed to be in chaos since I was a child. There was a time that things were so bad while I was in high school that I went to live with some other woman for a while."

"Did you know her?"

"Of course I did; she was like family. Really, she was like a second mother who was always there for me when times got tough."

"How tough were things for you?"

"Well, there was a time when things were so tough. My mother and father had owned a business and house at one time, but they managed money poorly. We were not living a realistic lifestyle or maybe I should say, we were not living within our means."

"How do you mean, Monica?"

"Let me just put it this way, Derek. Things got so bad that we lost our house and lived in the store for a while. I was so embarrassed. I did not want my friends to come visit me anymore. I would lie about why we didn't live in our house. I was at the point that I became depressed. This is when I went to live with Ms. Hazel for a little while."

"Now, this was just the beginning of things Derek."

"What is that supposed to mean?"

"My younger brothers were not in tune with the reality of life and never developed any responsibilities. They would talk down to me, trying to tell me what I should and should not do with my life. I would get a lot of hostility, insecurity, and jealousy from my family whenever I was out enjoying myself or my life in general was going well. For every positive step I took forward, they would attempt to pull me back two steps. There have been times that I felt as if my whole family was dysfunctional. I am just trying to live my life, being able to adjust to different occurrences within my life and my family."

"Don't take this the wrong way, Monica, but there are times that you must think for yourself. It sounds as if you are allowing yourself to be controlled in an emotionally abusive way. Never ignore the joy of your own life, especially when it's time for you to invest in the enjoyment of your life. You will regret waiting later because of the things you let pass you by."

"I am very much aware of this, but it's so hard for me, Derek."

"One thing you will learn about me is that I'm real. Please don't mis-understand or take anything I say the wrong way. I do not share things to be hurtful by any means. It sounds like the only thing being developed here is insecurity—a lack of independence and poor decision-making.

There is nothing wrong with being supportive of family, but family must also know when to be supportive of you. They must be willing to accept your happiness and respect your decisions. Hey, you are a thirty-four-year old sharing many of your life experiences with me. What you're sharing with me tells me that you are not pleased with your situation."

"To be honest Derek, I'm not happy with my situation, but what do I do. I know I constantly complain about being so unhappy living with my family. My mother and brothers seem to always be criticizing and judgmental about my life, telling me what I should and should not be doing. I am thirty-four years old. When I go out at night and spend time with friends, I finally feel like I'm being more active with my own lifestyle, instead of sitting home playing the role of a servant. When my family is not exactly thrilled with some of my own personal decisions, they rebel like children." "What do you mean they rebel?"

"Nobody will do the house cleaning or any of the other household duties." As Monica continued to share with me, I could hear her voice starting to tremble until finally, she broke down and cried.

She looked at me and said, "I'm sorry for putting all this on you. I know this is something you did not ask for. I'm sure you do not want to be involved with someone with so much drama in their life. What really hurt me was that one day last week my own mother was calling me names and talking about me. She was doing this to make me feel guilty for not being home with her more. She was telling our neighbors that I'm running the streets like I'm some sort of tramp or whore. She would preach to me about God and people need to attend church, but she does not even attend church." I looked into Monica's face and saw her watery eyes as we sat there in silence for a few seconds, which felt like several minutes.

I grabbed her hand and said, "I listen to you share your heart with me. I feel special that you are comfortable enough with me to be so open and honest."

"Well, I feel that since we are spending time together, and we have this relationship that you should know all about me so there are no surprises."

"You know I appreciate what you're saying and understand where you're coming from. First we should continue getting to know each other as friends before we start to discuss or define our relationship. I feel your pain, and to be honest you should have broken those ties with your family a long time ago. As I sit and listen to you speak, Monica, you are answering your own questions, but there has been no follow-through. In life and especially our own personal lives, we should be part of the solution for building or rebuilding our lives."

"Yes, I know, but things get so hard and crazy at times."

"Do you like to read, Monica?"

"Yes, I do. I like various books: mainly inspirational, romance, and books that are based on reality, and some fiction because some fiction I find to be true."

"Good, because there is a book by Darius Prince called, *What Are You Waiting For?* I found this book to be inspiring in many ways. It's an easy-to-read book that you could read in a few days. It's one of those books that you take with you as a guide to refer back to now and then."

It's been a couple of days since I spoke to Monica. I hope she is doing all right. The last time we spoke, she had a lot to share. She has to make some challenging and difficult decisions about her life. So, I decided to give her a call. "Hello, Monica, how are doing?"

"I'm doing well. I'm sorry about the other evening. Honestly, I did not think you would call me after my meltdown."

"I'm not that kind of person. I'm here for you unless you choose not to have me here. I respect your space, and there is no need to apologize. Hey, you have a lot going on in your life. You need to take time and sort some things out. Sometimes we just need to be with the right person who is a good listener. Just take it one step at a time, and it will all start to come together."

"Thanks for being there for me, Derek."

"Not a problem; that's what friends are for. How are things *really* going for you?"

"Well, I don't know."

"What do you mean you don't know?"

"I mean sometimes I get so lost and confused that I don't know what I should be doing half of the time. I have too much negative energy around me at times, and it weighs me down. Home is not home for me. My twenty-five-year-old brother who is living at home with my mother and me is immature and acts like a child at times, which just gets on my nerves. He is always looking for attention. For example, today he went as far as wanting me to go with him to the mall to get a shirt.

I told him, "No, I do not have time. There are other things that I need to do. He got an attitude and said, "If I were Derek, you would go. You make time for him, but you cannot make time for your family anymore. You don't even spend time with Mom anymore. She has to take the bus or a taxi to work now." "My mother is a matured woman who is healthy and very much capable of getting back and forth to work on her own. She was doing it way before I decided to get a car. I am not about to become anybody's personal taxi service and disrupt my personal life in the process. There are times I will take her and pick her up. I just cannot do it all the time."

"Wow, good for you, Monica. You have to start somewhere in taking back your life."

"That night we were talking, Derek, you assisted and motivated me to start trying to do things differently."

"I know; you don't have to thank me. I just do what I do."

"Hey, let's get serious, you did not really do all that much, so let the air out of your head. I will admit that I do owe you a small percentage of the credit, but mainly it was that book you told me about: *What Are You Waiting For?* It's a moving and inspiring book. It's as if the author is reading you, understands and knows you."

"Well my friend, I'm glad that the book has assisted you in some way. I'm happy that I was able to assist in some way, too."

"What are you doing tomorrow evening, Derek?"

"I don't have any plans."

"Then let me take you to dinner tomorrow evening at 6:30 p.m."

"You want to take me to dinner—wow, I feel honored for a guy that only assisted with a small percentage in motivating you in a small area of your life. What would I have been rewarded with if I was the author of that book?"

"Well I guess you will never know because you are not. Anyway, I have to go, Derek; I will see you tomorrow evening. If you do not mind, will you pick me up?"

"No problem, and have a good day, Monica."

The next evening I was on my way to Monica's to go out for dinner. While en route I was thinking about her and how she seems not to know what to do about her family situation. She has to figure out what direction she wants to go in life. She seem as if she is really trying and knows what she wants, but does not have the courage or heart to just do it. I arrived at Monica's house, and she was sitting on the porch looking just as beautiful the day I first met her. I thought in amazement at how so much could be going on in the life of such a beautiful-looking woman. We went to this jazz restaurant that has a very pleasant and relaxing atmosphere. We had to wait to be seated, so we sat down in the waiting area and started talking.

"Hey! Over here, Derek." I looked over, and it was my good friend, Tim. Tim and I went way back. We went to the same high school and even spent a few years working together. Tim was there with his girl, or I should say one of his girls. They walked over to us.

"Lynn, meet my good friend, Derek. Derek, this is Lynn."

I extended my hand saying, "it's a pleasure to meet you, Lynn. May I ask, where did you picked this guy up?"

"Well, Derek, he picked me up. He seemed to be all right so I figure I would give him a chance."

"Seriously like you said, Tim is all right."

We laughed, and Tim stood there with a smile on his face and his hand on my shoulder and said, "Oh, you guys got jokes."

"Excuse me and forgive me for being so rude, let me introduce you to Monica."

"Hello Monica," replied Lynn and Tim.

"Hello it is nice to meet the two of you."

"Hey Derek," "Yeah, Tim,"

"It's really busy in here tonight."

"I see."

"Lynn and I have been waiting for a table for about twenty minutes."

"Well we just got here. I'm thinking about going somewhere else."

"Derek, let's wait awhile because I never been here."

"You sure, Monica, we can always come back another evening."

"I'm sure, besides we are already here. By the time we go to another place it will be late, and we could have been seated here."

"Come on guys, you don't have to argue. Tim has a solution to your dilemma."

"What is your solution?"

"Now, Derek, me being the caring gentleman that I am, I would like to invite the two of you to join Lynn and myself. We could get a table for the four of us because we will be seated before you. We will probably even be served and out the door before you get seated."

"You are probably right. It sounds like a plan to me; are you okay with this, Monica?"

"Sure, Derek."

"How about you, Lynn?" asked Derek.

Before Lynn could answer, Tim said, "Of course she is because I already said so."

Lynn gave Tim a look, and he quickly added, "I'm only kidding. Do you mind babe?"

"I don't mind." We all chuckled.

"Tim, you need to man up you just backed down, and Lynn did not even have to say a word. She just gave you the *look,* and your tail curled up between your legs. I don't know man, I used to look up to you. Lynn you are the woman. In fact, I think when Tim grows up, he will want to be like you." Lynn and Monica laughed looking at Tim.

"Oh, you still got jokes, Derek."

"We all know who runs the show, don't we, Tim?" said Derek.

Before Tim could say anything, the waitress arrived to take us to our table. During dinner we had some good conversation. After dinner was over, we stayed and listened to the jazz group that was playing. Tim and Lynn went onto the dance floor. Monica and I sat at the table talking.

"Can I share something with you, Derek?"

"Of course, what's up?" In the back of my mind I've been thinking that we have had a very nice evening so far. Please let's not start talking about your family again because I'm starting to feel we spend most of our time together talking about your family.

"I wanted to ask you something about my other brother," *Oh no here we go,* I thought.

21

"Well, he moved out for a couple of months and now wants to move back home. However, my family and I are against it."

"What's making him move back home?" As Monica was starting to answer the question, Tim and Lynn were on their way back to the table.

Tim looked at us and said, "What are you guys over here talking about?"

"My brother wants to move back home, but my family and I are against it.

"Tim said, without hesitation, "then don't let him move back home."

Tim paused, tilted his head slightly to the right and looked at Monica, "Wait a minute, who do you live with?"

"I live with my mother and younger brother." Tim asked, "How old is this brother that wants to move back in?"

"He is thirty-two years old."

Lynn asked, "Isn't he too old to be moving back home?"

"Yes, he is too old."

"How old are you, Monica?"

"I'm thirty-four, Lynn."

"Why are you still living home? Is something wrong with your mother? Does she has some sort of health problem?"

"No, she depends on me. I help her out a lot."

"Have you ever lived on your own?"

"No." I could tell by the looks on Tim and Lynn's faces that they were wondering what is going on with this woman. There is something wrong with most people who live home at that age.

I wisely interrupted, "So Monica, what is it you wanted to ask about your brother?"

"Well, he is moving back because he does not get to spend his money the way he wants, and he is saving for his wedding, but no one is willing to help him move, not even any of his friends."

"I know you are not going to ask me to help."

"Well, would you mind helping him, Derek? He needs some help?" I'm thinking to myself your brothers need help, you need help, and your mama needs help.

"I'm sorry, Monica I do not know your brother like that. For me to help someone move it's usually because I have some sort of relationship with them."

"What about you, Tim?"

"What about me? What about leaving me out of this? Seriously, I can't help your brother move; I would not feel comfortable." My mouth dropped. I could not believe she asked this person who she just met two hours ago to help her brother move.

Looking at my watch, I said, "It is time for us to go."

On the drive home I had different thoughts running through my mind. "So, how do you honestly feel about your brother moving back home?"

"Honestly, I do not want him to; there was always something wrong when he lived at home before. Let me tell you how it was when he was living home." *Here we go again, but I asked for it.*

"He would borrow things without asking and deny it if you confronted him about it. He would not even return what he borrowed. He lived off of everyone and did not contribute in any way. He would boast about all the money he made from his job. However, if he owed you money, it was like pulling teeth to get it from him—if you were lucky enough to get it at all. He would brag in our faces about what he was going to buy and how good he was doing for himself, not taking in consideration that the rest of us were working to pay bills. Then he started going to church. He would go around, portraying this image of a Christian person. My other brother, mother, and I would sit around discussing how he was such a hypocrite, a fake, and a phony. The girl he is planning to marry is going to be in for the surprise of her life, especially once they are living together. She will get to know his true colors. He is planning to move with her down south. We are all looking forward to the day of his wedding and him moving away."

"Wow, it seems as if there is a serious strain in the relationships in your family."

A few days later while cooking dinner I started to think about all that Monica shared with me, especially about how her family takes advantage of her. I came to the realization she was just like her family and she did not even realize it. She acted the same way her mother did, which was needy. Monica and I had dated about seven months. Seven months of special moments and quality time was invested.

One evening Monica and I were at the mall, walking around. "I see that Derek."

"You see what?" "I see those other women looking at you."

"I have no control over what other people do with their eyes. Just like I have no control over what you do with your eyes."

"And what is that supposed to mean?"

"It means what I said."

"Well I do not like it, the way they look at you; it makes me feel uncomfortable."

"Are you ready to go?"

"Yes!" While walking to the car, I was thinking even more about this relationship. Monica and I have feelings for one another. We developed a wonderful friendship in the process of spending time together. However, Monica had no control over her life or the direction she wanted to go. In fact, her whole family was ganging up on her, dictating and controlling her life, making her life uncomfortable. The drive home was quiet; the conversation was limited. We arrived at Monica house, and I walked her to the door. "Let's sit on the porch and talk before you go in, Monica;

there is something I want to share with you." I looked over at Monica and took a deep breath and said to myself, *it's time to man up*. "Monica, over the past seven months you have shared a lot with me regarding you and your family. As I listened to you with care and compassion, I have heard the challenges and difficulty you are faced with daily. This is making it difficult for you to take a new role in your life, but it is time for you to live your own life, make your own decisions, and be happy. Nobody can do this for you, but you. If you do not take responsibility for your life and choose to live your life in this current state, your life and relationships will continue to be challenging and difficult. Most importantly, your soul will never be at peace."

"I know, and I'm trying; it's just so hard."

"We have had a great time together, but you're not ready to move on and grow with someone. You're tied to your family. I love you enough to be honest with you." I could see the water develop in the wells of Monica's eyes. As I watched a tear roll down her face, I reached over and hugged her.

Monica put her head on my shoulder and whispered in my ear, "I love you, Derek, more than you'll ever know. Thank you for being so caring, loving, and most of all for being a friend."

Somebody, Anybody, Do Something

O ne summer day while I was sitting in church, I realized there had been no mention of the annual church outing. These outings were times when friends, family, and church members would all come together. It was like a family reunion, giving the children something special to look forward to. I could remember as a child, my friends and I looked forward to this event. It was a special day at the amusement park, a time to enjoy the rides, eat cotton candy, hot dogs, hamburgers, and all sorts of other good treats. This was a time when you felt the love of friends and family in a fun-filled environment. Anyway, I went to the pastor and asked him the reason why there was no church outing taking place this year. The pastor said, "Well, Derek, nobody organized anything."

"Pastor you know that for many of the people that attend this church, this is a big tradition. Why did they forget about this tradition of all traditions?" The pastor just looked at me and chuckled. "Pastor I am serious; these outings were all about the children and young people. When I was a child growing up in this church, there was an outing; it was a tradition. You know what they should do, Pastor?"

"Please tell me what they should do, Derek."

"They should hold a fundraiser and raise additional money to help with the cost."

The pastor looked at me and said, "That sounds great. That is your vision. Now all you need to do is follow through with it." Now I'm standing there saying to myself, *What does he mean, this is my vision?* No, this is my idea, a suggestion to have something for our children.

I was expecting the pastor to say, "This is a good idea. I will pass it on and see what we could do about it." But, no, he didn't; he said, This is your vision, now go for it and make it happen."

****

As I was leaving the pastor's office, I saw James, Sheryl, and Barbara sitting in the church lobby. "Hey guys, what are you up to?"

"Nothing much, just talking about fun summer things we want to do," said James.

"You look as if you have something on your mind," said Barbara.

"I was just talking to the pastor, and there's no church summer outing."

Sheryl replied, "Are you serious, Derek?"

"Yes, I am."

"Did he say why there's not an outing?"

"Well, guys, he said that nobody planned anything."

"So, we should organize a church outing for everyone to enjoy, especially the children," said Barbara.

"You know this requires a lot of work, and once you start there's no turning back."

"We know, James," said Sheryl.

"There's Carolyn, who sings in the choir with me. Maybe she will be willing to assist. Hey Carolyn, come here. I want to ask you something."

"Hi James."

"Carolyn, we decided to come together and organize a church outing."

"Great! When I heard that the church was not having a summer outing, my first thought was how disappointing it would be for the children not to have that great experience we had as kids."

"Okay guys, if we're going to do this, we have to start immediately. We only have a few months in which to work, so we have to start organizing. We have to make contact with the appropriate people within the church to establish dates and finances. We will have to contact the amusement park and work on fundraisers."

"Wow, Derek, it sounds as if you had this all planned out," said James.

"Let me put it this way; it's my vision coming to fruition."

"What do you guys think about selling T-shirts as part of the fundraiser?"

"That's an *awesome* idea, Carolyn," said Sheryl.

"I have a slogan."

"What is it, Barbara?"

"Carolyn, on the back of the shirts we will put the church name, and on the front it will read, 'How Much Does It Cost to Be a Christian?'"

"I love it," replied Carolyn.

"I love it too, Derek, and I will get some of the youth together and have a car wash," said James.

****

"Hey, guys, this turned out to be a great event, everything turned out wonderful."

"It sure did, Derek; we were especially blessed with beautiful weather today," said Barbara.

"You ladies did an awesome job with the shirts. They sold like hotcakes," said James.

28

"Don't forget about the car wash; you guys did a great job washing all those cars," replied Carolyn.

"We can't take all the credit. The youth played an instrumental part," said Derek.

"I must say, overall the planning and manual labor involved made this a success."

"I couldn't agree with you more, Sheryl," said Carolyn.

"This is a special day; just look at the children running and playing and at the adults spending quality time together, playing horse shoes and board games, laughing and eating together having good conversation."

"Well, Derek, with that being said, I think we should go and eat," said James.

"I'm right behind you. Are you ladies going to join us?"

"I am," said Barbara.

"I'm going to sit here and continue to take it all in, what God has done to make this such a great day," said Carolyn.

"You go ahead. I'm going to sit here and keep Carolyn company," said Sheryl.

****

Sheryl and Carolyn became good friends, developing a special relationship. The next day Carolyn and Sheryl got together for lunch.

"Carolyn, why do you sound as if something is weighing on you?"

"What are you talking about?"

"Yesterday, at the outing, when you made the statement about taking it all in, you said it as if your joy is coming to an end."

"My joy has been smoldering."

"What do you mean?"

29

"Sheryl, I'm separated from my abusive husband. He physically beat me in front of the children and verbally abused me in front of our friends."

"I'm so sorry, Carolyn. I did not mean to pry."

"No need to apologize; you showed me that you're a caring person by reaching out to me."

"How did you manage?"

"Things had gotten so bad in my marriage that I kept a knife with me. I would tell myself, if he hits me again I'm going to kill him. Then I took a look at myself and realized, this is not the person God created. He is not worth going to prison over, and my children do not need their mother in prison. I'm thinking of doing things that are not of me. So, I had to leave him. I was very much afraid for my life and the lives of my children."

"Where did you go? How did you do it?"

"I decided to move out one day while he was at work and went into a domestic violence shelter for woman and children. Nobody knew I was in a shelter. After leaving the shelter I rented my own apartment, but I still remain in fear of my husband."

"Carolyn do you have an order of protection against him?"

"Yes, I do, but those things don't seem to hold any weight unless something serious happens like me ending up dead."

"How do you feel being in your new home?"

"I like my new home and had a security system installed on my apartment because of my fear. I also sleep with a bat next to my bed."

"It's terrible that you have to live this way. I mean, being in fear, having no peace or any sense of feeling safe."

"You know, Sheryl, the only time I have to myself to feel free from my troubles is when I attend church, choir rehearsal, and when singing in the choir. I love to sing."

"Yes, I know I heard your voice, and you are gifted with a beautiful and soothing voice for singing."

"I look at church as one of many places that is considered a safe haven. That church is a place where I should be welcomed and loved in the way God intends for us to be loved."

"What are you talking about, Carolyn?"

"What I have experienced at church at times was more heartache, pain, and rejection by members in the choir who call themselves Christians. Some of them would talk about me constantly during rehearsal. I feel as if I'm being treated like an outcast."

"Why do you say this?"

"Sheryl, nobody would talk with me or give any support, inspiration, or comfort even though they knew I was going through a troubled time in my life."

"Wow Carolyn, my heart goes out to you, and I mean this sincerely. I would see and hear some of the members talk about others, so I can imagine what they may be saying about you at times."

****

One Sunday Sheryl and Carolyn were sitting in church, waiting for the service to begin. While waiting they overheard a couple of members talking about another member. Sheryl looked back and said, "God does not like it when we oppress those that are oppressed. We should be lifting up one another and assisting those that are in need."

"Hey, Sheryl, you are bold."

"What are you talking about?"

"Your approach in how you confronted the people that were gossiping behind us in the church. They did not even respond back to you."

"I had a calm and peaceful demeanor during my conversation, and I was being polite and respectful. Carolyn, enough of that church talk; what is it that you want out of life?"

"Well, my dream is to move out of state to get away from my husband. I want to start life over again without being judged and criticized for not being perfect for the mistakes I made."

"Well you know Carolyn, we all make mistakes, and it does not make you a failure."

"Yeah, I know, I guess my most challenging problem is the struggle I'm having with my children's father. I'm tired of going back and forth to court to get child support, trying to establish visitations in a safe and suitable environment for my children. During visitations with their father, he leaves them with other people to supervise them. He does not spend any time with them. He doesn't drop the children off on time, or he only keeps them for a few hours when he is supposed to keep them for the weekend. I do not trust him at all. I do not have any contact with their father because I fear for my own safety."

"How do your children get to their father for visitations?"

"This is another battle I have. I made arrangements to have someone pick up the children and drop them off at a designated location. He was not willing to cooperate. He wanted to come to my house and pick up the kids and drop them off. I was not even going to entertain that suggestion, so the arrangements were made through the court."

"I bet he didn't see the court taking control coming?"

"Not at all and when the judge said that the court would assist with the visitations arrangements, the children's father did not like the sound of that. He showed his true colors, and the people at the court were given the opportunity to see what I was talking about."

"In what way did he start to show his true colors?"

"That man started yelling and cursing up a storm. He criticized the judge's decision and how the judicial system operates—that it's a big business just to keep people employed. The judge kept asking him to control himself. Then security got involved, and they escorted him out the courtroom. The sad thing about that whole scenario is that I felt sorry for him."

"You should have pulled out your cell phone and recorded a video of that moment."

"I am blessed to have a good job and the opportunity to continue my education. I'm focused and applying myself in my academics and doing extremely well. I'm blessed to be receiving additional support from family and friends to assist with daycare."

"This is awesome. See—there is light at the end of the tunnel."

"I know there's light at the end of the tunnel. My light fades in and out at times."

Sheryl laughs. "See, you still have a sense of humor, which is great."

"I do, but I still struggle when it's time for the children to visit with their father. I don't trust him. By him still seeing the children, it is like I still had to see him, too."

****

One night at about 2:00 a.m. ,Sheryl was home in bed sound asleep. Buzzzzz ... buzzzz ... buzzzz. "Who in the world could be at my door at this time of night?" Sheryl pushed the intercom button and yelled, "Who is it?"

"It's me Carolyn." It was Carolyn; her voice sounded as if she was crying and scared. So, Sheryl let her and the children in. Carolyn was an emotional wreck.

"What happened? What's going on?" She was crying and talking, but not making any sense. "Have a seat while I take the children into the spare bedroom."

33

"Carolyn's broken voice says, "thank you." I came back into the living room. Giving Carolyn a glass of water and napkin, Sheryl sat down next to her.

"Okay, relax, take a deep breath and drink some water. Now take your time and tell me, what happened?"

"Okay, the children's father, Kenny, had threatened to come over to my house and kick my ass."

"What? Carolyn I am totally confused. Start from the beginning telling me how this all came about."

"Well, Kenny called me asking if he could come over and see the children, and I said, no because it was too late and besides they were asleep. I could tell by the sound of his voice that he was drunk. Kenny started arguing with me, saying that he could come over and see his kids anytime he wanted to. I kept telling him that it was too late and the kids were asleep. He said, why can't I come over you have your boyfriend over? I told him I do not have a boyfriend. I told him that I was tired and did not want to turn this into a big argument." Carolyn paused, and it seemed as if it was for several minutes.

"Carolyn, are you okay, was that it?"

"No, Kenny said, "Well, I'm coming over anyway. I'm going to punch you in the face for not letting me come see my kids." I was just thinking of all the abuse I dealt with and was tired of it." Carolyn was sitting with her head in her hands and sobbing. She looked up at me and said, "I did not know what else to do or where to go so I came here because you live close by."

"This is fine, you and your children can stay the night and sleep in the guest room. You will need to notify the police, file a complaint, and get an order of protection. We must have hope and pray that within time this storm will pass so you can have a peaceful life."

"You know what I really need, Sheryl?"

"What is it you need?"

"I wish I had the money to get a divorce because then I would not feel that we were still connected; it would only be about the kids. I have this friend who is a lawyer; actually he's a friend of my family and he would do the divorce for one thousand dollars."

"Right now, Carolyn, that is not important. You need to get some rest and come up with a safety plan until you can get your divorce, relocate, or whatever it is you want to do. Before you get some rest and I go back to sleep, let's pray. Father, we come before you with humble hearts, broken, hurt, confused, and afraid. We all have our moments in life when the storms come, and we become impatient, wanting the storm to leave immediately. Father, we ask for patience and peace as Carolyn and her children go through this storm. I pray that you show Carolyn the way she should go as you guard and protect her heart. Provide her and her children with angels, so they will have the safety and peace they so deserve. Father, this I pray in the mighty and wonderful name of Jesus, Amen."

****

"Hello Carolyn, I know it's been a couple of days since we talked. I wanted to give you some time to yourself."

"Thanks, I needed the time because I did not want to be bothered. I did not even want to go to work. I just wanted to crawl in a shell and disappear."

"I'm sorry you felt that way. How are you feeling now?"

"Actually, I'm doing and feeling a lot better. I must admit that the tape of that night rolls in my head now and then."

"Well, have you heard from Kenny since that night?"

"No, he was drunk and probably thinks if he calls me, I am going to have him arrested."

"You know you still should get that order of protection."

"I have taken care of it. I do have to look out for the safety of my children as well as myself."

"I talked with Derek, about your situation. I hope you don't mind."

"No, I don't, I believe God brought all of us together as a team for a reason."

"I agree with you one hundred percent. I can't talk long because I'm at work. What are you doing at 6:30 this evening? Derek and I want to stop by and talk with you."

"I will be home, so stopping by is fine. I will talk with you later"
"Okay, bye."

****

"Have you talked with Carolyn?"

"I talked to her earlier in the day, Derek, and she's expecting us to be at her house at 6:30 p.m."

"Great, then we should get going because it's 6:00 o'clock now."

*****

"Hello Carolyn."

"Hi Sheryl, Hi Derek, I just got home from running errands. Have a seat."

"You know Carolyn, people are still talking about those shirts from the fundraiser."

"Really, they were nice shirts, Derek."

"I still have people asking if we have any extra shirts," said Sheryl.

"It turned out to be a great day and a great time, especially for the two of you, who seemed to have become very close and special friends."

"It was a beautiful day, and Carolyn and I became very good friends, Derek."

"Yes, good times," said Derek.

"So Sheryl, what is it that you and Derek want to talk with me about? I know it's not about the fundraiser, unless you're planning another event."

"No fundraiser, I was thinking about the night you arrived at my house. You shared with me about being able to take steps in the right direction in order for you and your children to start feeling safe."

"Yes, I remember sharing all of that information with you, but I do not understand where you're going with this."

"Just like you, I believe that God brings people together for a reason, and sometimes only for a season."

"I'm confused," said Carolyn.

"Derek has something he would like to share with you."

"Okay, Carolyn, let me get to the point. I made a call to a friend that works for Legal Aide. I informed them about your situation, from what little I know. They're willing to meet with you and provide you with legal service free of charge."

"Oh my, are you serious?"

"Yes, I am."

"I cannot thank the both of you enough."

"Thank Sheryl, she was concerned and it was on her heart to assist you."

"I really appreciate the both of you. How can I ever repay you for being so caring? Thank you, Sheryl, for being a true friend."

"Just embrace this special moment, God brought you this far because he has a special plan for you and your children," said Sheryl.

"Carolyn, you've been a blessing to us."

"Thank you, Derek, those words mean a lot to me. I see that when we are being patient and faithful, God will answer our prayers."

"Faith is the substance of things hoped for and the evidence of things unseen," replied Sheryl.

"I realize I have a testimony about going through a storm—a testimony that could assist many women who are going through domestic violence."

"Yes you do, and I'm going to connect you with a woman at the church for counseling service. You have to work on connecting to your soul. Well, I have to go, but if you need anything don't hesitate to call."

"I won't, Derek, and thank you so much."

"I will talk with you later, Derek. I'm going to stay and talk with Carolyn and have a cup of tea."

****

"Hello Sheryl."

"Hi Carolyn, how are you?"

"It's been a productive and healthy month for me. I want to talk with you and Derek when you have free time."

"Actually, Derek, Barbara and James and I are together, here at the church."

"Oh, that's great. Are you in a private area to put me on speaker phone?"

"I'm sure am."

"Hello guys, it's Carolyn."

"Hello, Carolyn."

"Guess what, guys?"

"What?" Said Derek.

"Come on, guess,"

"You got a promotion," said Barbara.

"No."

"What is it?" Said James.

"Come on, guess,"

"Will you just tell us?" asked Barbara.

"Okay, party poopers; my divorce is finalized."

"Congratulations, and I pray for continued peace and happiness in your life," said James.

"I'm still trying to get full custody of the children so I can move south."

"Just continue to pray, Carolyn. Let go and let God guide you through this. He knows how to make an ugly situation into a beautiful beginning."

"You guys are the best, and you truly know how to spread Christ's love the way food provides nourishment to the body. Your inspiring, supportive, and encouraging words nourished my soul. The kind of love you showed me touched my soul, and I'm very grateful. Because of that kind of love, my soul will humbly reach out to others with the same kind of love."

Getting Acquainted

———————◦———————

God, I felt as if I have spent the past few years of my life catering to other people, assisting others with putting some sort of meaning back into their own lives. This is an exhausting process emotionally, mentally, and physically. I'm feeling drained. I'm at that point where I need a time out and don't want to be bothered by anyone. This is very much time needed and time I deserve. I know this time will allow me to mature and grow into my spiritual life.

God is definitely working in my life. I'm feeling good about all aspects of my life including family, friends, and job. I'm living a balanced and focused life as a single man. I'm an active member in my church. I work out routinely, managing my finances, cooking and eating healthy nutritional meals, and spending time with my daughter and other family members. Most of all, I'm serving God, and serving those in need. I have never felt so good about my life and what God is doing for me. I can see life and the direction I am walking so clearly. I am investing time reading and studying the Bible, attending various church functions throughout the area whether on the weekends or weekdays. I try to put God first in everything I do whether it is assisting or just listening to people.

I enjoy listening to people teach the word of God and how to apply God's word to our life. I remember attending this Christian seminar for singles at one of the local churches. When I was registering, I noticed there was this one woman who was assisting with the registration process. I found her to be attractive. We spoke briefly, but not about anything in length or anything that would say this conversation could go any further if we had more time. Well, it was time for the class to begin, and there were about thirty people in this meeting, which was very inspirational and enjoyable. The discussions were real and true because they made you think about life and how do you want to live your life. Once the seminar was over I took the opportunity to engage in more conversation with this woman. "Hello. How did you enjoy the seminar?"

"I enjoyed it very much. I wish it was longer."

"Before you continue I would like to say, excuse my poor manners."

"What are you talking about?"

"Well I did not formally introduce myself to you. My name is Derek."

"Nice to meet you Derek. My name is Donna."

"Glad to meet you, Donna. Before I interrupted you were saying something about the seminar should have been longer."

"Oh yeah, Derek. Yes, I wish it was longer. There was so much information that was not covered, and the information that was covered felt rushed."

"I felt the same about being rushed."

"Even though some of the principles are practical, there just seemed to be more information that had been left uncovered. Well, Derek, it was nice meeting you. My friend is over there, waving to me. That must be mean she's ready to go."

"May I ask you a quick question before you go?"

"Sure, what is it?"

"Are you dating or have a significant other in your life?"

"No and I do not."

"Would you be interested in getting together one evening to talk more?"

"Of course I would; let me give you my phone number." Donna was attractive, but I questioned whether she was my type of woman. I figured I would take the opportunity and at least get to know her.

Donna and I spent a good amount of time talking on the phone before we went out. As we all know, first impressions of people are usually good and you don't really get to know someone until you invest time in them. Well, in getting to know Donna, I acknowledged and saw a lot of things that were going on in her life. She definitely could use some assistance, and it wasn't anything unmanageable. She has a son that is nine years of age, who presented himself as a polite and respectful person. He was a skinny kid with a big head for his body. I was moved with compassion as I got to learn more about Donna, and my heart went out to Donna and her son Jeff. What I observed was a young woman that lacked structure, stability, guidance, and lived an unbalanced and haphazard lifestyle. I believe that God puts us in places and with certain people for a reason, even if it's only for a season to serve His purpose. This is why we should make the most of that season. In order to make the most of the season we should treat each day as if it has its own purpose.

During the time Donna and I spent together talking about life, I found that the things she wanted out of life were realistic. However, her method of doing these things was not realistic, so we talked about different ways and methods to make those things realistic. I guess I viewed this as a challenge and a test for me. Yes, for me to accomplish the task of getting Donna to see and develop her life, as well as accomplish tasks in a realistic manner. "You know, Donna, steps are involved in order to accomplish our tasks and reach our goals in life. The steps that we take do require patience and understanding."

"I am very much aware of this, Derek. I have been patient and understanding in knowing that I have to move out of my apartment."

"What are you talking about? Why are you moving?"

"The owner is selling the house, and the buyer wants the house empty before purchasing. This means that I have to find a new place to live."

"What does that have to do with taking steps in life?"

"Come on, Derek, you are a smart guy. There are steps I must take when looking at apartments."

"This is true, Donna."

"So, I have this whole step thing under control. It's just a basic and practical principle."

"Any luck with finding an apartment or any prospects."

"No prospects, but I was looking at houses. Unfortunately, I do not have the money to buy a house or good credit to be approved."

"Well, Donna, it does not sound as if the step thing is just a basic and practical principle."

"Why do you say this?"

"Well, you said that you do not have the money to buy a house or good credit to be approved. Those two things right there are two very important steps. When it comes to certain things we are trying to accomplish in our life, we cannot just ignore certain steps."

"Then let me put it this way, Derek: my belief is that I strongly believe God will bless me with a house."

"I agree with some of what you're saying. God will bless you with a house. However, you must realize that if you do not have certain things in order in your life, God will not bless you with more than you can handle. Let me explain to you the work that's involved in order to be blessed with what God wants you to have."

"What kind of work are you talking about?"

"Well, you will have to take a look at your finances and budget. You have to satisfy whatever bills you need to pay off." Donna did not believe that there is some work in her own life that she must do to be blessed with materialistic items. She's a person who knows what the Bible says but does not apply it to her life in order to have a productive life. She believes that the way of establishing a true relationship with God and people is by attending church functions and volunteering to be part of any event that the church may have. This type of behavior kept Donna from dedicating time with her son, assisting him with his school academics. Jeff, a bright and intelligent boy, is in the fifth grade. He does well in his academics but probably could do a lot better with more support and encouragement. Instead of Donna dedicating and investing time with Jeff, so he could become a better student, she would rather drag him around to the things she wants to do without realizing that she was neglecting his needs.

One day I was at Donna's house and I decided to have a conversation with her about her son. "Donna, can we talk?"

"What is it you want to talk about?"

"Well, Donna, I hope what I'm about to say doesn't offend you."

"I guess you won't know until you say it."

"Your son, I mean Jeff, should be challenged and pushed more with his academics. He is a very bright kid, but he seems to do only the bare minimum or nothing at all."

"Oh that's it. I thought you were going to say something off-the-wall or bizarre. I'm comfortable with constructive criticism and any support or insight that would help my son. I'm always willing to listen."

"This is good information for me to know and will store it in my mental rolodex."

"To be honest, Derek, when it comes to Jeff and his schoolwork, I lack patience. Jeff acts out at times, and this frustrates me."

"You're the parent, and Jeff needs to learn about earning things and rewards."

"That's the other problem I have."

"What problem?"

"I must admit that I give Jeff what he wants. I guess when he acts up, it is easy for me."

"You know you're doing Jeff a disservice due to no fault of his own. As parents, it is our responsibility to invest time with our children and to see that they practice and utilize the tools they receive from school. From the look on your face I'd like to say that you're agitated and angry, so I will drop the subject."

"No, that's not it. It's okay. I'm fine. Really I am!"

"Let me put it this way, Donna, I feel that there is more to this situation than you want to talk about. I hope you don't feel as if I'm intruding or judging you."

"No, it's nothing you said, it's just that ....."

Donna sat there in silence for a few seconds, but before she could say anything I said, "Hey do you want to get something to eat? I'm feeling very hungry."

"Yes that would be nice. I'm hungry, too." I felt I needed to change gears to assist Donna with shaking whatever had her in such deep thought. So, to put her mind into a peaceful state, Donna, Jeff, and I went to dinner. While at dinner we conversed about funny and humorous things we had seen or experienced. I told jokes and acted silly. Donna and Jeff laughed, but Donna had a look of embarrassment on her face.

The following week, Donna found an apartment to move into and asked me and a few of her friends to assist her with the move. The day of the move was a very interesting day because she asked about eight of her friends to help her move but did not have much of anything packed. "So, Donna, did you forget to pack or did you forget that you were moving?"

"Well I did pack some things, but I have been very busy all this week."

"Well this three-or-four-hour move is going to be an all-day project, keeping people from doing other things they want to do."

"If you have something else you need to do, you can leave whenever you need to, Derek."

"I need some help with getting some boxes out of my car, Donna. Would you mind assisting me?"

"Yes I will, let me put my shoes on."

When we got to the car, I leaned against the car and looked at Donna and said, "If you looked, you could sense and see some of the frustration and disappointment on some of the people's faces who are upstairs assisting with the move."

"They look fine to me."

"Come on now, this is like inviting people to your house for dinner and then expecting them to go buy the food and cook it. Don't take this the wrong way, Donna. My impression of you at this time is that you are an unorganized and inconsiderate person. This leads me to wonder what you have experienced in your life to make you function this way and even think the way you do."

"Why do you say this, Derek? I know my life is not the best, but I'm doing the best I can with what I have."

"When I look at you this very moment, I see a beautiful woman who is a single parent crying out for help but doesn't know how to ask."

"The sad thing about what you said, Derek, is that you're right. I struggle miserably with opening up and asking for help."

"Why you struggle with asking for assistance?"

"I guess I don't want to feel like a burden to anyone. I'm embarrassed knowing that as a grown woman. I'm relying on others to help me."

"It appears that you have very good intentions in all that you do, but you struggle with the basic concepts of life. Trying to balance your own life and putting some structure and stability in the life of your son are challenging tasks for a single parent."

"There are days I just want to throw in the towel and call it quits."

"Then why don't you call it quits?"

"I wake up every day, thanking God for renewing my spirit. I tell the devil he's liar, and he will not kill my joy."

"This is good to hear, Donna; when you have God on your side you can never call it quits."

"Yes, I know. I have learned to turn my worries into prayers. When I start to worry, I stop and pray."

"Yeah, prayer works for me all the time. You know true peace comes from knowing that God is in control."

"You know, Derek, I could have reacted and said things out of anger, but I respect you for being you, a kind, caring, and considerate man. I know that you see my life as dysfunctional and unorganized. Let me tell you what I do know. I know that I have no set schedule or routine for my son to follow as regards to bedtime, doing homework, or with doing chores. For a child his age, he does not have any stable friends. I want a lot for my son and myself."

"Do you really think what you want is a lot, Donna? I could remember growing up at your son's age and having some very close friends. Today we are still friends."

"To some people, it may not seem like a lot, Derek, but to someone like me it does. It also seems so far away. You don't think I want my son to have stable friends to grow up with?"

"No"

"What do you mean no?"

"No, I mean yes, I know you want a lot for you and your son."

47

"I know my son's life mirrors a lot of my life."

"In what ways does his life mirror yours?"

"Well, I'm very much aware that I have friends, but no close friends. My friends consist of people that I attend church with. Some of these individuals just come and go."

"Yeah, I know how some church folks can be. Their friendship is not true Godly friendship."

A few days later I received a call from Donna, asking if I could pick her up from work. "Hello, Donna, how was your day?"

"My day went well, but I really need a car."

"Are you planning on buying one anytime soon?"

"God is good, Derek. I have this friend at church, and she is buying a new car. She's going to give me her old car because she wants to bless me."

"Okay, that is nice of her to give you her car."

"I can't believe someone is actually going to give me a car. I am so excited." "That is wonderful, Donna. God works in unexpected ways at unexpected times in our life. Embrace this as an opportunity to get ahead in other areas of your life."

"What do you mean, Derek?"

"You forgot about the conversation we had the day you were moving. The conversation we had about planning, organizing, and balancing your life."

"No, I did not forget."

"Well, this is one of those opportunities to start taking back control of your life. Look at it this way, you could take the money you would have spent on a car you would have purchased to take care of your financial situation. Don't just look at it as having extra spending money."

"I know what you mean; I'm not looking at this as having extra money. I'm planning on using the money to pay down some bills. There are so many other things that I am trying to accomplish. I look at this as God giving me the opportunity to focus on a particular area of my life so I can start living a more balanced life."

One Sunday afternoon I was sitting in the house watching the Lakers' game. My cell phone rang, and I answered; it was Donna. "Hello, Derek, what are you up to?"

"I'm watching a basketball game."

"Who's playing?"

"The Lakers and Nuggets"

"Why don't you take a break from your game and come outside."

"Why what's up?"

"Just come outside. I want to show you something?"

"Give me a few seconds; I'll be there." I walked out of my front door and saw Donna standing next to a car.

"So what do you think of my new car?"

"Hey, this is a very nice car. Wow, this car is in great shape. You can definitely tell that the owner took very good care of this car. I'm surprised the owner did not trade it in or sell it."

"I was surprised too; let's go for a ride."

"I'm watching the game with friends."

"Come on catch the highlights on the news besides the Lakers are going to lose anyway."

"Hey, if you keep talking like that, you will be riding solo. Let me run back inside, and tell them I'll be back in a few minutes."

While riding, I decided to start a little conversation with Donna. "I don't think I ever asked you this question, why didn't you have a car?" Donna got a little quiet and had a look of embarrassment on her face and slowly said in a soft tone.

"Well, I was laid off from my job because the company downsized. I had a car, but unfortunately I had bills. I was looking for work and keeping up on my bills with the money I saved, but it was starting to go fast. I got behind in my car payments and sold the car. With all that I have been through, my credit started deteriorating. So, I'm in the process of working on repairing it, and this is my top priority."

Donna and I were starting to spend a lot of quality time together and as we spent time together, I started to see a person who was living a life of happiness. I also saw a caring and generous person. For some odd reason, this had drew my interest in Donna more than any other woman I had ever dated before. I don't know if it was because she appeared to be in need of some special support and guidance and did not have the resources or family support to assist her. She did appear to be genuine and a spiritual person with a good heart. I was able to see her maturity when challenged with adversity. As time went on, our relationship continued to grow and we became closer. We shared in many conversations on different subjects relating to the Bible that grew our interest and desire to want to build on our relationship. We spent time going to movies, having dinner, and sharing in attending spiritual functions. We were growing as friends even though there would be times we had our moments of disagreement. I can remember one time when we were on our way home from a movie, and Donna brought up a discussion about God's plans for our lives. "You know that God has a plan for our lives, Derek, and as long as we are obedient He will bless us."

"Share more of this with me about what you mean."

"This is how I see it, as long as we follow the word of God, good things will always happen in our lives. God will continue to provide for those that keep their faith in him."

"I agree with what you are saying, Donna, but I believe that there is more to this than what you are sharing. You have to be doing something productive with your life that is pleasing in God's sight. God is not going to give you more than you can handle. You have to be able to manage what you have before he adds anymore to your life."

"Yes, that is true, but."

"Wait! Hold that but, we will come back to that. Let me share something with you, Donna. You want to buy a house, your credit needs to be repaired, and you have bills. First of all, you have to start getting your credit and finances together, which you have been doing. God knows that if you get these things in order, you will eventually be blessed with a home. God is not going to give you a house, knowing your credit and financial status is not together. God knows that there are a lot of responsibilities that come with a house, such as financially maintaining the home and other responsibilities that require you to have some financial balance in your life."

"Well Derek, I'm a firm believer that if you just believe in God and pray, then everything that is going wrong in your life will be taken away."

"Don't you know that a 'doing' man is a blessed man? Don't get me wrong I strongly believe in God and prayer. That God wants us to continue to work on those things we pray for in order for us to see where we are going and to continue our faith in him."

"I understand what you are saying, but I know that requires patience."

"Thanks for reminding me, Donna."

"What are you talking about? Remind you about what?"

"You used the word 'but' and I asked you to hold that but. Now we are going to discuss your but."

"Well, I hope you referring to the word 'but' and not literally my butt."

51

"Funny and no, we are not going to talk about your butt. We are going to talk about the word 'but,' the conjunction. Why do you look disappointed?"

"Just go and say whatever it is you're going to say, Derek."

"I was just going to share with you that when we use the word 'but,' it usually has a more valuable meaning than we realize."

"I don't follow you."

"When a person is speaking and then says, 'but,' this usually means, "Behold the Untold Truth."

"Interesting, I like that. This is really going to make me pay close attention to when people speak."

One evening, Donna, Jeff, and I were watching television. Donna looked at the time. It was 9:00 p.m. "Jeff, it's time for you to get ready for bed. Don't just sit there as if you don't hear me."

"Okay, Mom."

"No! Right now! Don't try and show off because I am not in the mood."

"Jeff! Get up and go to bed right now! I am tired having to go through this with you! I am tired of you not listening to me when I know you hear me! I keep telling you that this being disrespectful towards me is going to stop!" Jeff got up, started walking towards his room. He first went into the bathroom, but the only thing about this is that Jeff was taking his time and spent about an hour just preparing for bed, which really made Donna upset. At this point I told Donna and Jeff that it was time for me to go home. I would talk to her tomorrow.

While I was driving home I asked myself *Is this someone I want to invest or spend any more time with*? I realized that Donna had some things going on in her life, but there was still this part of me that felt bad about Donna and her situation. I had seen a lot of things that a lot of other people had not seen or knew about her, especially her immediate family. One thing I noticed about Donna was that she would always say that everything was going well. When she talked to people, especially family, there were times that things were not always going well, but I guess this is something we all do. The last thing anyone wants is for people to worry about them. While driving home I received a call. "Hello."

"Hi Derek, it's Donna."

"Hey, is everything alright?"

"Oh yeah I just wanted to apologize for Jeff's behavior. He gets moody and in a funk at times, especially when it starts getting late."

"You don't have to apologize. I know how kids can be. This is when you need to reach deep down inside and find patience."

"Isn't that the truth!"

"Donna, you have a close relationship with your parents and other family members."

"Yes I do; I love my family."

"Then why don't you share with your family about some of the challenges you are facing for some additional support? They may be able to assist by talking with Jeff. Providing some outside support that could be beneficial to you and Jeff."

"I don't know Derek. I guess I don't want people to worry about me."

"You know people don't have to know what is going on in your life to worry about you. Sometimes what people observe is enough to make them worry about another person. Your family may be worrying by observing your mood, response and reaction. Sometimes this leads people to think the worst of a situation when things are really going well."

"Thank you for being so caring and considerate, Derek. Talk to you later; good night."

"Good night, Donna."

Once I arrived home I turned on some jazz music before I took a shower. After my shower I noticed a message on my answering machine. "Hello Derek. It's me again and me is Donna. Hope I am not being a pain. Would you give me a call when you get in?"

"Okay, let's see what is going on now."

"Hello"

"Hello, Donna, I'm returning your call. Is everything all right?"

"Maybe I'm being paranoid or worrying too much, but ... or should I say, behold the untold truth? Are you all right with what took place with that whole situation with Jeff?"

"Yes, believe me I'm fine, Donna. I work with families that deal with a lot worse. I have a daughter, and sometimes we go through our moments at times. Let me share something with you, Donna. From what I observed, you may want to try and do things differently with Jeff, but I warn you, it also seems as if Jeff is set in his ways so he will challenge what you try."

"Yes, he is set in his ways, and I lose my patience."

"Can I share a scripture with you?"

"Yes, go right ahead."

"This is a scripture that I enjoy and assists me in many areas of my life such as getting through the day, bringing me peace, and comfort into the night."

"Do not be anxious about anything, but in everything, by prayer and petition, with thanksgiving, present you requests to God. And the peace of God, which transcends all understanding, will guard your hearts and your minds in Christ Jesus."

"As I sit and listen to you read that scripture, I know that God will guard my heart. For some reason I tend to find myself worrying more than I know I should."

"Then let me share something with you about worrying. Worrying could hamper your efforts."

"What do you mean by worrying can hamper your efforts?"

"Your day would be unproductive, uneventful, and long. Worrying is less helpful than anything else and shows a lack of faith in God and what he could do for you, resulting in you doubting yourself. It's as if you're giving up. God does things in his timing, not ours, so we must learn patience." Donna laughed. "Why did you laugh?"

"I didn't mean to laugh it is just that patience is what I lack, and I am trying hard to work on within myself."

"I am going to share my heart with you, Donna. You are a nice and caring person. What I am about to say is not anything to offend you, and I am not trying to sound mean; it's about love. Patience is not the only thing that you need to work on,"

"I know, Derek."

"I learned that we must turn our worries into prayers. That when you start to worry, you should stop and pray. True peace comes from knowing that God has it all under control."

It was Wednesday evening and I attended Bible study with Donna at her church. The pastor was good with teaching the word and realistic with the teaching, so that you were able to apply his message to your life. The way the pastor spoke, it was as if he was speaking directly at you and at the same time trying to intimidate you. As I observed the service and the people, it appeared that some of them worship the pastor. During the service, I noticed that a lot of parents brought their children. The children were in the back of the church trying to do homework or sleeping. I was thinking that these kids should be home doing their homework, studying, and in bed at a decent time. It was obvious these kids were not doing homework, but what kid can when they're sitting with friends? It was obvious why Jeff was struggling academically and only meeting and not exceeding expectations. It assisted me with understanding that Donna's priorities were not her son's academics. The service ended at about 9:00 p.m. People lingered around talking as if their kids did not need to get home for bed and probably did not have dinner. "What time are you going to be home?"

"I will be home in a little while, Derek."

"You might not want to stay out late. Jeff has school and homework."

"He's used to this. He will be fine."

"Okay, if you say so."

"Before you leave, I want to introduce you to a few of my friends."

"All right, but I have to get home." I met several of her friends that evening, and some of them asked if I would be joining their church. I replied that I am happy at my church. It seems as if I was being recruited to join a special club. Then I was out the door for sure this time.

When I arrived home I received a call from Sheryl. "What's up, and I feel privileged to receive a call from Ms. Sheryl."

"Oh, stop it. I was just calling to see why you were not at Bible study this evening."

"I went to Bible study with Donna."

"Hey, you are not planning on leaving our church are you?"

"No, I just wanted to check out the Bible study at her church."

"Well, I just want to let you know that people were looking for you and wondering if you were okay because you never miss Bible study."

"Sheryl, I am doing well and there is no problem. I have to go because I am hungry. I will talk with you later. One more thing Sheryl, I appreciate the call and it is nice to know that people still show a concern for others."

Today is Thursday. Where does the time go? Donna invited me to attend this formal engagement. The event started at 7:00 p.m., and Donna is scheduled to meet me at my apartment at 6:00 p.m., but as with some women she was fashionably late. When she arrived, she still had to do some minor things to be fully ready. I started to feel agitated and angry because she is taking her time. Then she said, "Hey, I am always running late." In my mind I am thinking, *Don't be late, not be ready, and then start bragging to me about how you're always running late.* When she was finally ready, she said, "You are a very patient man."

"I'm patient, and you were testing my patience. I would like to say that you're worth the wait. You look fabulous and that is a beautiful gown."

"You probably did not know I do like to dress up."

While sitting at the dinner table I noticed Donna would light up when spoken to and sat with a straight posture. Not taking anything away from Donna, she is an attractive and nice person. I'm sure that she means well in all she does. The person I saw looked the part. I guess my question was: is she willing to play and live the role? Was this a desperate person who craved attention and needed to have people in her life to feel some sort of acceptance? I saw this as a means for giving her confidence about herself. Our dinner was served, and dinner was very enjoyable. She presented with such etiquette and sophistication. I mingled and met some new and different people. I met some people at the event that I thought I would not see there. Donna and I spent time dancing, enjoying each other's company. I could feel her energy while we danced. There was a feeling of peace and happiness. "I'm ready to leave Derek; it's getting late. I have to get up for work in the morning." On the ride home we chatted in the car with a little background music, just low enough so that we could hear each other while talking. "I really enjoyed myself, Derek. This was a different type of evening for me."

"Different can be a good thing, and it's good when we do or try something different—I mean, being able to experience different things and being able to say you experienced it or tried it. You will not know if you like it or not, and yes, there are some things that you know you just won't like without trying it."

"I agree with you there because there are things I know I just won't even attempt to try or even think about trying."

"If you take a look at this world and all the many beautiful, wonderful and enjoyable things God put here for us to enjoy, we truly don't appreciate them. Some people turn their nose up at God's beautiful creations or take them for granted. There are so many people, places, and things we could learn so much from." Donna looked at me as she grabbed my hand while I was driving and said,

"Like what?"

"Like jazz music, plays, art, and hiking in the mountains. We could learn from people who live in other countries and the sacrifices they make. Their ways are so different from ours. They're so happy and at peace with less. People live a simple and traditional lifestyle in some countries. Then you look at our lifestyle, how complicated and dysfunctional we live. We think we have it all, but, in reality, we spend our time creating new and advanced problems."

"I guess you have a point. I never thought of it like that. I can see what you mean even when God brings people together, and sometimes it is just for a particular reason and season. I guess we don't know how to enjoy the moment and the relationships we have. God is awesome. Derek, for me just to sit here and know all that He has done for me, like how He brought us together, not knowing the reason why or how long the season is going to last ....."

"That is the ultimate question, Donna: What's the reason and how long will the season last? The good thing about this is that we know for relational reasons, but for what kind of relationship?"

"Yeah, that is the question, Derek. What I do believe is that in time God will reveal this to us."

"Of course he will; we just have to be ready to accept whatever it is."

"Well, we are here; let me walk you to the door. Time flies when you are in good company."

"I guess I should take that as a compliment, Derek."

"Oh yes, you should. I truly do not know where this is going or where it's supposed to be going, but you are a special woman." I lifted my hand in a way to let Donna know to place her hand in mine. Then I leaned into her to give her a hug and kiss.

"Good night."

"Good night, Derek; have a safe ride home." On the drive home I started to think. Yes, Donna is an attractive woman fun to be with and talk with. Meeting women that were sexually or physically attractive was not a problem. I just wanted to meet someone who is independent, secure within herself, and wants to have an effective relationship. I wanted to meet someone who wants to travel and grow together physically, mentally, emotionally, and spiritually. I was not looking for the perfect woman like some women talk about the perfect man or Mr. Right. When it comes to relationships, there are many outsiders ready to tell you who is right or who is not right. Hello, Mr. Right—and just who is Mr. Right? And for the guys, who is Ms. Right? We do not know ourselves, and for that matter, our friends and family members do not know, either. Realistically, there is no Mr. or Ms. Right; there is no perfect person or flawless person.

The weekend arrived I invited my close friend, Kevin, and his wife, Cynthia, over for dinner. The four of us got along very well together. I thought that it would be nice to get together with another couple for a relaxing evening and some mature adult conversation. I finished preparing dinner. We sat at the dining room table and shared in some idle conversation. After dinner, we went into the living room and a conversation about beginnings and ends erupted. "You could never have a beginning unless you bring closure to the end thing that has taken place in your life," stated Kevin.

Then Cynthia shared, "You must also have peace within yourself about what has taken place before you can move on."

"If you have God in your life and cast all your cares on him, you will be fine," Donna shared. I sat back and listen to what was being shared.

Kevin looked over at me and said, "Derek, what are your thoughts about beginnings and ends?"

I sat in silence for a few seconds. I closed my eyes briefly before I focused my attention on them and with a look as is if being deep in thought, I said, "Are you referring to anything specific when you say beginnings and ends?"

"Yes, relationships, whether it's dating, marriage, co-workers, family, or friendships you develop over the years," said Cynthia. I looked at them with this look as if being deep in thought, with patience and giving consideration with my choice of words.

"Okay, beginnings can be a beautiful thing as well as endings, but we also know as mature adults, that in some relationships, endings are not always so beautiful. So, I can say I agree with all of you to a certain extent. What's important is that we learn how to fill the voids in our life before beginning and especially after ending any relationship. Also, you need to allow God to take precedence in this process so those voids are spiritually filled."

Donna asked, "What do you mean?"

"What I mean is that we go through life experiences and relationships in many fashions, some healthy and some not so healthy. For some people, the unhealthy relationship could turn out to be a traumatic experience. Now this is the time when you must examine yourself, really examine your heart, and ask yourself.

"Have I repaired and filled that new pothole that has been developed within me? Is my soul whole and does it have a home?" See, we go through life not filling the voids or, we can say, potholes, in an efficient and effective way. Some will use the Bible as a crutch, only fooling themselves. You read a certain scripture in the Bible; or something related to the Bible has been shared with you that relates to or defines your situation. You say, 'Yes that's it! I needed to hear that I'm going to be okay. 'Now another question you must ask yourself is, 'Am I really going to be okay?" With a smile on my face I looked at each of them and said, "Listen up my friends. We all go around with these voids in our lives. We use people and things to fill them, which is only a patch job so the voids are not being completely filled. You are allowing these voids to be temporarily covered with the possibility of being reopened, resulting in more damage occurring and making the void even bigger." I paused as I took inventory of the room and said, "Are you guys with me?" I got some lazy like nods and a "Yes," but I was feeling within my heart that they were listening but not hearing me. So, I looked at them with a smile on my face and said, "Let me use this analogy. The void in your life is like a pothole in the roadway. So when a road has a pothole, the hole is usually filled by doing a patch job, but, in time, this hole starts to reopen because it was not filled completely and it do not blend in with the road. By not blending in with the rest of the roadway, this pothole is noticeable and as time goes on it start to crack and reopen. The hole is patched again and again; it continues to reopen and sometimes it gets bigger because it's no longer connected to the roadway. So, the right way to fill this pothole is by stripping the roadway totally and taking the time and patience to repave it from beginning to end, knowing that the road has been fully and completely repaired with no patches. Just like the void in your life, you need to take time and be patient with yourself and with God to allow the pothole, or void if you prefer, in your life to be stripped and filled, at the same time making your soul whole and giving it a home. We should not use people or things, remember, because people and things come and go. They're more prone to reopening that temporarily patched void with the possibility of allowing it to reopen causing more damage and hurt. This occurs by not allowing time and patience to completely repave our roadway. Realistically, most people look for other people or things to fill the void or pothole in their life. When something is said or done that relates to a past experience, it becomes a trigger; meaning you have not truly taken the proper step to fill the void. Now you're back at stage one and probably in a worse condition. This is how I view beginnings and endings because most people today bring their ending into a new beginning with unfilled voids or potholes. We must realize that voids leave us with a feeling of emptiness that is intolerably painful. We are hurting, and we are willing to do anything to eliminate that discomfort even if it is a temporary form of relief. Let me tell you something we will use whatever we can to fill that void even if it is the temporary love of others, sex, anger, drugs, alcohol, or even work. Well, let me put it to you this way, when it comes to beginning and endings, we need to respect the saying, 'Don't open any new door until you close the other door'; and most importantly, you want to be able to say, 'My soul has moved forward to being whole."

"This is true," they said while nodding their heads.

"I never looked at it in that way," said Donna.

"You're going to be a pastor someday," replied Kevin.

"You think so?"

"Oh yeah,"

"And why do you say this?"

"I say this because you take into consideration the well-being of others. You are a good listener and envision life in a way that makes others feel comfortable with their life circumstances."

"This does not mean I need to be a pastor, besides, we have enough already."

"I just mean the way you say things when you speak helps people see and understand life, even themselves, in a different way. Your words are felt and you talk with great compassion, sincerity, and concern. When you speak to people you speak from the heart." When Kevin made that comment, Donna and I smiled, then laughed a little.

"What are you guys laughing at?" asked Cynthia.

I looked at Donna and said, "You share that thought with them."

"When Derek and I were getting to know one another. We were out having dinner, having good conversation. He looked at me, and said, 'Share your heart with me.' The first time he asked that of me, I became nervous. I thought this man was asking me to share some personal and intimate feeling. He laughed, then said, 'The expression on your face is priceless. When I talk with people, I always try to share with them from the heart not that it has to be anything of an emotional feeling or personal."

"Wow! That is deep, Derek," said Cynthia.

"Personally, I believe this is an effective way that we should communicate with one another. The words that come from our mouth should be shared with peace, kindness, patience, understanding, sincerity, and love," said Derek.

"When Jesus would communicate, He did so with compassion, love, care, and sincerity even when he was not pleased by the decisions of others," Kevin said.

"This is true; God knows our heart better than we do. I believe if we pay more attention to our heart, the decisions we make and how we handle situations with others will always be done in love, regardless of the outcome. It's easy for us to share what we are thinking, but is it easy for us to share what's on our hearts? What is in our hearts is usually the truth. What we share is most likely a thought to avoid sharing what is in our heart," replied Derek.

"You think in a way that the majority of people do not," said Cynthia.

"When listening to another person when they're sharing something profound and meaningful, not with just with your ears but with your heart, you can feel that person's pain almost the way they do. The most of the people I have met through my counseling experience had some sort of traumatic experience. This lead to some sort of pain that some people do not recover from. Listen up, guys! The bottom line is that we are not perfect, but the hurt we cause one another could result in a lifetime of pain. Once whatever was said or done is out there, you cannot pull it back. This reminds me of this saying I once read. The author who wrote it is unknown, but it went something like this: 'Four things you cannot retrieve; the stone after the throw; the word after it is said; the occasion after the loss, and the time after it's gone."

"I bet you're a good counselor because you listen and take your time when speaking," said Kevin.

Looking at Kevin with a smile on my face I said, "I'm not just a good counselor. I'm a great and effective counselor. I just do what I do because I'm just an ordinary somebody trying to help somebody. Let me reiterate I'm not perfect. I do not even look to being right with the things I do or say; I try to be effective."

"That makes sense," said Kevin.

"What makes sense," asked Cynthia.

"What Derek was saying about being right in comparison to being effective. You know most people become angry or depressed because they focus more on wanting to be right rather than on being effective."

"Yeah, Kevin! That is true! Trying to be right all of the time when you are doing something is pressure; its hard work, and this is not being effective. This is the kind of pressure that nobody, I mean nobody, needs to place on themselves. There is a challenge you face with being right, the challenge is being right and not to hurt others. Anyway, the next time anyone of you are with someone, look at them and say, 'share your heart with me' and see what kind of reaction you will get." Cynthia, who was sitting listening very intently was caught in the moment. "Share your heart with me, Cynthia." She opened her mouth, but nothing came out. We laughed; she had this expression on her face as if she was a deer caught staring into headlights.

"Funny, we got jokes, Derek."

"I'm only kidding I just wanted to demonstrate the kind of reaction people will give you. To be honest not many people are comfortable with themselves in being able to share in this type of manner. Some of us have taken the word *love* out of the context that God has defined it as being used for; I'm comfortable with this because it's part of my spiritual relationship with God. I appreciate that God allows me to be realistic in a caring and compassionate way."

"You know something? Throughout this whole conversation I did not even hear the music playing," said Kevin.

"That's because God wanted us to hear something more important at the present time," replied Cynthia.

We all agreed by saying, "Amen."

Where Is the Love?

———————◦✦◦———————

I t was Sunday morning. I awakened to the sounds of comforting and relaxing music. I enjoy starting my mornings off with a prayer and music. Sometimes this does not happen, but I try. I took inventory of my life. I realized I have developed and grown in my spiritual life. There was this fire and excitement in me, knowing that God is using me and that I'm able to serve him in whatever capacity he guides me. Being single assisted me in being focused and living a balanced life. To have a woman in my life was not a priority. I know women come and go, and there were no guarantees. The only guarantees in life are taxes and death. Taking a look at the clock, it was approaching that time for me to get ready for church.

My Sunday school class consists of a good group of people with different personalities. Ms. Wilson is an awesome teacher who is a highly respected woman. She is real with you, caring and compassionate. If you were out of character, she had no problem letting you know. She is one of those old-school Sunday school teachers from head to toe, and she is sharp and witty. She stays abreast of current events that are taking place in society. She knows her Bible and loves the Lord. She really invests in her class by coming up with different teaching methods that assist her class with staying grounded. I understand her focus is for us to build healthy relationships with one another. She develops questions pertaining to the

Sunday school lesson and then presents them to us. What makes this interesting and funny is that you get to see who studied Sunday's lesson and who didn't. Those who did not study would look around the room for those who did study to sit next to them. When it was question-and-answer time, it was all good because we were like one big family and tried to help each other out as much as we could. When class was over, we would sit around and chat for a while, knowing that we were to be in the sanctuary with the rest of the church going over the morning review. This time of socializing usually did not last too long because someone from the church would come over and break things up. We would walk over to listen to the morning review. After the review of the lesson, it was time to prepare for church service, and this would start with morning devotion. It appeared that those leading the devotion acted as if nobody wanted to sing, but once they got rolling, you could feel the spirit of the Lord. People would say a prayer and share a testimony before the church service began. The choir and trustees would do their walk down the church aisle, with the pastor bringing up the rear. After going through the routine and dramatics of service as things are listed on the program, it was time for the pastor to preach. A lot of the members were not fans of the pastor and would criticize his preaching and even him as a person. They showed very little respect for the man, themselves, and God. There would be people in the back talking constantly while he was preaching. Some would just talk about him in general as if they're at some sort of social function. Sheryl would tell me what some of the members who sat behind her would say. She found it embarrassing to repeat. Sheryl was a nice woman but could be a feisty woman and loved to debate with you. I would tell her she missed her calling; that she should have been a lawyer. She was one who did not hold her tongue. If an inappropriate, disrespectful, comment was made, it had to be acknowledged and confronted immediately. So when those individuals were making the rude remarks, she told them that if they have a problem with something the pastor is doing, they should go and talk to him instead of gossiping and talking about him behind his back. This is when I first learned of the feisty Ms. Sheryl and that once she got rolling, stand back! When I start to see that initial spark that ignites the feistiness in her, I will immediately change the topic to something less controversial.

Service was over, and after every service we go through the routine of greeting and giving people hugs and kisses. I remember going to give this older woman a kiss on the cheek. She turned her head as if she was trying to kiss me on the lips. I think she was trying to slip me her tongue because the corner of my mouth was wet when I pulled away. Then I went over to give this other older woman a kiss. I observed her push someone away when they approached her. I decided to let her be, but this also validated my thoughts that people are people, and it does not matter if they are at church or in a club. I met people at clubs who were truer and more real than those in church. There were times I would look at church people as phonies, you know, perpetrators. Don't say you don't drink, but when you are at home, at a social event, or even during dinner you have a drink or two, but when the Pastor comes around you are too afraid to drink. The funny thing about this is that I see some of these same individuals out at the sports bar some weekends getting their drink on, but I do not judge. Just be mature, responsible, and drink in moderation. This doesn't mean you have to drink to get drunk, and then you find yourself out of character. It's perfectly fine to drink; don't indulge and don't overdo it. This goes for anything—even for food. If you have an addiction; going through recovery, use wisdom, and avoid any and all. God wants us to be real and please Him and not to be fake in trying to please people.

I remember this one gentleman named Bill who attended the church. Some Sundays, Bill would come to church smelling like liquor. He would even bring his bottle to church functions. He wanted to be involved in several areas of the ministry. See, I knew Bill from the past. I know people can change, but he did not change. He was a heavy drinker when I met him. Sorry to say, he was a fake and still remains to be a phony.

One day I decided to give Bill the opportunity to show me that my opinion of him was wrong. I asked Bill to assist me with repairing one of my computers. He assisted me all right. This guy tried to rip me off and steal from me. The computer needed a motherboard, which I purchased for $50.00. I knew this was the part that needed replacing. He told me that he could get me one for $250.00. Now, I knew this guy was trying to run a game on me, so I went to get my computer from him. When I arrived at his house, he was trying to take parts off my computer to upgrade his.

His lame excuse, "I'm trying to make sure that the motherboard was the actual problem." From that day on I never asked Bill for anything else. What makes this so unfortunate is that he was an intelligent and talented man but was still trying to get over on people. Now this helped me to understand why God had to have His Son save us from our sins because, no matter where we are in our Christian life, we will continue to make mistakes that cause us to sin.

James, Sheryl, Barbara, and I went out to dinner after church service. James was a talented man. He could sing and had a lot of energy. You could not help but notice him because he would be getting his dance on in the choir, having a good time. He definitely made church, church. Anyway, while sitting at the table James started to sing. People just looked at him, but they were enjoying listening to him sing. He was not being rude or loud as if he was trying to draw attention to himself. He was just loud enough that those who were around him could hear. The song he was singing was Fred Hammond's, "Jesus Be a Fence"—one of my favorite songs.

He looked at me as if to say, "Derek, I know you know this song" waving his hand for me to join him.

I looked at him as if to say, "That's okay," but that was my song so I caved and sang. Sheryl and Barbara were looking at us, laughing and rocking to the song. Then all of us started laughing. This was good fun; there is nothing like having fun with friends you have love for and are comfortable being around.

"Hey Sheryl, do you remember the time when we were leaving church? You were walking towards your car. I made the comment that it's been awhile since you organized anything for the youth."

"Yes, I remember that day. You need to be careful how you talk to people, Derek."

"See guys this is the same kind of rambling reaction I always get from her. One time she even made some sort of comment about taking the plank out of your own eye before making comments to someone else." I laughed and said, "Hey girl take it easy, I'm only joking with you; take it down a notch or two."

"Wait a minute Derek! You did not say it like you was joking."

"Yes I did! You did not hear me because you just kept on rambling on about something else. I kept saying: 'Sheryl! Sheryl! Sheryl!' I called your name about three times before you responded. Then you said, 'What!' Then I said, 'I have to go, but you may continue that conversation you are having with yourself in your car' and you started laughing."

"Yeah whatever, I don't remember it being that way."

"I'm surprised that you remember it at all." Then there was Barbara: a very intelligent young lady who was working on her master's degree. She wanted to be a veterinarian. I was impressed, but she comes from a wealthy family. You would not know it by the way she carries herself because she is down to earth, supportive, and helpful. Then there are times you could see the immature side of her, so you had to be careful of what you said to Barbara or how you said it.

One day while in front of the church, Barbara, James, Sheryl, a few other people and I were outside talking. "You know what I would like to add to the church, Derek?"

"What is that, James?"

"I would like to hear and sing a different style of music. The hymns are nice and all, but we need to get some contemporary sounds in here for the upcoming generation. You would enjoy a different sound, right, Barbara?"

"Oh yeah. I would like to hear more contemporary music—at least a song or two now and then."

"I know what you like to listen to, Barbara."

"What do you know, Derek?"

"I know you probably want to hear some hip hop or rap; that's what you listen to in your car." Barbara blew a gasket. Her eyes told it all as they increased in size. All I could see was a fiery furnace. For a moment I felt like the Hebrew brothers, you know, Shadrach, Meshach and Abed-Nego.

Yes, the fiery rage came out, "I do not! Listen! To that kind of music! I do not! Know! What you are talking about! You can go get in my car right now, and you would not hear nothing like that."

"Come on, Barbara, let's keep it real. It's okay if you listen to a little hard core rap and heavy metal."

"I listen to that genre of music myself as long as it's clean. You know you sit in your car leaning to the side bobbing your head from side to side. You know when you're at home you're in the house dancing; you're probably pop locking, doing the wop, running man, and some other dances."

What made this entire conversation funny was that Barbara was taking

71

this very seriously while the rest of us were laughing. Then Sheryl came to her rescue.

"It's time to go. Let's go! We have to be somewhere."

Barbara walked away with Sheryl looking back at me and yelled, "I do not listen to any of that music!"

"Hey, right now you and Sheryl are going to have a jam session. When you put that key in the ignition and turn it on. You're going to hear the music before the engine."

Later that evening, I received a call from Sheryl."Hello."

"Hi Derek, it's me, Sheryl."

"What do I owe the nature of this call?"

"It's about Barbara—the way you kept picking on her was not right. I talked to her while we were in the car. I told her that she has to take it easy and that you and James were only joking with her, mainly you!"

"You know why she was acting that way?"

"Why was she acting that way?"

"She does listen to that type of music." Sheryl started laughing. "Why are you laughing?"

"Well she does listen to rap music."

"Honestly, Sheryl, I do not care that she listens to a different style of music. I like different genre of music myself. It's nothing to be ashamed about. What she should be ashamed of is that she is not being true to herself. She can tell us whatever her heart desires, but the bottom line is that God knows the truth. People should listen to a variety of music, as long as the music is clean, loving, and fun; and not degrading, putting down women, men, races, or nationalities."

"I agree with you one hundred percent; besides, we should not deprive ourselves of all the beautiful and wonderful things God has put on this earth for us to enjoy."

"I will call Barbara and apologize. I will let her know I was only having fun with her and did not mean anything by what I said. I will apologize for James, too."

"Why are you apologizing for James?"

"I initiated the whole thing, and it got a little out of hand."

"Oh! Just a little, you were about to get a taste of some of her ninja moves," she said, laughing.

"Okay, a lot."

One evening on my way home from work, I received a call from the pastor, "Hello, Derek. This is Pastor."

"Hello."

"Derek, could you contact a group of individuals to meet and talk about starting a children's church. I have a list of people I would like for you to start with." He gave me the list of names, and as I looked over this list, I said to myself, "This does not look good." Some of these people were more problems, if anything, and to try to work with them definitely would be a major challenge. I smiled and chuckled to myself and said, "God, you have a sense of humor." I called each individual on the list and asked if they could meet with me at the church. Some were willing, and some were hesitant. When I shared the vision with some of the individuals I called, they responded with a rude and sarcastic "No!" Those who were being hesitant were the ones that I viewed as being potential problems.

On the day of the meeting, I shared the agenda and purpose of the meeting with these members. "Well some of you may know why you are here. Some of you may want to know more about why you were asked to be here. The pastor asked me to meet with you because most of you work with children and youth. The possibility of starting a children's church is being taken into consideration.

One of the members said, "It's about time!"

"How about giving me some feedback if this is something you feel is in your heart for us to do."

Another member stood up and said, "I feel this is great and is something that the church needs. We need to start praying for this ministry in that it would grow and be an uplifting ministry for our children."

"Thanks for the positive feedback. I believe this will be an inspiring ministry for the children. I have another question; is anyone willing to be the secretary and take notes of our meeting?" I waited for several seconds, which seemed like minutes for a response, but nobody volunteered. "Well I see no one is willing to volunteer. Well I feel in my heart that Sheryl would do an excellent job at keeping the minutes for our meetings." Sheryl looked a little surprised when I nominated her.

In a low and unclear voice she said, "I will do it if nobody else is willing to do it."

Another member asked, "Where do we start?"

"To get a vision and idea of what we want our children's ministry to look like, and to get it up and going, we, as a group, will go and visit other churches to observe their children's church ministry," I said. So we visited three different churches and it seemed as if everyone had their own way of running their children's ministry. Basically, there was no structure for these children's church ministries. The other concern I had was how we would fit this into our church service. At our next meeting, the group and I discussed some training options to assist with the implementation of the children's church.

One of the members said, "I think it would be important if we research current training material to give us an idea of what direction we should head in."

Another member added, "I think we should meet as a group every two weeks to discuss the direction that this ministry is moving." You could feel and see the excitement within the group. There was a strong desire in wanting this ministry to grow. Being part of something new and different gave them extra fuel. While we were meeting, a member of the church entered the room.

This member stated, "I hear you're planning to start a children's church ministry."

One of the group members said, "Yes. Is there something wrong with that?"

"No. There is no problem with you wanting to start a children's church ministry. As the Sunday school superintendent, some of the other church leaders and I know that some of you are not certified as teachers. It's the church policy for you to go through the training class before you can be considered to teach children,"

I responded, "This is ridiculous; how could you allow politics and the church's bylaws take precedence over the Bible."

"No, we just want to make sure we are consistent and keep things in order."

One member of the group said, "Excuse me Ms. Superintendent, I know personally there are some people teaching Sunday school classes for many years who have not taken these classes."

"Well, I don't know about them because they were teaching before I was offered this position."

The member responded by saying, "Then you need to go do your homework and make sure that all your teachers are in compliance with what you are asking of us. Besides, the training you're asking of us is not required to develop a children's church. Some of us within this group who are teachers, Ms. Superintendent, are certified. Now do you want me to testify?"

We laughed and the only response from the superintendent was, "Here is the information for you to study for these classes." She left the room and we looked through the information she handed us.

I looked at the first packet of information and shared my findings with the group, "I know some things don't change, but this information is dated back to 1979 and here we are in the year 2015."

Sheryl asked, "So what you guys think?" Before anyone could get a word out, Sheryl said, "This is what I think. Right now this experience is putting a bad taste in my mouth. My level of respect for the leaders in this church makes me wonder if they really care. The things people will pull in order to prevent God's work from being done. This is all about God and the children, not us or others."

I quickly shared my thoughts, "I agree with some of things you said; unfortunately, there are people too stubborn and selfish to see the bigger picture. They're not able to see the forest from the trees. I think we all should go home and pray for this ministry and that God's will be done. Let's pray before we leave."

That same evening I was home cooking dinner I received a call from Sheryl.

"Hello."

"Hi Derek, It's me Sheryl."

"Well to what do I owe the nature of this call? Wait a minute. Let me guess. You're still upset about what happened at today's meeting, that we invested a lot of time in visiting churches and other functions researching this project."

"Yes, I'm very angry. When we were in the beginning stages of developing this ministry, nobody, I mean, nobody came to us and said anything about needing additional teacher's training. Someone could have, at least, had the common courtesy to meet with us and shared that, before those of you who are not certified get started with investing all your time in developing this ministry, you will be required to take the training for new teachers."

"Hey, I agree with you a hundred percent and felt this was something the superintendent should have mentioned on day one," responded Derek.

"This should have been handled in an orderly fashion. Just sitting here talking about it, I feel the anger and frustration starting to rise in me."

"Well Sheryl, on a different note, where are you from?"

"Changing the subject, Derek?"

"Well, change can be a good thing sometimes."

"Anyway, I'm from Virginia and lived in the New York area for the past five years. I'm an independent single parent and do not need a man to support me."

"So you're saying you're young, single, and free?"

"Yes I am; when the time is right the right man will come along. I'm not like some women that will go out of their way putting their kids second to have a man."

"Thanks for sharing, Sheryl; I only asked where you were from, but I do appreciate the extra."

"See what I mean? You try to be nice and share information with someone, and they take it as if you talk too much."

"To be honest you do like to talk. It's as if you got this motor mouth thing going, except there is no on and off switch."

"Oh, we got jokes alright wait until you need me again, and you know you will."

"I just mean that you have a special and unique way of communicating."

"Just stop while you are ahead, Derek; you're digging a hole so deep that God will not be able to find you."

I laughed, "Okay, okay! On a serious note, you said you are a single parent."

"Yes, I am."

"I agree with you that children should be first when you're entertaining any relationship. When children are involved, time should be spent investing in your child because this is their time. That's regardless whether the child is in a single or two-parent home."

"I do try, or at least, I like to think I try and invest time with my son."

"I'm sure you do Sheryl; I am not saying this for you to second guess or doubt the kind of relationship you have with your son. The way society functions, trying to have a trustworthy and healthy relationship is a battle within itself."

"This I know too well. These days life is scary. You could be with someone for ten years and find out that this person had another life or family, is not who they say they are, or is an abusive person. It's challenging enough just to meet someone in the traditional way. Now, you have more people putting their trust in the Internet to meet that special person, which I find to be very risky."

Then Sheryl switched gears on me. "Hey, what are you listening to? I hear music in the background."

"I'm listening to jazz. I like various kinds of music R&B, Gospel, Christian, Blues, Pop, Soft Rock, and Classical. I'm open minded and willing to try something once, depending on what it is."

"How about old school music, you have any of that?"

"Of course what do you want to hear? I probably got it." She started naming songs and artists. I went into my collection of music and started popping out songs as she requested: Cyndi Lauper, Jackson 5, Marvin Gaye, Sarah Vaughn, Prince, Commodores, Hall and Oates, she even asked for the Beetles. "Hey Sheryl! I got it all and if I don't have it, I might just go and get it so I do have it."

"Alright; I'm impressed that you have such an extensive music collection."

"Come on; don't be impressed. That's an insult. Just compliment me on having a diversified music collection."

"Well then, if you want to be all diplomatic about it, I compliment you on having a diversified music collection. Hold on Derek, there is someone at my door."

"Sure not a problem,"

"Okay, I'm back. It's my neighbor Terri."

"Go and entertain your company. We'll talk later."

I hear a voice in the background whispering, "Hey Sheryl who are you on the phone talking to? Don't you know you have company?"

Sheryl replied, "Be quiet! Besides, you are not company. If you must know, I'm talking to a friend from my church."

"Is he cute?"

"Behave yourself or I will have to send you back home! We work together on one of the church's ministries. He has a lot of old school music."

"Oh yeah! Does he have the Temptations, Smokey Robinson, Stevie Wonder, Blondie, Elton John, and Phil Collins?"

"Yes, yes, yes, yes, yes, and yes! I have them all!" I played a few songs for her. I can hear them yelling and screaming into the phone.

Next thing I knew Sheryl's friend was on the phone, "Hey you have to make me a CD."

"Okay, I can make you a CD."

Sheryl was back on the phone, "I apologize for my friend's rude behavior. If you don't want to, you do not have to make her a CD."

Terri shouted, "Don't listen to her! I want the CD!"

"It's not a problem. I will make the CD."

"Hold on, Derek, someone's trying to get my attention." Sheryl became quiet, and I heard whispering in the background but couldn't make out what they were whispering about. "I'm back, Derek; may I ask you a question?"

"Sure. What is it?"

"Are you single?"

"Yes, I'm not looking to start a relationship because I do have a friend."

"Is the friendship going anywhere?"

"To be honest, I do not know for sure."

"Who are you dating, Sheryl?"

"Nobody, I'm not dating or have any special friends."

"Hey, on another note, Sheryl, I have to cook me something to eat. I will talk with you later."

"Wait, you cook?"

"Don't sound so surprised. I do cook, especially if I want to eat. Is there something wrong with a man cooking?"

"No, that is a beautiful thing. I think when a woman meets a man who cooks, it's a plus in a relationship."

"Well I have met women that could not cook to save their own life, so I guess it would be a plus."

"Now, why are you single, Derek?"

"We're back on this? It's by choice."

"Are you gay?" I laughed, "What in the world would make you think I'm gay or even ask that question? I'm far from being gay, and have no desire in finding out what it is like to be gay. No, I'm not one of those DL (Down Low) guys. Now don't get me wrong. I have nothing against gay people. Obviously, we are all different in many ways."

"Then why you're not married? I'm surprised that somebody has not come along and snatched you up."

"Well, it's not that easy."

"What's not that easy?"

"For someone to be snatched up and it's not easy to meet a woman. To find the one you would want to spend your life with is challenging."

"Have you ever lived with a woman?"

"No, in order for me to live with a woman, we would have to be married. I must admit, I do wonder if living with a woman before getting married would be beneficial. Even though I know this is not how relationships ought to be developed. It gives you the opportunity to get to really know one another. I feel after a couple of years you should make a commitment for marriage. Besides, relationships these days are so difficult and challenging because some people have their own agenda. These agendas put a different type of spin on the relationship. Then, before you know it, you and that person are going in different directions."

"That is true. Even if you were to meet someone in the church, you might encounter those challenges," replied Sheryl.

"Meeting someone in the church does not guarantee you anything. But honestly it could help. Besides we are not perfect creatures no matter where we are in our faith. Some people are more concerned about being with someone, when they should be spending time with themselves and God, creating a sense of peace and oneness within themselves. You know what I mean Sheryl?"

"Yes I know what you mean. Then how can anyone ever accomplish this sense of peace and oneness within themselves when they are more concerned about who or what they can have in their life?"

"I will be the first to say I'm not perfect, Sheryl. I made a lot of mistakes in my life and I will continue making mistakes. What I do know is my purpose. I know that if I ever do get married, the things I do will not be just for me, but also for the person in my life. I'm not looking or expect to have a perfect wife or relationship. I would like the relationship to be effective and for us to be walking in the same direction. We may even walk at different paces." Sheryl was quiet. I took this as a sign it was time to change the subject. "You know Sheryl I do not feel as bothered by what has taken place or the obstacles we encountered in regards to the children's church."

"There are a lot of children in the church who do not have much to meet their spiritual needs at their level."

"I know Sheryl, so why don't you share with me your true thoughts about this ministry and being part of the team."

"Let me put it this way, Derek, being part of the team is wonderful. I thank God for allowing me to be used and having a part with the development of the ministry. I would like to say thank you for being a friend. I mean, I meet a lot of people, especially guys who would start to show other interests in me, if you know what I mean. When I talk with you, you are all business and friendly. I'm comfortable calling you, requesting information for things that are going on at the church or other members' phone numbers."

"Hey! I have had my share of ups and down with women. So, I do not take things lightly when it comes to relationships. Hold on, Sheryl someone is at my door." "Hello, who is it?"

"It's me, Donna."

"Hey come in. I'm on the phone. I will be off soon."

"Sheryl, let me call you back later or I will see you in church."

"Okay bye." I could feel and see that Donna wanted to ask who I was talking with on the phone. She's is silent, looking around as if something is on her mind, and here it comes, 5, 4, 3, 2, 1.

"Who was that Derek?"

"It was Sheryl from church."

"Why is she calling you?"

"She is calling me because we are working on developing a children's church. The team ran into some obstacles with other members, and she needed to vent." Now I'm thinking, *Here we go.*

"Oh no, I do not like that because she is going to want more than that after a while."

"I work in an office where I am the only male with five other women. Is this going to be a problem for you?"

Donna paused looked at me and said, "That's different." I'm thinking, *Let it go, Derek*. She's jealous of the fact that another woman has called my house.

"Then what about your male friends who call you?"

"They're only old friends from years ago; this is okay."

"I don't know. Should we take a survey? Even though they're old friends, it's still the same concept. They're no different as friends, just like I say that Sheryl is my friend. You say you do not know Sheryl, who's my friend and what her intentions are. It goes both ways. I do not know your male friends and their intentions."

"They are like brothers of mine."

"Well, I don't know this and I never gave you a hard time about it because I trust and respect you. What you fail to see, Donna, is that I do not really care as much as you do about this situation. I would like for you to open your eyes and look at the whole picture. Now, why is it okay for you and not okay for me? What is the real difference and is it right and is it justifiable?"

"Out of respect for me and even more so for our relationship, would you mind not having other women call you."

"You know something, Donna? That is not a problem. I am going to share with you why it's not a problem. First of all, I do not want you to feel threatened and thinking another woman was trying to take me from you. Second, I don't want you to think I am some sort of player. Mainly this is about respect and love. It's my way of saying I care about you."

"Thank you, I appreciate your consideration, Derek."

"I try to give the woman, the respect and treatment she deserves, but once she crosses the line then we must reevaluate our relationship pertaining to trust and respect. One last thing, Donna: you need to keep in mind that I have no real control over if it's a man or woman who calls me."

Its nine o'clock at night. I'm lying on the sofa, watching television when my phone rang. "Hello"

"Hi, Derek, I just wanted to call to say, I apologize for the way I handled that situation at your house."

"We all have our moments whether good, bad, or indifferent, Donna."

"Yes I know, but I should have been more mature about the situation by trusting you. The way I handled the situation, I questioned the trust I have in you."

"Yes you have, I also think you should know that I have boundaries. My limits and boundaries all depend on how well I know the person. When a woman and I are in a relationship, I ask for trust, respect, maturity, a growing relationship, common sense, a good heart, and an effective relationship. It's not about who is right or who is wrong; it is about being effective."

"I understand the other things you're asking pertaining to a relationship, but what do you mean by being effective?"

"Being effective means working as a team, no game playing, and a willingness to sacrifice."

"It's not a lot, but it sounds like a lot."

"Maybe you should chew on that, and we can have another discussion at another time. Right now, I'm tired and ready to go to bed. I will see you tomorrow; good night."

"Good night, Derek."

****

Donna and I met after work for dinner. When I entered the restaurant, Donna was sitting waiting patiently. "Hi, Donna, how are you doing?"

"I'm doing well. I've just been sitting here waiting for you."

"I hope you were not waiting too long?"

"No, I was only here for about ten minutes. I gave your name for the next available table."

"Okay. Hopefully the wait won't be too long. Anyway, how was your day?"

"I had a very good day. I woke up well rested. I'm all caught up on my project at work. This gave me time to do some miscellaneous things. I had the opportunity to see why so many of my co-workers are behind in their workload."

"What do you mean?"

"I stay busy while I'm at work. Some people spend their time socializing and hanging in other people's office. This is why they're so unproductive. Overall, it was a peaceful day."

"I'm glad to hear it, Donna."

"What about your day?"

"My day started off well but ended as a disappointing day."

"What happened that made it end as a disappointing day?"

"Well, Donna, I went to work and looked at my appointments for the day. I had a couple of clients to meet for a family therapy sessions. My ten o'clock appointment arrived, and the session was very productive. Then a little after twelve o'clock, I went to the gym to work out. I returned to my office about 1:30 p.m. I prepared for my two o'clock appointment. The two kids had arrived shortly after I did, so we were just waiting for their mother. Before we knew it was 2:45 p.m. and the caseworker for the kids returned to pick them up. She asked, "Where is their mother?" I said, "She was a no-show today, which is unusual, because she has not missed an appointment. She is good about calling if she will be late."

Donna asked, "What happened to the mother; did you ever hear from her?"

"Hold up; I'm getting to that. Anyway, while I'm sitting at my desk writing up a report, I received a call about five o'clock from a different caseworker. She asked me if I heard what happened. I said, no, and she continued saying, the kids' mother was on her way to the visit as usual. She was crossing the street to catch a bus. She was hit by a car and died."

"Oh my, Derek; I'm so sorry."

"I just keep thinking about how her kids are going to feel. This really makes me think."

"What are you talking about Derek?"

"It makes me realize that we are not promised tomorrow, that we should be thankful for each day we wake up. We need to learn to enjoy each moment of our lives as if it's our last moment of life."

"Unfortunately, I don't think we do that enough. I think we spend more time complaining than anything else."

"You're right, Donna, and when I look at you, I ask myself 'What are her intentions? What is it she really wants from me?'"

"So, what answers do you come up with?"

"I tell myself, I know she wants to get married, but I guess I'm asking myself, am I afraid of giving up my freedom and my space. There is also that other part of me that wants to build, grow, and share my life with someone. I know we're not perfect in our ways or thoughts. We are not human beings, only humans becoming. I guess marriage is what you and the other person make of it."

"You seem to have something else on your mine, Derek."

"Actually I do, Donna."

"What are you thinking about?"

"You really want to know what I'm thinking?"

"Yes, I want to know."

"About marriage and us," Donna started to smile. "Can I share my heart with you, Donna?"

"Sure you can; you do not have to ask."

"I know we are not engaged and we talk about marriage. How do you or I know if two people are right for each other? Some couples get married based on the word of God and try to build the relationship on God's word. You and I know that realistically, when a major problems start to erupt in our lives., there is hurt and pain that could have a traumatic effect that could seriously scar the relationship. Then things become very difficult in the relationship. Then you ask yourself whether you can give anymore. This is why God had to have his son (Jesus) die on the cross for our sins. God knows that we are going to continue to make mistakes. We are never going to be perfect even when it comes to marriage."

"Yes, I agree Derek, as long as we have faith and stand on his word, everything will be all right." Derek chuckled. "Why do you laugh at me?"

"My half-hearted chuckle is not at you. The comment you made about faith and standing on God's word."

"So, what did I say that made you chuckle?"

"Nothing, it's just that it's true. What I mean is that, I understand what you said. If you take a look around, you'll see that's what all Christians are trying to do. Unfortunately, there are certain circumstances and situations that occur in our lives that tell us that it's time to move on. I see it like this, Donna; sometimes the things that we are trying to hold on to are sometimes the things that God is trying to pull us from. Not all things go according to God's plans because we as people will make anything happen according to our own plans." Donna's eyes started to look watery as if she's starting to cry. I felt her concern in my heart. "Why do you look sad?"

"It feels as if you are saying that you do not have an interest in me or our relationship."

"Wait a minute, Donna; don't take what I'm saying the wrong way. I'm not saying that I'm not interested in getting to know more about you, seeing where our relationship goes. I'm just being real. If you open the eyes of your heart, there are a lot of things that go on in our society that people do not want to admit to, even if they are grounded in the word of God. Sometimes, Donna, it is what is, but we will work so hard not to deal with the truth and live in denial." Donna starts to perk up there's a half smile on her face.

"I'm sorry, Derek. It's just that I allow my emotions to get the best of me to the point I would become easily frustrated and angry for minor things."

"What would you like to do, Donna?"

"I would like to do whatever you like."

"You don't want to do what I like to do, you want to do what I love to do."

"That's what I like about you, Derek."

"What's that?"

"The simple fact you know how to make me feel good when things seem to be down."

"Oh, this is what you like about me?"

"Yes,"

"I think you meant to say this is what you love about me." Donna had this big smile on her face.

Hostess yells out, "Table for party of Derek is ready."

One evening, I went to Donna's house to visit. Jeff was in the living room playing a video game. "Hello, Jeff."

"Hi, Mr. Derek."

"Jeff, have you finished your homework?"

"Mom, I will finish it later."

"Can I have one evening without having to tell you to do your homework?"

"Excuse me, are you guys hungry?"

"Yes, Mr. Derek, I'm very hungry."

"What about you, Donna?"

"I'm hungry."

"So why don't we order a pizza and while the pizza is being delivered, Jeff, why don't you do what your mother asked you to do?"

"What did she ask me to do?"

"She asked if you could please finish your homework. By the time the pizza arrives you will be finished. Before you go I would like for you to choose the toppings."

"Okay, I want pepperoni, sausage, peppers, spicy chicken, onions, and extra cheese."

"Hey! Great choices Jeff, this is going to be one tasty pizza. Now it sounds like both of us have work to do, Jeff."

"What work do you have to do, Mr. Derek?"

"I have to call the pizza shop and order the pizza. I have to make sure they add all the toppings you picked. I think I will do extra work. I'm going to go to the store and pick up some ice cream"

"Can we have cotton candy?"

"Cotton candy-flavored ice cream it is; I'll be back."

"Oh! Yeah! I'm going to go to my room and start my homework."

Donna stopped Jeff, "What do you mean start?"

"Mom, I have to finish what I didn't start."

"Never mind just go start what you didn't finish." Donna walked over to Derek and gave him a kiss on the cheek." Thank you. That meant a lot to me."

"Not a problem, you have to work with kids in a way, so that it appears, as if they're getting something for the work they do. It's like rewarding them. In reality you're not, because he has to do his homework, he has to eat and he's eating something that he enjoys. He thinks that he's getting something special for doing his homework."

"Hey, I like the way you think. You don't think that way with me, do you?"

"No I don't, but this does not mean that I may not do it subconsciously." An hour went by and the doorbell rang. "Donna, Jeff the pizza is here, get it while it's fresh and hot."

"So Jeff, are you still doing your homework?"

"Yes Mom, I was just finishing this last question, honestly."

"Great! The pizza is here, go wash you're your hands so you can eat."

"Okay, Mom."

"So Jeff, what are your plans after you graduate from high school?"

"I'm going to go college, but I'm not sure about what I want to study."

"That's right; my baby is going to go to college."

"That is great, but let me share something with you. When you go to college, you are expected to work and study. The work and studying you are doing now is just practice. In college you are going to be working two or three times as hard."

"Mr. Derek, I will be ready. I just get bored sometimes or don't like the assignments."

"FYI, Jeff,"

"What's FYI?"

"It means 'for your information'. I am going to let you in on a little secret."Jeff was very excited when Derek wanted to share a secret with him.

"Okay, what is it?"

"Your mother can't hear so come a little closer. I will whisper it in your ear."

"Okay, what is it?"

"In college, you will be given a lot of assignments and research projects you will not like. You will have to study subjects you do not like."

"That's no secret."

"So, what did Derek tell you?"

"He said in college I will have to do a lot of assignments I will not like and do research. I will have to study subjects I will not like." Donna laughed.

"So, Jeff, how are you doing in school?"

"I'm doing well, Mr. Derek, but I know I can do better."

"College is like having a job, Jeff. You have to be responsible and independent. You're the one that's going to have to be responsible for your success. You will not have teachers; you will have professors. In college when a student is not passing or going to class, nobody is going to call home or send a letters home to tell your parents. In college, when you're not meeting the academic requirements, they will kick you out or put you on academic probation."

"I'm planning on being an A and B+ student when I go to college."

"I'm glad to hear that you think positive and set goals for yourself."

"Well, guys, I hate to break up the conversation, but it is time for Jeff to get ready for bed."

"Alright. Good night, Mom. Good night, Mr. Derek, and thanks for the pizza and ice cream."

"Good night Jeff, I had fun and we will do it again."

"Okay, Mr. Derek."

"I'm going to head home myself because I have to get up early for work tomorrow."

"Yeah, I'm getting that tired feeling myself, Derek."

"Good night, Donna,"

"Good night, Derek."

While driving home for some mysterious reason the conversation we had while eating pizza stuck in my head. I could not believe that someone who wants their child to attend college does not invest time assisting their child with improving in their academics. It hurt me to know that there was something lacking in Jeff's life and the person who's responsible for him is not being real with him. Then again how could she be real with him when she is not being real to herself? Jeff does not have a positive role model in his life. I wonder what type of lifestyle Donna modeled for him. It seems as if Donna was more concerned with meeting her own needs then meeting Jeff's needs. It seems as if she puts him second, and he probably learns from other people or his environment. The sad thing about this is that I had met with several Jeff's for a living. Maybe this is why I'm so compassionate about the dynamics of this situation.

Donna invited me to go on vacation with her and Jeff to visit her parents, who live in the South. At first I was a little hesitant, but then I said yes, why not? I needed to get away. This also was as an opportunity for me to learn more about Donna and her family dynamics. It was 5:00 in the morning, and my phone was ringing. I was wondering who would be calling me at this time of morning. I rolled over and looked at the caller ID; it was Donna. I'm thought something must be wrong. "Hello, Donna, is everything alright?"

"Oh, everything is fine; I'm calling to see if you're up so we don't miss our flight."

"Our flight does not leave until 9:45 am, which is over 4 hours away, which means I have at least another hour or two to sleep."

"I'm excited and cannot wait to go see my parents."

"I'm glad you're excited and ready to go. So why don't you hang up, so I can get up soon and get myself together."

"Alright, I'm sorry for waking you up so early."

"I'm going to lay here and get another hour of sleep before getting up." When I finally did get up and got myself together. I picked Donna and Jeff up. We drove to the airport to catch our flight. I was in a calm and relaxed state of mind. Donna was still excited as if she had too much coffee. Jeff was excited about seeing his grandparents as well. It was a three-hour flight before we arrived at our destination.

When we arrived at our destination, Donna's mother was there to pick us up. Her mother presented herself as a down-to-earth and open-minded woman. Donna resembles her mother, but Donna's personality and character comes from a different species. "Hey Mom, where is Dad?"

"He went to the store to pick up a few things for the house. He will be at the house by the time we get there."

"Mom, this is Derek."

"Hello Derek, it's nice to finally meet you. I have heard a lot of nice things about you."

"Thank you, ma'am, and it's nice to meet you." Donna's mother drove us back to her home, which was a very nice home. As we pulled up into the driveway, Donna's father was standing outside as if he was anticipating our arrival. "Hello, Dad."

"That's all I get is a Hello Dad? No hug or kiss? I bet I could get more than that from your friend there. What's your name young man?"

"Derek, sir."

"So, Derek, you would greet me with more than a hello?"

"Well sir I could greet you with a hello, a solid hand shake, and a brotherly hug."

"At least I know you are not afraid to show me some love."

"Oh Daddy, stop it you know I'm going to give you a hug and kiss because you are my favorite Daddy."

"Why? Do you have another Daddy I need to know about?"

I laughed, "Don't laugh, Derek; that only encourages him. Dad, stop saying things like that in front of Derek before he thinks something is wrong with us."

"No, it perfectly fine; you're family. I enjoy your father's humorous personality."

"See he's fine and he likes me. Derek, you will never guess what she asked of her mother and me."

"What did she ask of you?"

"She wanted us to pretend to be a fairytale-like family for you."

"Daddy, stop; that's not true."

"Donna, it's okay, Derek is comfortable with us as we are. He knows I'm only joking." "Hey little man, I didn't forget about you."

"Hello, Grandpa."

"Jeff, how are doing?"

"I'm doing very well."

"That's what Grandpa likes to hear. Doing well in school; keeping your grades up?"

"I'm doing better, Grandpa."

"You wouldn't lie to your grandpa, would you?"

"No sir."

"You know Grandpa has one of those hearts that cannot handle lies, especially from his favorite grandson."

"Grandpa, I'm your only grandson."

"See; that's why you're my favorite."

"Donna, your mother and I are going to take all of you out to dinner tonight."

"That sounds good to me."

Later that evening when we returned home from dinner, we were in the living room talking. Donna's parents are generous, caring, and giving people. They treated us to dinner, made sure that our basic needs were met, showed great hospitality, opening their home up to me and making me feel right at home. They shared with me stories about Donna growing up as a child. Donna's mother loved to laugh and was very energetic woman filled with life. One thing that I noticed was that when Donna's mother was not happy about something she would let you know. Her father had a good sense of humor and likes to joke. There were times that Jeff demonstrated some behaviors that Donna would not address.

Her mother would look at her and say, "No, no, no; if he was living with me he would not be getting away with any of this nonsense."

Donna's father said, "Jeff, if you were living with me, you would not behave and talk the way you do at times. You're a good person; try to be that way, always." He would correct Jeff with an explanation. Jeff would apologize for his behavior.

One morning after breakfast, Donna's mother told her that they're willing to keep Jeff for a week when we return home. Donna's father said, "We would like to give you a break. Besides we're planning to visit family, and Jeff could come back with your sister. She said she's planning to visit you after we leave her house. We already spoke with her and made all the necessary arrangements."

"Thanks Mom and Dad; this is great of you."

"We are very happy to see our grandson and we love him," said her mother.

The week went by fast, and Jeff was home with his mother. Donna shared with me that she and her sister were talking. Her sister shared with Donna that Jeff had demonstrated some disappointing behaviors towards his grandparents. Jeff was very disrespectful towards his grandmother. Donna's sister shared with her, "One day Jeff was given a directive by

Mom and refused to follow her directives. Mom said to Jeff, "If you are not going to do what you're told, I'm going to beat you with this belt. "Jeff replied, "You are not going to beat anybody with that belt."

"Where was Dad when all this was going on?"

"Well, let me finish. Dad was in the other room and heard everything. He entered the room and said, "I cannot believe what I am hearing. You are talking this way towards your grandmother. We love you, Jeff, and there is nothing we would ever do or say to hurt you. There is no reason in the world for you to be blatantly disrespectful towards us."

"You know, Sis, that if you or I did something like that we would have gotten our butt whipped."

"Oh, Jeff did not get off that easy. Dad did whip his butt. He also had him doing all kinds of work around the house. What could have been a pleasant vacation for Jeff turned out to be a learning vacation."

"You know, Sis, sometimes I just don't know what to do about the decisions he makes. I think he is angry about not having his father around. I'm also concerned that this is going to push Derek away."

"Don't think that way. Derek does not seem like the kind of man that would distance himself because of Jeff."

"I guess you may be right. He is a wonderful man, and he shows an interest in Jeff."

"Who you need to be worrying about, Donna, is Mom. She is very hurt and upset by Jeff's defiant behavior. She just could not believe he would display that kind of rude and disrespectful behavior towards her." Later that day after hearing what took place with Jeff and his grandparents. I stopped by to visit after work.

"Hello, Derek."

"Donna, do you mind if I spent some time with Jeff alone to talk."

"No, I don't mind at all."

Jeff and I went to get ice cream. We sat and talked about respect while eating our ice cream. "I heard what happened between you and your grandparents. Were you feeling unhappy about something?"

"No,"

"Did someone do something to you that you didn't like or made you feel uncomfortable?"

"No,"

"You are a smart young man Jeff, and since I've been around you. I know you know how to be respectful of people, you should always respect your grandparents. If it were not for your grandparents you would not be here today having this ice cream."

"Mr. Derek, what do you mean by that?"

"Well, Jeff, let me give you a short and quick history lesson on mothers and grandmothers of the past, also known as Big Mama."

"No more Big Mama's exist today, do they, Mr. Derek?"

"Unfortunately no, not too many mothers and grandmothers today are like my mother and your grandmother. Anyway, Jeff, a grandmother or Big Mama is someone you should always respect. They're the foundation for raising children and the glue for keeping families together. Grandmothers are the ones you can count on when everyone else turns their back on you. They're right there, waiting, arms open wide, and ready to take you in anytime. Big Mama will be there for you when your friends are nowhere to be found. They will always love you no matter what you do or going through. Jeff, has your grandmother ever done anything or said anything to you that hurt you or made you feel bad?"

"No, she and my grandfather have always been good to me."

"You are a smart young man. What do you think my next question is going to be?"

"Why did I talk the way I did to my grandmother and treat her bad?"

"Yes! Those were the questions I was going to ask. I told you that you were smart."

"I don't know."

I believed him because I feel Jeff was just displaying behaviors that he observed and how he probably has been treated throughout the course of his life. Derek looked at Jeff and said, "You and I have something in common."

"What is that?"

"I only knew my grandparents on my mother's side. I never had the opportunity to get to know my father's parents because they died before I was born. Jeff, you are a good person. You just missed out on something that other kids had the opportunity to experience, but it comes in other ways. I'm going to be honest with you. I know some of your frustration and defiant behavior comes from not having a healthy relationship with your father. I know that not having a strong relationship with your father does not help. Do you see your father much?"

"He shows up once in a while, and when he does, we only spend a couple hours together. The last time I saw my father was probably a month ago. He and my mother do not speak, and sometimes I feel it's because of me. I hate my life and wish I was never born."

"Whoa whoa, whoa! You should never think or speak that way of yourself, *ever*! You hear me, Jeff?"

"Yes, I hear you."

"You were born for a reason and purpose. Only God knows your purpose, but as you grow and mature and stay on the right path, you will discover your purpose. Life is about who you are, not what you are."

"Later that night Donna asked, "What were you and Jeff talking about?"

"We talked about respect of other people, especially his grandparents. We talked about his relationship with his father."

"His dad is barely around and does very little to help support Jeff. I get child support, but that is much of nothing, and sometimes it is nothing because Jeff's father cannot keep a job."

"I hope I'm not making you feel uncomfortable about talking about Jeff's father."

"To be honest, Derek, I'm ashamed and embarrassed to talk about Jeff's father. I do get angry for allowing myself to get pregnant by him."

"I'm being sincere when I ask about Jeff's father. What is going on with his father?"

"What do you mean?"

"I mean is his father involved in his life?"

"You mean Martin."

"Is this the name of Jeff's father?"

"Yes, I call him Martin because he is not a father."

"Martin is in and out of Jeff's life. Martin comes around now and then. He is not consistent and does not invest any quality time with Jeff. I believe this is why Jeff behaves the way he does at times. Jeff is a wonderful son; he is good in school. He is well liked, by his teachers and peers."

"Have you ever sat down with Jeff's father, I mean Martin about Jeff's unusual behavior."

"I tried to talk with Martin about a lot of things, but he just ignores me and walks away. Martin is more interested in being on the streets, selling drugs, and this is something I do not want to expose Jeff to. I do not want Jeff to grow up thinking that selling drugs is the way of life. Don't get me wrong, Martin and I had a good relationship once upon a time, but he changed. He decided he did not want to work anymore and started hanging with some of his old friends that were always up to, no good. Next thing I knew, he was selling drugs while we were together. This eventually caught up with him and his friends, resulting in Martin spending time in prison. He would write me letters while in prison, asking if Jeff and I would come visit him. I was not about to bring Jeff to a prison to visit his father. If he wanted to be with Jeff, he would not have chosen selling drugs, and hanging with his friends over Jeff. It's not like we were hurting for money, and if we were, it still didn't make it right. Derek, if Martin did not make the choices he did to end up in prison, he would not have to worry about his relationship with Jeff."

"So, did Jeff ever write Martin? Did Martin ever write Jeff?"

"No, they did not write each other."

"Did Jeff know that his father was in prison?"

"He knew his father was in prison but did not know why he was in prison. Once Martin was released from prison, he was different. I was different. I had matured and invested more time into my spiritual life. I'm cordial and polite with Martin when he stops by the house to spend time with Jeff."

"Do you and Martin talk at all?"

"To be honest, it's pretty much 'Hello. How are you doing?' Nothing more or less; he is not reliable, and visits sporadically, so I do not entertain or engage in any real conversation about Jeff."

"Do you think if you shared more with Martin, he might be more willing to make himself available?"

"I don't know."

"My point exactly, you don't know, if you at least made the attempt you would know the outcome. If Martin did not show anything different at least on your end you could say you tried."

"I guess I have not tried because Martin hurt me, and I'm still angry."

Quality Time

———————◆———————

There's nothing like spending time with Mom and enjoying her wonderful cooking, and there's nothing like Mom's Sunday dinner. Kim and I look forward to Sundays. I invited Donna and Jeff to join us on this one particular Sunday. My family greeted Donna and Jeff with open arms. "Hello, Donna. I am Derek's mother—welcome."

"Thanks for having us, and this is my son Jeff."

"Hello, Jeff, and welcome. You make yourself right at home." My sisters were setting the table when we arrived. My brothers-in-law were watching the basketball game. I peeked in the kitchen and saw that the food was ready.

As my sisters were preparing the table, I said, "I am right on time."

My mother responded, "Yes you are; now go and get the extra chairs for the dinner table out of the living room."

"Sure Mom; what's for dinner?"

"Food, Derek, go and get the chairs and when you are sitting at the table, you can see what's for dinner."

"Hey, Sis?"

"Yes, Derek."

"Why is it that the good-looking one in the family is always treated unfairly?"

"You want to know something else, Derek?"

"What's that, Sis?"

"If you do not go and get those chairs you are going to be the hungry-looking one in the family."

"Wow! It's like that; can't a brother get some love?"

"I know a brother who better go and get those chairs."

"Alright I'm going."

"Now that we are all at the table I would like to thank the good-looking one of the family for getting the chairs."

"You're welcome, Mom."

"I am also going to ask the good-looking one of the family to bless the food."

"That's must be me," said Jeff. We all laughed.

"I mean the other good-looking one, and thank you, Jeff," said Mom.

I blessed the food, and dinner was served. The table was covered with everything from macaroni and cheese, baked chicken, rice, vegetables, rolls, yams, roast beef, and a lot of other good food. Even though we were months away from Thanksgiving, the variety of food made it seem like it was.

After dinner was over and all the cleaning had been done, my sisters and brothers-in-law were getting themselves together, preparing to go home. Kim and Jeff were sitting in the living room, watching television and talking. Donna went into the living room and joined in their conversation. Meeting for the first time, Donna and Kim seemed to interact well. I went into the kitchen to talk with my mother.

"Are you doing well, Derek?"

"Yes, how are you feeling these days, Mom?"

"I'm doing very well. I talked to your brother the other day."

"How's Pete doing? I have not heard anything about him recently."

"He said he's doing well."

"You know, Mom, I don't understand. Pete is an intelligent man who never had a problem getting a job. He used to take very good care of himself. He was married to a beautiful wife and had three lovely children. Yes, I know the drugs and alcohol were major contributors. Unfortunately, he allowed drugs and alcohol to take over his life. Then he started committing crimes, going in and out of jail. It seems as if all of this erupted when his best friend Bruce died."

"Yes, I know Derek, he still needs the support and love from his family."

"A family that was always bailing him out of jail, visiting him, and giving him money when he was in need. This is an ongoing problem for Pete, and some of the family is getting tired of him calling when he's in trouble and looking for money. You were constantly there for him, Mom, and he would just take advantage of you."

"I must say, Derek, like the rest of the family, my patience is getting very thin and I'm becoming weary."

"While we talk, can I help myself to some of your delicious sweet potato pie?"

"Go right ahead, Derek."

"Thank you. You keep on complaining about the things Pete continues to do. I know Pete is your son and my brother; you and dad raised him no differently then you raised the rest of us. We were taught to be responsible, right from wrong, and being careful about the choices we make in life."

"I know Derek; I just don't understand why he continues to do these things. It's as if he never learned from his mistakes, especially when they're the same mistakes."

"We all make mistakes in our lives, and we are going to continue to make mistakes, but what's important is not that we just learn from our mistakes but how we come up out of our mistakes is just as important."

"Derek, I want you to remember that making mistakes does not make you a failure."

"I know, Mom."

"I don't want Pete living on the streets. I just want to know he is safe."

"Pete is a forty-five-year-old man, Mom. He made a choice to live the life he is living. This is not how his life started as a child. You and Dad did not use drugs, drink any alcoholic beverages, or smoke. The both of you worked to keep food on the table, clothes on our backs, and a roof over our heads. You would buy us things that we wanted even if you did not have the money just to see us happy. As a parent I understand, I truly see and understand the sacrifices you and Dad made for us. I understand there comes a time in your child's life where you must be there for emotional support and guidance, but you must also be realistic and say to yourself, I must now let go even though it's hard. Pete has to start helping himself before anyone else can help him. Mom, like you always told me, you can lead a horse to water, but it does not mean the horse is going to drink. Even though Pete still goes through his trials and tribulations, he still has a supportive, loving, and caring family that he can spend time with whenever he chooses."

"Yes, I understand and now he's in prison for a good amount of time. He's doing more time than some people do for murder."

"Mom, Pete is in prison for the choices he made. Unfortunately, we live in a country with a disappointing and dysfunctional government as well as a dysfunctional judicial system. There are people who have killed other people and gotten less time than someone selling drugs. Hey, we know selling drugs is wrong, but we also know drinking and driving drunk is wrong, too. I always ask this question, Mom: Why our government allows drugs to filter into this country with all the high technology equipment they have? The government can zone in on anything they want when it's for their convenience. They can zone in and watch people change their clothes and even tell what size underwear they wear."

Mom laughed, "You are silly, Derek."

"You laugh, but you know this is true; they should know what is coming into our country with all this high-tech security at ports and in other countries. You mean to tell me they know nothing? Then they think they have done something when they take a few people off the streets with a large or small quantity of drugs. They have not even put a dent in what has already entered our country and what still remains to enter our country. These guys on the streets are just pawns. When our government is willing to address the true root of suppliers and how drugs are entering in our country, then they can say checkmate, game is over. The people on the streets do not have opium plants growing in their yards. Our government does not seem to have its priorities in order. This drug issue appears to be more like a big business; it's all about the money. Its greed; it's about how much money they can fill their pockets and bank accounts with. This makes our government the true kingpins."

"Slow down, Derek; take it easy. You are getting very upset. We as people have to be strong and resist the temptation of using and selling drugs."

I looked at my mother and said, "It is not that I am upset; I am saddened and disappointed, knowing that we live in a dysfunctional society and it does not matter who is president or what politician is in office. There is nobody in any political or law enforcement office who is truly willing to attack this problem. It does not feel as if the decisions they make are in the best interest of the people. They would rather waste our tax dollars on a billion-dollar aircraft, cloning, and the dumb beetle, which does not serve any purpose. You or I will never ride in these aircrafts or spend money on cloning. In my opinion, Mom, our government is just a legal and legitimate hood with educated and proper-speaking suits with money. The other day I was watching the news, and they reported that this guy killed this man and burned the body. He told the police where the body was and was given only ten years. He literally took a life and destroyed the body in the worse way, imaginable. That person was a life that cannot be brought back or rehabilitated, the family members will not see this person ever again, and this person did not have a choice to say no. We even have some doctors selling drugs; they're only licensed drug dealers. Then we have male and female teachers taking advantage of young boys and girls. They do not get much time for violating a child for this matter. Most female teachers are only given a slap on the wrist. Hey, statutory rape is statutory rape. You know what makes this funny?"

"What?"

"The constitution states that all men are created equal but forgets to mention that some men are created more equal than others."

"All I ask of you, Derek, is that you just make an effort to keep in touch with your brother. Just so that he knows you are thinking of him. This may assist him with getting through the time he has to serve."

"I usually write him a letter or send him a card of inspiration. I sent him a book."

"What kind of book?"

"An inspirational book of encouragement, the title of the book is *What Are You Waiting For*? Pete wrote me and told me he was going through a new transition in his life. I felt the book would inspire him in his new transition. He sent me a letter with a positive attitude and focused mindset."

Here is the letter he sent me.

Hey Derek, How are you doing? I hope fine. I'm doing okay. I was a little down for a while, but I got through it. What really helped me was the book you sent. I received it early this week, and when I started reading it, I gained a great amount of insight about a lot of things that I must address. The funny thing about the book is that a lot of the things that the author points out have crossed my mind. I'm a prime example of one who procrastinates. I've wasted too much of my life, but that's neither here nor there. It's time to close that chapter and start a new one. It's time for me to be a true survivor and not a street survivor. I feel that I now have the proper attitude and open mind in order for me to succeed. I was definitely waiting, for what I don't have a clue. I know one thing for sure, I refuse to lose my self-unity. You know something, I feel funny inside. It's not a bad feeling; it's sort of peaceful like. You know what I mean? It's weird; I've never felt like this before. When I read the book, I took my time not to rush through it to feel what the author is saying. I read a chapter a week for understanding and meditation. I have internalized it. You know the one thing I can honestly say is that through all my trials and tribulations, I never lost my spirituality. Even though I knew I was doing something wrong, I always had the feeling God was watching me. God was always on my mind, and it frightened me. I guess that was His way of watching over me until I came to my senses. I swear that every time I was among the wrong people or sold drugs, He would pop up in my mind and that disturbed me. I know that He has plans for me. He kept me around for a reason. I'm blessed and very grateful; I took life for granted. I thank you to for helping me. I was stumbling along, and you helped clarify what I wasn't seeing clearly. I love you, Derek. I love each and every one of my family members. Anyone else would have given up on me, kicked me to the curb, but all of you stuck by me. By reading this book I find it much easier to deal with situations that I created. Something I never took a look at was my emotional side: the anger, confusion, and depression. That is a very important piece for me. That was a major problem for me. I tended to let my emotions get the best of me, but not anymore. My emotions have been getting the best of me for a great many years. I told myself that as long as I maintain a positive attitude, keep an open mind, and take control of my emotions I would be just fine. With the mindset that I have now, I feel invincible; I feel fabulous. I feel so good that it's unexplainable. I'm at peace with myself. You really helped open my eyes and mind. Well I've got to go, but I'll be in touch. Love, your big brother Pete.

"It's nice of you to still keep in touch with your brother."

"Well, Mom, I just hope and pray Pete examines himself and starts putting the pieces of his life back in order. Wow! It's getting late and we should be getting ready to go. Let me see what those guys are up to in the other room."

"Derek,"

"Yes, Mom,"

"I want to tell you Donna is a nice and beautiful-looking woman."

"Thank you and your sweet potato pies taste great, as always."

"Is Kim still going to stay with me tonight?"

"Yes, I am Grandma."

"Well, Donna, you're home, Have a good night, Jeff."

"You have a good night, too, Mr. Derek."

"So, are you going to spend a little time with me before going home?"

"Yes I will visit with you for a little while. I know I spent a lot of time talking with my mother."

"That's fine besides I was sleeping. I can see that Kim is Daddy's little girl."

"Yes she is. Kim and I invest time with each other, whether it was going to the movies, shopping, amusement parks, or spending time with family. We spend quality time together watching videos, playing video games, going out to eat, doing schoolwork together, or just talking. To be honest there are times I wished her mother and I were more mature when Kim was born. Every child deserves the opportunity of living with both their parents in the same household. Regardless of the situation, all kids want both parents in their life or to be together as a family."

"I can relate to what you are saying, Derek. There are times I would reflect on when Jeff's father was in our lives. Jeff was happy. Now it just seems to get harder by the day since his father is no longer around and shows up only sporadically. What hurts the most is that I wonder if Jeff will ever get through his pain. I know it was difficult for me, but I got through it."

"Unfortunately, as adults, when we go through breakups, separations, or divorce, the children will suffer more than anyone else in the relationship. As adults we go on with our life by entertaining new relationships, making ourselves happy, but failing to take in consideration the happiness of our children, who truly suffer, as you go on with your life. This is why it is so important that when a couple is together that they are mature and responsible to discuss the children and be true to themselves and their situation."

"This I know too well; you don't have to tell me, been there and done that. Jeff keeps me so busy that I sacrifice so much for his happiness. I'm waiting for the day when he is old enough to be independent, so I can start doing some of the things I desire. There were times I would go back and forth about having another child, but the truth is that I do not have the energy. I also need to work on some personal areas of my life, especially my career. The areas that I must work on will not benefit just me. I'm always thinking how it will benefit Jeff."

"I know what you mean; I believe it is important that we are able to give our children the attention they deserve. My daughter is a bright and beautiful young lady. I love having the opportunity to watch her grow, and especially being part of her life. Someday it will all gradually end, because she will become more independent, which will be a good thing. Then she will be off to college and entering adulthood. Yes, we even have our moments of debates and disagreement. We talked about her feelings regarding her mother and how she feels about her mother and me not being together. I'm pleased and happy that Kim and I have such a great relationship. I'm very happy she has a great relationship with her grandparents, aunts, uncles, and cousins. She's well connected to her family. At the same time I understand her pain. It hurts me just knowing that she's not happy, especially in an area of her life she deserves to be happy."

"It's just not fair to them, Derek."

"No it's not; they have to suffer because of the mistakes and choices we make as adults. It's not just our kids; it's all kids that have to go through this experience."

"You know Derek, I never thought about that with Jeff."

"Thought about what, Donna?"

"The importance of Jeff's relationship with family and relatives, his relationship with his father is not all that great and that bothers me."

"If you think it bothers you, just imagine how Jeff feels. Well, it's getting late, and I have a long day tomorrow. I should be heading home."

"Thanks for visiting with me."

"Not a problem and I will talk with you tomorrow."

I worked as a counselor for this camp. I enrolled my daughter so we could spend more time together. I saw this as a great opportunity for us to spend the whole summer together. Getting up every morning, preparing lunches, and getting ready for our day was a special time for me. Driving to camp together allows us to have one-on-one time. Even though she was not assigned to my group, we still had fun. She was listening to music with the other campers and counselors and, getting to see her father act silly and have fun. When not at camp, I washed her hair and took her to have it braided, which I found to be an enjoyable and interesting experience. Kim would say, "Dad, you are all right for my dad and all."

"What do mean that I am all right?"

"Yeah, you're all right, because I have some friends who are boys, and their dads do not spend time with them the way you do with me. The time we spend together, the special things you do, are just as special for me as they are for you."

"Well Kim, I must invest spending this time with you now. There will be another phase in life when you are all grown up, and you will not have time to spend with your old dad."

"Not true, I will always have time for you no matter how old you get; besides, you are old now."

"Hey, I may be old, but one thing I want the both of us to do."

"What's that?"

"I would like us to be able to share special moments together, have good memories of the things we shared together, so we could look back and laugh. Remember, that life is not always about how much we do, or how much time we spend together, it's about the quality of time we spend together."

"What do you mean, Dad?"

"Spending quality time with someone is a way of showing a special kind of compassion—showing a special quality of care, attention, respect, consideration, time, and love."

"Is this something we do with all people we are close with, like family and close friends?"

"No, this is not always done with the people we are close to, Kim. For most people, it's a lot easier to express their true feelings, care, and love for their child, than for most people to share with another adult."

"So, are you saying that it's a lot more difficult for you to talk to other adults, Dad?"

Laughing, "No, Kim, that is not what I am saying. As time goes on, you will learn that with some adults it is challenging just to find the right words to express yourself, without sounding as if you are offending that person. The words we use, and what we say, could make a world of difference in our relationship with people."

"Dad,"

"Yes Kim,"

"I love you,"

"And Daddy loves Kim."

Kim laughed and said, "You are silly at times."

"I may act silly, but I do love you Kim. We do not tell one another that we love each other every day, but we do express how we feel and love one another in other ways."

"What are some of those ways?"

"Sometimes this is done by giving a special card that says it for you."

"What kind of card are you talking about?"

"For example, the card you gave me on Father's Day. I do not know who wrote the card but it said:

[set as extract]A good father is one that gives his children the freedom to be themselves and inspires them to strive for their highest and best. You may not get your share of praise for all the things you do, but I hope you know you're loved a lot by all those close to you, and hope you know that everyday you're wished the very best of all the special things in life that make you happiest.[end extract]

"Yes, that is a special card. When I read it, I just felt everything inside the card spoke of you, and it felt right for you."

"This is what I mean: some people don't express themselves well with their own words, but rather in other ways."

"Can I share something with you, Dad?"

"Sure, what is it?"

"You're the best, and I love you."

Donna and I were out having dinner. While eating my salad, I had this feeling that somebody was watching me. Before lifting my head and making eye contact I said, "Something wrong? Is your salad okay?"

"My salad is fine, but something is wrong. I mean, nothing is wrong; there's just something I want to tell you."

"Then share with me, what's on your mind?"

"Do you remember that day when you were with your daughter, and I started acting like I had an attitude."

"Yes, what's the problem?"

"There's no problem; it's just something that I have to get over. I was feeling jealous of your relationship with your daughter. I never had a relationship like that with my dad, and I wish I did. My father was not there for me like you are with Kim. I'm just jealous of the relationship. It's nothing you are doing wrong. I just wish ..." Donna became silent.

"What is it that you wish?"

"That I had the bond and experience Kim has with her father."

"I'm not completely following you."

"What I mean is that, when I was growing up I wish I had a special bond with my father."

"I will always do special things for my daughter because she will always be my little girl, no matter how old she gets."

"I know that. When I see the both of you together it just makes me realize how much I missed in my childhood with my father."

"I hope the things I do don't trigger unpleasant memories."

"No, that's not it at all, when I'm with you I feel good and at peace."

"To be honest, Donna, I could tell that you had tough and unpleasant experiences. This is an area of your life you're going to have to strengthen, and this is only going to happen when you start putting in the work."

"This is true and there are some things I have not gotten over."

"Stand back! I'm going to shock you."

"What are you talking about?"

"Well, I know this is going to be hard for you to believe, but even I, Derek Johnson, have been through some challenging times. I know what it's like to be down in the valley, but I also am aware of what I must do to get back up on that mountaintop. Besides I'm not your past. The people you had unpleasant encounters with are not me. So every time I do something for you, and if you look at me as if I'm part of your past, this relationship is not going to work. I'm willing to be here for you in any way I can, but I cannot answer for the things that are going on in you. If there are unresolved issues dwelling inside you, you need to start dealing with them now." Donna sat in silence and so did I. I reached across the table and took Donna's hand. "I'm going to be honest with you about a thought I have."

"Okay, what is it?"

"For a moment I had the thought of reevaluating our relationship to being strictly friends. Then there is that part of me that loves and cares for you. You're a special person with a good heart with good intentions."

"Just to hear that from you means a lot to me. Thank you, Derek. It makes me feel good and appreciated."

"Well that is how you should feel. This is why I have the type of relationship with my daughter. I treat her in a special way. I want her to know how a man should treat a woman. I tell Kim that the way I treat you is the way you should expect a man to treat you. I tell her that I'm your father. I do not put my hands on you. You should never allow a man to raise his hand to you or even attempt to hit you. She will be able say to any man that you have to be able to at least treat me the way my father treats me. This is why I feel it is important for men to spend time with their children whether they live in the same household or not. Our children today need guidance and protection. They need to be shaped and molded in how to be treated as young men and women who know how a man and woman should treat one another, and how a man and woman should conduct themselves, at all times."

"Kim has a very special father. I do struggle at times with my past. I have not been through a lot. It's just that what I have been through, is just enough to bring some discomfort within me at times. It makes me question people's intentions, and if they truly love you in the way God expects us to love one another."

"If you do not mind, may I share something with you?"

"Sure, go right ahead,"

"Well, Donna, whenever I go through something or whatever I've been through. I know that God works in our lives to let us know we are cared for. This I view as love becoming a mixed up and confusing word with little meaning."

"I'm not following you. What do you mean?"

"People are confused about love, and that love is the greatest quality among people. Love is all about God. No one is ever going to be perfect, so we must learn to accept and love others in spite of their faults. When we see fault in others we should be kind, patient, and gentle; unfortunately this is a challenge most of us face because we're really self-centered and not Christ centered. Keeping this in mind, we have to set boundaries to be effective in this area of our life. We should not allow ourselves to be responsible for others' decisions. But also in life when dealing with people, there are some do's and don'ts, which could alter a relationship and either make it or break it."

Donna sighed and said, "I did not mean anything by how I reacted, and I also did not mean anything about what I shared about my past experiences. Those things are not there anymore, and I have moved on. Just the father and daughter thing gets to me. I want you to know that I never go backwards, Derek."

"Sometimes we must look back in order to get things right in the present or at least not to repeat our past. When we go back it's because sometimes there are things, circumstances, or people that we must go back and face in order to make the present the way God intended it to be for you, while at the same time you may also be fulfilling your purpose in life. What do you think would have become of the prodigal son if he did not go back? He went back to make things right in his life in the way God has planned. He understood where he went wrong and asked for forgiveness. I'm sure the next time he ventured out, it would be different.

We should not allow pride or selfishness stop us from doing what God has planned for our lives. Now just imagine how things could have turned out if Moses did not keep going back to God, even though he did not want the responsibility he was called to. The Israelites would have never been lead to the Promised Land."

"I completely understand what you're saying."

"Just don't miss the forest for the trees, Donna. You don't want to be a person who's not able to let go because of your pride, putting you in a position to pass up opportunities." Donna was sitting with her head down. "How are you feeling, Donna?"

"I feel fine, and yes, I'm listening to what you're saying."

"Listening is good, my question to you is, do you hear me?"

She smiled and said, "You are so patient and understanding."

"It's not about me; it's about God, in how he uses me, and how he works in me."

It's New Year's Eve, and I invited Donna over for dinner, so the two of us could bring in the New Year together. "Hey, Donna, it's only 6:00 p.m. You're early for dinner."

"I wanted to get here a little early to assist you with dinner."

"Thank you for being so kind and considerate. I greatly appreciate you taking the initiative, and for being so thoughtful. For the record, let the wonderful aroma show that I have dinner all under control. All I will ask of you is to have a seat in the living room and enjoy this glass of wine. So now, go and relax, listen to the music, and enjoy the beautiful bouquet of flowers."

"Since you insist, I guess that's what I will do."

"Yes, I do insist, and since the food is almost done I will join you."

"Have you ever heard that the person you spend New Year with might be the person you could spend the rest of your life with?"

"No, I have not, Donna, but I do find that to be interesting. Are you trying to tell me something?" Derek laughs.

"No, I did not mean anything by it. I was just making conversation, and I find that to be an interesting statement."

"Yes, I find it to be very interesting myself. I think the food should be done. Are you ready to eat?"

"Yes, I'm hungry."

"Well then let's go sit. The table is prepared; it's only missing the food and you."

"Wow! This looks great. Wow! I'm impressed."

"I'm glad to get two Wows of approval from you. It's nice to know that I'm making a good impression, but you should not be impressed. Just put this in your photographic memory and mental rolodex that I have romantic qualities. I can cook, be considerate, and show great hospitality. Most importantly I'm able to Wow you!"

"I sure will, if the food tastes as good as the looks of the table and the ambiance of the room. I will put this into my memory video display to play over and over again."

"Okay, Ms. Food and Ambiance critic. Let's eat before the food gets cold. I don't want that to be part of your review."

"Will you bless the food, Derek?"

"Lord, we give thanks for the food we're about to receive, that the meal you provide to us will nourish and strength our body. I pray for those who are less fortunate than us and that you will provide and guide them to place of comfort. Father, this I ask in the name of Jesus, Amen. Donna, are you okay?"

"What makes you ask?"

"Well, when I looked across the table you appeared to be in deep thought."

"Yes, I'm all right. I was just thinking about all the time we've spent together over the years. There were times I thought you and I would not make it this far."

"To be honest, sometimes I thought the same thing. It takes a lot for me to lose interest."

"Wow! Dinner tastes great."

"I'm glad it passed your taste test and got your Wow of approval, so dinner must be good."

"No seriously, this is really good, but what type of things would make you lose interest in a relationship?"

"I guess something that is traumatic: a lack of trust, betrayal, abuse ... it's hard to say because I have not experienced anything in a relationship that had any sort of mental or emotional impact on me."

"Would you immediately abandon the relationship or try and work things out?"

"Some things are hard to answer, Donna, because every situation is different. I mean, I can say one thing now, but if I'm actually in an unhealthy relationship I may respond differently. If we're working together, being supportive of one another, we'll have to pray that everything will be fine and seek counseling. We can continue the conversation while I clear the table."

"Let me help with the dishes."

"You don't have to there is not much for me to clean."

"I still want to help. I will wash the dishes while you put the food away. We will get the job done quicker, and then we can relax."

"Thanks for helping with cleaning up, now would you like to go into the living room?"

"Sounds like a plan to me. What time is it, Derek?"

"Well from my clock on the wall the time is 10:55 p.m. Why did you ask?"

"I was thinking that we could watch some of the New Year's Eve show."

"Sounds good to me; then we will not miss the coming in of the New Year. Let me turn off the music and turn on the television."

"Do you watch the New Year celebration shows, Derek?"

"Yes and no, what I mean it depends on where I'm at and what I'm doing. Donna ..."

"Yes, Derek,"

"There is something I would like to share with you."

"What is it you want to share with me?"

I looked into Donna's eyes and said, "I want you to know that I love you and respect you as a woman, as a woman should be respected and treated. I know we have our differences at times. I know that you don't have everything together in your life in the way you would like it to be, then again none of us do. I would be greatly honored if you would allow me to assist you with that part of your life."

"What do you mean and in what way?"

As I got down on one knee, I pulled a ring out of my pocket. "Would you be willing to share your life with me? Share cooking breakfast with me, and share my last name with me by being my wife?"

Donna looked at me with her mouth hanging open. It appeared that her mouth was moving, but no words were coming out. She then looked at the ring with a surprising look on her face and said, "Yes, yes, I would love to be your wife."

"Thank you for accepting my proposal."

"Wow! I was not expecting this. I mean, I did not even see it coming. Wow! I'm overwhelmed with excitement and joy."

"Listen, I know you have a good heart and that you mean well in all that you do. Life is challenging for all of us, Donna, whether we want to admit it or not."

"I'm still in amazement, and this ring is so beautiful."

"I'm pleased to know that you're satisfied with the ring."

"I'm more than satisfied. Can I share something with you?"

"Sure, Donna, what is it?"

"Just for the record, one of the most important things to me is trust. I'm not just saying this because of this moment. I feel trust is important in any type of relationship."

"I agree, and once the trust and respect is broken, it causes hurt and pain in the relationship. The relationship may never be the same. Realistically, Donna, no matter how much a person apologizes or comfort they provide—yes it may help to soften the blow and that person may get back on track and even start taking responsibility for their life again—it does not erase the memory or any other emotional scar that resulted from the incident that took place." As we sat taking it all in, we both heard the countdown as we were about to enter a New Year. We both started to count down with the clock, "10, 9, 8, 7, 6, 5, 4, 3, 2, 1: Happy New Year!" Donna and I hugged and kissed wishing one another a Happy New Year.

On New Year's Day, Donna and I called our families wishing them a Happy New Year and sharing with them our New Year commitment. I did the honorable, noble, and traditional thing by asking Donna's parents for her hand in marriage and their blessing. They were honored and pleased, giving us their blessing. "When does this end, Derek?"

"What are you talking about?"

"That was very special and respectful of you to ask my parents for their permission and blessing."

"This is about the respect I have for you and your parents. It's important to have their approval and blessing, knowing they accept our relationship. I never take for granted when I'm dating, that it necessarily means your parents approve of me or my parents approve of you. When you plan on marrying that person, you may hear the parent's true feelings about the person. What I like about your parents, Donna, is that they're down-to-earth people and keep it real with you."

"Yes, I do have great and wonderful parents."

"We are going to make mistakes. We are not perfect creatures. It's very important that we have a strong relationship with an openness to communicate. You look as if you're in thought, Donna."

"I'm still taking it all in. I also have things on my mind."

"What's on your mind?"

"Don't take this the wrong way, Derek. I believed that we will have a wonderful marriage. I also know that there will be hurdles and obstacle."

"Of course, Donna, I do expect us to have our challenges and ups and downs. For example, I know of your financial situation. I believe if we are disciplined and respectful of this relationship, we can get where we need to be in order to enjoy the beauty of marriage and have less concerns about our finances."

"I believe it's possible because I'm willing to give my all, no matter what, Derek."

"I know it can happen and more if we remain obedient. Be responsible, do things in an orderly fashion, and work together as one, not as individuals. There will be times when we will be tempted to get off course, but we will have to remember to be responsible and to keep one another on course, working as a team."

"Yes, I do agree, that keeping one another accountable is very important, especially if we want to maintain a positive and healthy relationship."

"We must not overlook communication, Donna. Communication is a key part of any relationship; communication will assist with having an effective relationship. I'm going to communicate something to you right now."

"Okay, communicate."

"I'm going to let you continue to call your friends and family, while I watch some football."

"Oh, I see; you're giving me a taste of what I have to look forward to?"

"Yeah, just a little taste, just as you are giving me a taste of how much time you spend on the phone."

"I'm only calling a few family members and some close friends, for your information."

"Then you're communicating to me that this is a woman thing."

"Oh, we have jokes now; when are you going to tell your friends?"

"I will tell them soon because some of them will be taking part in our wedding ceremony. I could see that this is a special time for you; I am glad to see you feel and look happy."

"You know something, Derek? I'm very happy."

"So am I."

"So Derek, do you want to pick a date for the wedding?"

"Whoa, slow your roll. First, let's enjoy this evening and this moment. Second, why don't we take our time and enjoy being engaged? We can gradually plan to get married in a year."

"Well, I was thinking six months."

"I'm not looking to rush this. Why don't we just enjoy the moment and besides it takes time to plan a wedding. We need more than six months, especially since we are paying for it. We do not have the money to make this happen in 6 months. You have to learn to be patient. Allow your heart to be led in the right direction, because the way you want to go about doing this, it's all about Donna."

"No, this is not true; I'm just so excited."

"Let's not miss the forest for the trees." She looked at me with this puzzled look on her face as if she did not know what I meant but would not ask me to explain. "Let me share something with you, Donna."

"Okay, go ahead."

"People tend to feel the need to rush things in order to get what they want, failing to realize that when they try to make something happen before its time, they could be setting themselves up for a disaster to occur. See, most people miss the abundance of joy in their life because they fail to realize that life is about stopping, enjoying, and embracing that special moment that takes your breath away."

"I must admit, I could get caught up in the moment and rush through it, Derek."

"Being able to appreciate and embrace that moment is a wonderful thing. People go through so much in their life just to make it from day to day. I went through my share of struggles just to be where I'm at today. I feel good about myself: my life and the accomplishments that I have made over the years. I do not have much, but what I do have is a lot."

"I completely understand, Derek. I continue to work on those areas of my life and others. I'm working on how to approach certain situations and circumstances. For some reason I get ahead of myself instead of enjoying those special moments, as you put it. Just to let you know: I am appreciative of you, all the other wonderful people God put into my life, and the things he gives me to make it from day to day."

"I'm very appreciative and thankful for what I do have and for what I don't have. There are nights, Donna, I would pray. I would lie in bed, and cry tears of joy for all that's God has done for me and for all that I know He will continue to do. All I ask of you is that you work with me as a team so that we're effective. It's not about being right or wrong; it's about togetherness. There are sacrifices that are going to have to be made, and we cannot be selfish and just think of ourselves."

"What are you talking about, Derek?"

"All the things I have and the things I do were not just for me, but also for whoever became a part of my life. If you're in this just for self-gratification or think that you don't have to work for anything, you may want to rethink about keeping that ring." I reached out and gently grabbed Donna's hand, looking at her and said, "What I say, and what I do, I mean well. It's done with love and respect for you and for us as a family. You and I are mature enough to know right from wrong. From your experiences and mine, there are some things we should not even entertain or allow to disrupt our mission and goals. Of course, there are areas in both of our lives that needs to be worked on. We have some financial problems, and this will be our first area of focus. Within a matter of time we will be house hunting."

"There is something I would like to discuss when you're done, Derek."

"Okay, I'm done; what it is you want to discuss?"

"I want to have a child. Do you want to have more children, Derek?"

"No, I understand where you're coming from in wanting to have that family connection thing in all. Having a child is not the answer. Why do you feel you would like to have another child?"

"I always thought that when I'm married, I would like to have a child."

"Donna, I have a child and you have a child. I do not think this is something you may want to entertain or jump right into. Both of us spent time in our life making so many sacrifices for our kids, and now that they are getting older. We are just starting to get our lives in order and building healthy relationships. We will be able to provide for them the way we always dreamed."

"I know what you mean, and I understand, Derek. I would like to provide and invest in Jeff's life differently. He deserves more than what I've been able to offer him."

"You know if we have another child within the first few years of this marriage, Donna, it will make things more challenging than they have to be. A lot would have to be sacrificed because having kids today is very challenging emotionally, mentally, physically, and financially. Personally, I do not want to go through every day of my life, worrying about another child's safety like I do with my daughter."

"Well, it seems as if your daughter turned out fine."

"Now, it has become a little easier because she is older and moving on in her life, but to start over with a baby ... this would be very stressful for the both of us. We live in a society in which safety is always a concern. I would worry about the child going to school and even going to the doctor. I do not want to worry every day that when I leave my house, about whether I will see my child again. Having and raising a child is hard, and you should know this from your own experience."

"I do know because Jeff's father is here, but not here, if you know what I mean. I just dream of having a child with both parents being together."

"There is nothing wrong with wanting that as part of your life. Just to let you in on a well-known secret, you could have that without having another child."

"What do you mean, Derek?"

"I know Jeff is not my biological son, and Kim is not your biological daughter. The four of us will have to learn how to become a family, a family that is comfortable with one another. This is a process in itself that takes time and patience. Answer this, Donna, what is it that you want in your life that you do not have?"

"There is a lot I desire; what would be first on my list is knowing that my son is taking care of, being debt free, having a house, and being able to travel."

"Being that our children are getting older, we are that much closer to doing those things and then some."

Donna looked at me and let out this long sigh as if she was unloading a breath of relief." You know Derek, I never looked at it in the way you explained it. I do agree with what you are saying; I have made some major sacrifices in my life."

"It would be great, Donna, to be able to do more without struggling. We're at a point in our lives that we are still young. Both of us experienced some things that we know we do not want to revisit. We want to grow and start meeting our own needs. It's a beautiful thing when you're able to share this with someone that wants to have an effective relationship that is in one accord."

"May I ask you a question, Derek?"

"Sure."

"I hear you use that word *effective* very often. I'm confused about how it applies to relationships."

"Well, let me share this with you. With an effective relationship comes communication, love, unity, sharing, caring, and a long-lasting relationship. This is how God wants us to be toward one another: helping our mate in a way that says I care for you and truly love you and not to do anything that will hurt one another that could have a tragic effect in the relationship."

"So, that's what being in an effective relationship is all about?"

I closed my eyes, looked up and took a deep breath and said, "Yes it is, Donna; yes it is."

A wedding date has been agreed upon and Donna was in full force. She was working on all the arrangements in order to make this happen. She was displaying true dedication and focus on this wedding. I admire her dedication and discipline in wanting to make this a beautiful and special day. I hope she put the same kind of effort into our marriage as the energy, focus, time, respect, consideration, and details that she was putting into planning this wedding. "Hello."

"Hello Derek, what are you doing?"

"Hi, Donna, nothing at the present time. Later this evening I'm taking Kim and one of her friends out to dinner. Do you need me for something?"

"I was thinking that it would be nice if we could go to this store and look at some items for the wedding."

"Sure, I can do this with you; it's still early. I have some time to spare." We arrived at the store, and Donna's level of excitement rose after viewing the different wedding items.

"What do you think of these as wedding favors?"

"We have to buy favors for people who are attending the wedding?"

"It's our way of showing appreciation to those who took time to celebrate our special occasion. They could take it home in remembrance of our special day."

"Yes, I know, Donna."

"You sound as if you do not have any interest in being here with me."

"Honestly, I would be lying if I said I'm interested. I'm not into this; this is not me. What I mean is this shopping and looking at wedding decorations."

"They're not decorations; they're called favors."

"Sorry, favors."

"Well, if this is how you felt, why did you come?"

"To spend time with you. Besides, I did not know if I would have any interest. I'm sorry; this is all new to me, and I'm starting to feel overwhelmed. There are just some things you don't know if you will like or not until you try it."

"I'm finished looking; let's go, Derek." Donna stopped what she was doing, left the item on the counter, and stormed out the store. I followed behind her as she walked at a very fast pace.

"Donna, Donna, Donna!"

"I hear you! What, Derek!"

"Can I have your attention for just a moment? I apologize if I said something that offended you; I was just being honest. This is what you're going to get from me." Donna stood next to the car not saying anything or acknowledging my presence. "Maybe we should not get married. The reason I'm not making a big deal about the wedding arrangements and plans ..."

I paused for a few seconds, and as I was about to finished my thought, she said, "So Derek, what is the reason you are not making a big deal about the wedding?"

"My reason is because our wedding day will come and go. When it's time to take on the real challenge, meaning the marriage, I hope you're able to display this same type of energy and focus. Weddings only last for a few hours; behold the untold truth: a marriage is supposed to last a life time."

"I guess it's different for a woman than for a man, Derek. This is a day that most women dream about. For women, planning the wedding becomes a big and special part of our lives."

"If you feel in your heart that this is not right, speak up now, and let's not waste any time. I will be all right, Donna."

"I'm sure you will be all right."

"What is with the attitude and sarcasm? Don't you realize that we are not going to share in the same interest in many other things?"

"I know we are going to have different interests, Derek, but you could have at least amused me."

With a smile on my face, I looked at Donna and said, "True, maybe I should have pretended and allowed myself to be tortured." Donna cracked a smile while still trying to maintain a serious look. As I gradually moved close to her and gave her a hug. "Well, since we've resolved our differences, let's go." Donna stood there with a look on her face of disappointment. I waited to see if she was going to respond, and it seemed as if I was waiting for an hour.

"So, that's it; you're ready to go?"

"Yes, I'm ready to go back into the store. For the record, you can manage the wedding arrangements with your friends. I will handle the tux arrangements for my friends."

"Do you really want to go back into the store?"

"Yes, Donna, there are times we will have to learn to compromise and come to some sort of agreement."

I took a day at home to relax, catch up on some reading, while listening to music. Occasionally a thought would come to mind, and I would focus on that thought. Ministry kept coming to mind, so I gave thought to the time I spend in ministry, working with people. Obviously, God was doing some awesome things in my life, guiding me to be productive and positive in my responsibility with working with people. I had this overwhelming drive and ambition to be a high achiever for God. Yes, the thought of getting married entered my mind. I asked myself, is marriage where God wants me to be? Presently, I'm happy, focused, balanced, and purpose driven. Man, just being able to relax like this, I could feel and see the joy in being able to do whatever it is that God asked of me. I would get this feeling as if my heartstrings were being tugged on as if I was supposed to be somewhere else and as if I was supposed to be strengthening and developing another area of my life.

"The other day, Donna, I was home relaxing and the thought of God's plan for my life, entered my mind. I was having this unusual feeling in my heart."

"What were you feeling?"

"One thing that entered my heart is that I do not think I should be getting married."

"What do you mean, you don't want to get married?"

"I said, I don't think! Think! I should be getting married. I'm so happy and focused with the ministry work I'm doing. I do not believe God wants me to depart from it."

Donna had a worried look on her face, "So what are you saying Derek, that you do not want to marry me?"

"I'm not saying I do not want to marry you. I'm trying to be respectful and obedient in making sure that I do not disappoint God."

"You know what I think, Derek?"

"What?"

"I think you are just getting cold feet! And you do not want to marry me!"

"Wait a minute; you do not have to get so emotional. Listen and hear me, I love you. If I did not love you, I would not be sitting here sharing this with you. Besides, I'm only being real and true to my heart. I'm sharing my heart with you. My intention was not to make you feel sad and cry."

"If you don't mind, Derek, I'd rather not talk about this any further. My mind is cloudy. I can't think or comprehend anything right now."

"I understand, Donna; I apologize for all the confusion I caused."

"Stop with all the damn apologizing, will you?"

The next day I received a call from Donna."Hello Derek."

"Hello, Donna, how are you feeling today?"

"Better than I did since our conversation yesterday. I want to apologize for my behavior, and for not taking the time to listen and understand what you were trying to share with me."

"There's no need to apologize, Donna."

"Yes, I do; I know it had to be very difficult for you to share that with me."

"I could only imagine how you felt trying to absorb it."

"I just had to talk with someone, Derek. So, I called my mother for some understanding about what you shared with me. I clearly understand how important the service you are providing to God is to you."

"I appreciate you taking the time to understand, Donna."

"Just to let you know, Derek, I do know people who are married and active in their church's ministry together."

"Yes, I know this to be true, but this does not mean that this is something for all couples. Please do not do or say something you think I want to hear in order to marry me. Honestly, as we go through this process, and if you have any doubts, we should talk about them."

"What do you mean, Derek?"

"I mean if you feel differently than I do about anything we discuss in regard to having children, finances, or anything recently mentioned in the many conversations we shared, please say something."

"No there is nothing, but is there anything you want to share since you brought this up."

"No. We are just fine."

"For the record, this is why I love you, Derek."

"Why?"

"You are open, honest, and straightforward, even about the difficult things you share with such great compassion and care."

"I'm not out or wanting to hurt anyone. This is why I'm careful about my choice of words, and what I allow to come out of my mouth."

"Touché, Derek."

No Second Chances

66 "Dad, what do you have planned for today?"

"My plan for this morning is to wash and wax my car."

"Are you going to do it yourself or take it to the car wash for them to do?"

"Kim, let me tell you something, washing and waxing your car is not just something you let anyone do. This is something that a man takes pride in, like a woman with their hair, nails, shoes, purses, dresses, and makeup."

Kim laughing, "You're silly."

"You get the point I'm making. Besides, this is another way for me to have time to myself. Do you have plans for today, Kim?"

"Nikki invited me to go to the movies this evening. Do you mind if I go?"

"No, I don't mind; I like Nikki. Just let me know what time the two of you are going. How you are getting there? What time are you going to be home?"

"No problem; can I have some money?"

"I knew there was a catch." After Kim and I brought each other up to date on our agenda for the day, I went outside to wash my car, but I decided that I would drive to the car wash and vacuum out the inside first. As I pulled up to the car wash, I noticed a couple of my friends, Don and Kevin, cleaning their cars. I parked my car. Walked over to them, we greeted one another with a handshake and brotherly hug. "How are you guys doing today? How are you feeling Don? I have not seen you in a while."

"I could complain, but that does not do any good."

"So, how are things going with Donna?" Kevin asked.

"Now who is Donna?"

"Donna is a young lady I met a while ago, Don. We have been spending a lot of time together."

"I know, because in order to meet with you, I have to make an appointment," said Kevin.

I laughed, "Come on it's not like that at all. You know I work and spend time with my daughter. There is only so much time in a day and only so many days in a week."

Don jumps back into the conversation, "Now! Who is Donna? You know I, I can't keep track anymore. You do not have a problem meeting women."

"The problem is not meeting women," I said, as Kevin chimed in and both of us said in unison, "it's meeting a mature and respectful woman." They both laughed.

"Let me share something with you guys," I said.

"Well then, share," said Don.

"Gentlemen, sometimes the unknown always looks good until it becomes the known."

Don stood in between Kevin and me. He put an arm around me and the other around Kevin, "you know something, Derek; you're right. Speaking from experience, I met my share of irresponsible and insecure women."

"Of course, Don, we all have, but if you really want the truth ..."

Don asked, "What is the truth?"

I looked in Kevin direction, "Well Kevin, FYI, Don's been trying to keep this a secret. He is the man and always has been the man. When I grow up, Don, I want to be just like you."

Kevin laughed and Don looked at me and said, "What are you talking about, Derek? You're older than me."

As we were talking and joking around, Kevin said "Hey! Isn't that Martin, the father of Donna's son?"

"Yes that's him," I said.

"Before he got caught up in that drug game, his life was together. I feel bad for the man. He did time in prison for being at the wrong place at the wrong time. Our judicial system doesn't care about who they lock up. They just want people to think they're doing their job," said Don.

"Today you're guilty by association or as they like to call it, conspiracy. The laws in this country work when our court system wants them to work, but they do not work for all. Ever since Martin was released from prison, he never has been the same. It seems as if prison made him worse," said Kevin.

"Hey, like I always said, they say that all men are created equal, but some men are created more equal than others. Gentlemen, I will talk to you later. I want to talk with Martin about something."

"Okay, Derek, we will talk to you later," they replied as I ran across the street. Martin was probably about forty yards away before I called out his name.

"Hey! Martin!"

He looked back at me. "What's up?"

"Do you have a few minutes for me to talk with you?"

Martin looking me over and said, "Aren't you the guy dating my son's mother?"

"Yes, my name is Derek, and I want to talk to you about Jeff."

"Is Jeff okay?"

"Yes, he's fine."

"So then what do you want to talk with me about?"

"First, let me ask, how you are doing?"

"I can't complain. I'm making it, you know, trying to keep my head above water. You said you want to talk about Jeff?"

"I don't know what happened between you and Donna, but I do know that Jeff really misses spending time with you. He really needs you more then you realize. When it comes to children, Martin, they want to have a relationship with their parents, no matter what is going on in their parent's life. Whatever circumstances or situation that has taken place, it does not matter to them."

"I know what you mean, but ever since his mother and I parted ways, she does not make things easy for me. She makes me feel unwelcome, as if she does not even want me around. I went through some challenging times in my life. Every time I take one step forward, I feel as if I'm being pulled back two or three. Let me give you a full picture of where I'm coming from and where I have been trying to go. I was incarcerated for five years for a drug offense that had nothing to do with me. I was still attending college. I had my bachelor's degree, and was in the process of earning my master's in business administration before I was incarcerated. When I was released, I was put on parole for another two years. I was told that I could be released early for good behavior or if deemed rehabilitated. After spending time being incarcerated, you need rehabilitation. You come out of prison worse off than when you go in prison. Your whole entire life is altered. I was nervous about coming back out into society. I lost touch with Donna and Jeff. She did not want to have anything to do with me. I have to deal with this difficult job market on top of having a felony record. I had a difficult time with finding a job, or should I say, I had a difficult time in anyone willing to hire me because I had a record. Finally, I was hired at this warehouse, but that only lasted for about seven months because there was a big layoff. Then I was hired at this telemarketing company, which we all know is a dead-end job. Then, finally, this facility maintenance company hired me. I'm still currently employed there. I keep my resume out on the market. I receive calls, and I am invited to interviews. The interviews would always start off well. Employers are impressed with my experience and resume. During the interviews they would say, "You're definitely qualified for the job." However, once I tell them I spent time in prison, I feel this big dark cloud enter the room. They act as if that is not an issue, but if they could hear themselves and see the expression on their faces, the truth is revealed. I feel a difference in the interview. A few days later I would receive a letter in the mail stating that even though I have the qualifications and experience, they selected another candidate they felt was more qualified for the position."

"I can't say I understand, Martin; then I would be lying. I have never spent time in prison, but I have met people who have shared some similar experiences. To be honest it's unfair, but we have more criminals in our political offices and in law enforcement agencies that get away with a lot and cover up a lot. I respect you for hanging in there the way you do, Martin, doing what you need to do to keep straight, living an honest life, and taking care of yourself."

"I have my days when I get easily frustrated and want to give up, but I have faith that eventually things will turn around for the best."

"Hey, that's a great attitude to have; I admire your attitude."

"What gave me hope was this one particular interview I went to. Before any questions were asked I told them, 'With all due respect, I want to be honest and straightforward with you, and I ask that you're the same with me. I want you to know that I served time in federal prison. I paid my debt to society and then some. Obviously, you think I'm qualified for this position because you would not have invited me for this interview. I would like to put something on the table before we go any further. I was incarcerated for five years for a drug conviction. Honestly, I never sold drugs; I was just guilty by association. With that being said, if my past is going to be the deciding factor in you hiring me or not. There is no need to continue with this interview. I don't want to waste your time or mine just going through the motions.'"

"Wow! Bold move, but I like it! So, were you offered the job?"

Martin looked at me with this intense look on his face and said, "Yes, I was offered the job. I'm the manager of this facility maintenance company. Even though this is not the job I want, it is better than nothing, and it is allowing me to get myself established. Even though I have this job, I still interview. I found in some interviews with employment agencies and companies, they typically do not offer me a job once they conduct a background check. I hear people talk about the idea that we live in the land of second chances and that all men are created equal. This is not true for all men because some men are created more equal than others."

"You could never be more right."

"This is how I think and live life, Derek."

"I don't understand what you mean."

"I don't care what anybody says. Most of our society does not forgive, and there are no second chances for a lot of men like me out there. My second chance will only come by the grace of God. I did not allow the system to break me because some guys will go back to criminal activities. While in prison, some guys learn to become a different type of criminal because they're constantly reminded of their crime. Our correction and law enforcement systems are not meant to help anyone, they are only meant to belittle people. Some correction and law enforcement officers are deceitful, abusive, and demeaning. The only difference between them and the guys who are incarcerated is that they have not been caught. They ask you if you have been rehabilitated while in prison. Prison does not rehabilitate or correct; it just punishes. Inmates will always be guilty; they have no voice, and no one is really listening. If they want a person who is incarcerated to feel rehabilitated, they would not place you hours away from civilization, making it challenging for families and friends to visit you. After you do get out and you're placed on parole, parole officers are just waiting for you to make the smallest and tiniest mistake, so they could send you back to prison. They want to place all these restrictions on you that are unrealistic. My parole officers gave me a curfew and told me I could not travel outside of certain areas. They had their foot on my neck, telling me I needed to get a job and become a productive member in society. At the same time, I have been harassed for traveling in certain neighboring towns or counties for interviews. What really angers me is that I had to do time in prison for something I did not do. I did not have any drugs on me and never sold drugs, but I was accused of conspiracy. This was all because I spent time around guys that sold drugs. This is why my time spent, is to myself and by myself. Eventually, I know I will have to build that circle of trust."

"I did hear you did prison time for something that people felt you were falsely accused of."

"The funny thing was, before the judge read my sentence, he said to me, 'I'm sorry to have to give you this sentence, but it's the way the law is written. My hands are tied."

"It sounds like the judge knew in his heart it was not right. Man."

"He knew. I felt his compassion, and it was hard for him to look at me. I'm sorry, Derek, I know you don't want to hear about my woes."

"It's okay; I mean, I did ask to talk with you. Sometimes we just want someone to listen to us once in a while. Just try to spend a little more time with Jeff and share your heart with him, so he knows that you're there, even when you are not."

"As far as Donna and Jeff go, Martin, well, I can share this with you if you want to lend me your other ear."

"Sure; you got my attention and I respect the conversation we're having."

"You've been through a lot, and you know your situation better than anyone else. So, I would like to ask you a couple of questions. I would rather hear directly from you then anyone else."

"What are your questions?"

"What happened between you and Donna? Are you concerned about Jeff?"

"When I got out of prison I went to live with Donna and Jeff, thinking we could work on our relationship and be a family. I know Jeff needs his father; we're close. It hurts me just as much as it hurts him, not being able to spend time with him every day or the way I would like."

"What do you mean by this? You can see him anytime you want, right?"

"Yes I can, but it is not that easy."

"What do you mean it's not that easy?"

"There is a lot you may or may not know, Derek, but Donna and I went through a difficult time. This did not help me with what I was going through. It started when I was laid off. I was collecting unemployment, still assisting around the house with the bills. I was keeping up my end of the household expenses as much as I could. I was still diligently looking for work, sending out my resumes, and going on interviews. There were days Donna would talk down to me. I had enough days of people talking down to me when I was locked up. She made me feel as if I was not important and incompetent—as if I was not doing my job as a man. I would talk with Donna and tell her I'm doing my best. I would tell her that some of the words that come out of her mouth hurt. I spent time with Jeff, and it was quality and meaningful time. I assisted with dinner, Jeff and his homework, and other household duties. When Donna came home from work she did not have to do anything. Financially, we were doing well despite my being unemployed. It came to the point that I wanted a job, doing anything. I got tired of listening to her complaining about what I didn't do and what I should have been doing. At this point a job doing anything would have made me happy just to get out of the house. Finally, when I did get a job, she still was not happy. Now, don't get me wrong, I love the time I spent with Donna and Jeff."

"What do you think happened, Martin?"

"It was the stress, the stress from the arguments and being degraded. The worst feeling is when the woman you love is making you feel like less of a man. I started to drink more than I ever had. Before you knew it, I was so far removed from Donna and Jeff that I no longer felt a part of the family. So over the past few years, I just had been fading in and out. There are days I feel so ashamed to face him because I feel as if I failed, not just as a father, but as a dad. There was this one particular day I was on my way to visit Jeff. Donna was outside, and she made the comment, "Some role model of a father you are." That comment rings in my head when I think about Jeff even today. I never felt so little and helpless after hearing those words. Ever since, it's been hard for me to face Jeff. I wonder what his mother tells him about me. Deep in my heart, Derek, I felt Donna did not want me around because she was ashamed of being with me."

"I don't know, and I cannot answer that for you. What's important is what you share with Jeff about how you feel for him as your son. Jeff needs to hear this from you. This is on you, Martin. I just want you to know that he misses spending quality time with you. The one thing that I can tell you is that I can never be his father."

"I hear what you are saying, Derek. I greatly appreciate it and you."

"I'm just letting you know that you are not forgotten regardless of what you been through."

"Thanks, this means a lot to me."

"Not a problem, I'm glad that you and I were able to have this conversation. Oh, Martin, one other thing,"

"What's that?"

"We never had this conversation."

Martin winks at Derek, "What conversation?" We shook hands and embraced with a brotherly hug.

"I will see you around, Derek."

"Take it easy, and Martin."

"Yes."

"Don't lose the positive attitude."

"I never did, and besides I cannot afford any other attitude."

Keeping the Peace

———————◆———————

I t was a beautiful bright sunny, hot day and the big day had arrived. I was feeling excited, calm, and cool as usual. People were asking, "Are you nervous?"

I replied, "Not at all; I'm feeling fine." Friends and family came from out of town to celebrate this special occasion with us. It was a good feeling to see friends from college I had not seen since graduation. My longtime friend was my best man.

We waited in the back, chatting, "Are you feeling well, Derek? You ready?"

"You know me; I'm as ready as I'm ever going to be."

"Hey, its four o'clock, and your future wife is not here. Maybe you have one of those runaway brides."

"The only thing going on is that she is running is late as usual, which I expect because she is late for everything."

"Let's say, hypothetically, she did not show. She's now a runaway bride; how would you handle the situation?"

"I'm not concerned about her not showing, and if she decide to take a detour. I would just say run, Donna, run. Seriously, I would be fine, but at the same time hurt and disappointed."

The pastor poked his head in the room and said, "Gentlemen it's show time. I need you to come out and take your post."

"Pastor, you are definitely right about that," said Anthony.

"What are you talking about?" I asked.

"From this point on, Derek, get used to taking your post and waiting." The music started playing, and the bridesmaids and groom's men started walking down the aisle. The bridesmaids looked beautiful in their gowns. The groomsmen were looking very sharp themselves. The ring bearer and flower girl were cute. They hurried down the aisle as if they did not want to be seen. Then that song came on, the one that makes everyone stand to their feet as the bride starts to enter the room. Donna looked beautiful walking down the aisle. Once she made it down the aisle and at my side, I looked at her and said, "You look gorgeous."

"Thank you; you look very handsome."

"Thank you."

The pastor interjected, "Hmm, hmm, now that you two are finished gazing and complimenting one another, may I start the ceremony?"

"Sorry, Pastor, go right ahead."

"Thank you, Derek." The pastor read a couple of scriptures from the Bible. When he had finished reading the scriptures, he said, "Derek, will you repeat after me." I repeated the wedding vows. Then he said, "Now, Donna, will you repeat after me." Donna was standing as if she was in amazement, as if a deer caught in headlights. The pastor was standing there calling her "Donna, Donna; are you okay, Donna?" I applied a little pressure to her hand to get her attention. It was kind of funny; there was some laughter from the guests, and the pastor found some humor in it, as well. Finally, after getting her attention, she said her vows and we sealed it with a kiss.

Now, low and behold the untold truth: playtime is over, and now it is time to start working on the real deal. Don't get me wrong; planning a wedding requires a lot work, time, and preparation. I know some women will put their heart, blood, sweat, and tears into having the perfect wedding. Then you must ask the question: is one truly willing to put that same amount of dedication, preparation, heart, blood, sweat, and tears into the marriage that lasts longer than a day?

"Now that we are finally married, Donna, we should talk about the dynamics of the household and roles. I feel that the role of each individual should be fairly easy. Do you remember us sharing the many ways we would work together to complete some of the simple and basic tasks in our marriage and as a family, such as our expectations from each other, such as being responsible, mature, accountable, and most importantly supportive of each other to have an effective, loving, and caring relationship?"

"Yes, yes, and yes, I remember, Derek. We both know that there will be times of disagreements and having different views and opinions. This is not going to be perfect, but we want to be effective in all we do."

"I'm glad you remember."

One evening during dinner, Donna, Jeff, Kim, and I sat and talked about the children's roles in the house. Kim and Jeff were good students in school, and we were not worried about their academic accomplishment, but we would monitor their performance and homework assignments. Their main responsibility was to keep their rooms clean, schoolwork, study for tests or quizzes, and get to bed at a decent time. "Excuse me, Derek; dinner is ready. Would you let the kids know?"

"Sure, actually I'm just finishing up this report—perfect timing."

As we sat at the dinner table, we listened to the kids tell us about their day. "Hey, Mom,"

"Yes, Jeff,"

"I'm having some difficulty with my science and math classes. I could use some help."

"Derek and I could assist you."

"Yes, Jeff, your mother and I will work out a schedule, starting tomorrow."

"Great! Thanks a lot."

"How about you, Kim; anything you need assistance or additional help with?"

"No, Dad, I have everything under control. If something comes up, you will be the first to know."

"What days you want to assist Jeff, Donna?"

"Why don't you make up the schedule? The only night I ask to be free is the night I go to church."

"Okay, I'll put together a schedule, and for the record, it's important as parents to invest time in our children. One way of spending time with them is to help them with their homework."

"You don't have to lecture me, Derek."

"I'm not lecturing; anyway we could spend two hours a night assisting Jeff with science and math."

"That sounds fair to me." A month went by, and Donna was not sticking to her commitment to assist Jeff with his science and math. "I made plans to go help a few friends from church. Could you assist Jeff with his homework tonight?"

"It seems as if over the past few weeks you always have something planned. I will assist Jeff; he should not have to suffer due to your lack of sacrifice."

"I don't think he needs as much help as we thought."

"I'm the one making the sacrifices, so of course, you may think he does not need much help."

"What do you mean you're the one sacrificing?"

"Nothing; I don't want to have this conversation now, especially since I will be assisting Jeff tonight."

Jeff came home one day after school very excited. He came running into the living room and said, "Hey, Derek, I passed my math and science tests, and my grades went up in both subjects. I got a B+ in science and a B in math"

"Hey, congratulations, Jeff, I knew you could do it. You just needed to refocus and take your time. For your hard work and effort, you deserve a reward. This is to let you know that, hard work pays off and there are rewards for working hard."

Later that evening, Donna and I were in the kitchen cleaning up after dinner."Can we talk about something, Donna?"

"Sure, what's on your mind?"

"I did not like how you handled the situation with Jeff."

"What are you talking about, and what situation?"

"Jeff and his schoolwork; he needed our help!"

"I'm sorry, but sometimes I just don't have the patience."

"This is your son, and you must be patient with him for the rest of your life. Now if you're not capable of being patient with Jeff, what makes you think you could be patient with another child?"

"What in the world are you talking about?"

"You talked about wanting to have another child if you got married, and now you are married."

"I do not want to have any more children. I'm done! Jeff is eleven years old, and in a couple of years he will be in high school and then off to college before we know it."

"I'm confused; why you would tell me you wanted to have another child?"

"Having another child sounded like a nice thing at the time, you know, couples getting married and having a baby."

"Sorry, I do not know. Are you living in some sort of fairytale life? You just don't turn it on and off when it comes to having a child. You are talking about a life, a life you are responsible for developing, nurturing, and cultivating. When Jeff becomes an adult and he is twenty-five years of age, he will still be your child whether you accept it or not."

"I'm sorry I can't talk about this any further. This is making me very upset. Could we discuss this later, Derek?"

"Yeah, whatever; when you're ready to talk let me know."

"Excuse me, Derek, I want to discuss an issue with you that I've been trying to figure out over the past week."

"Okay, what's the issue?"

"I want us to sit down and talk more about our finances. I need some guidance and assistance."

"Not a problem, besides we need to start tackling some things to start getting ahead."

"As you know, Derek, my biggest hurdle is that I have this debt totaling $14,000.00, I just want to pay it off."

"To be honest, Donna, that's not too bad, and this could be taken care of in a couple of years, because you do not have a car payment. To assist, I will take care of the rent and insurance, as long as you take care of the utilities bills such as the cable, electric, and phone, which total to be about $375.00 a month if that, and we will work the groceries out together."

"This sounds good to me, and I can manage the $375.00 a month. Realistically, I should be able to pay my debt in off less than two years."

"If you do, that would be great. Keep me posted on your progress because there will be times when unexpected things will come up and throw you off."

"I will definitely let you know if anything comes up."

"What makes this a realistic goal, Donna, is that we do not have a lot of bills or unnecessary expenses to keep us in debt—especially, if we continue to live within our means. With that being said, I will continue to manage my own financial responsibilities, so you can focus on yours. I want us to have the opportunity to experience life and marriage as one, not as separate individuals. I want you to know that I'm here for you, and once we get over this small obstacle, everything else will be a joyful ride with only an occasional bump here and there, of course."

"You think we will have some bumps, Derek?"

"Of course, nothing comes easy, and no matter how hard you plan, there will always be a glitch here and there. I want you to know that I'm accepting your debt as my responsibility."

"Wait a minute, Derek, my debt is not your responsibility."

"Alright, what I meant to say is that I'm not making your debt totally my responsibility. This is my way in supporting you by managing other financial things you do not have to worry about. This is my responsibility whether you like it or not."

"No, I do not have a problem with that, Derek."

"Besides, I would like to start looking at houses in a couple of years."

"This would be great, and my debt should be paid off."

"I want you to know that I have been saving money to buy a home for a while. I want us to share in every phase and aspect of what it takes to buy a house together."

"Why do you want to wait? Why don't you just go and buy a house now?"

"I feel this is something a couple should experience together. If I wanted to buy a house by myself, I would not have waited to get married. Let me share something with you, Donna. The things that I'm currently doing in my life and the things I had done before I met you were not about me. I have a daughter who is my responsibility, seeing that her basic needs are being met and that she's safe. I also knew that someday, I would have someone in my life who I would want to spend the rest of my life with. I wanted to be able to make life a little more pleasant for that person. I also know that the things that God blesses us with are not just always for us as individuals. God wants us to take these things and prepare them in a way that we're able to give to those that come into our lives. For example, my going back to school and working on my master's degree is not just about me. Yes, it benefits me in a way with better job opportunities, and it also will benefit my daughter and you. When I was saving money to buy a house, I was not looking to buy a house just for me. I kept that in mind for when I bought a house. Even as a single person, I would get something that I could share with others, such as friends and family if I ever needed to. Don't worry, I will keep saving while you're paying down your bills."

"You know I would like to contribute anyway I can."

"How about for now we take this one step at a time? We know the first contribution will be focusing on paying off your debt. Donna, I love you; do not hesitate to share or ask me anything. I know this will take time, and one other thing God gave me, is patience."

"Good. I want us to experience everything in our marriage together as a family, Derek."

"All I ask of you is to give some thought about the direction you want us to move in our life as a family. Tell me what you would like out of this marriage because I'm no mind reader," said Derek.

One evening I arrived home from the gym about 7:00 p.m. I walked into the house and Donna was sitting in the living room watching television, and the first words that came out of her mouth. "Where were you?"

"Hello to you to, and how was your day?"

"Hello, Derek, and where were you?"

"I worked late and went to the gym. You know this is not something new."

"If you start coming home late like this, it's going to make me wonder if I can trust you."

I looked at her and was two seconds from going up one side of her and down the other for making such an insulting comment. So, I said to myself, walk into the bedroom, unpack your bag, and get ready for tomorrow. Then I went to take a shower and while in the shower, I was thinking, *Where in the heck did that come from, especially now? Of all the times I come home late, all of a sudden, she raises the question about being able to trust me. We're going to talk about this tonight.* Once I finished my shower and dressed. I walked in the living room. "Excused me, Donna, can we talk?"

"Why, is something wrong?"

"Yes, something is wrong. Why did you make that comment when I came through the door?"

"What comment are you referring to, Derek?"

"Don't act like you don't know. The comment you made when I walked into the house. 'If you start coming home like this it's going to make me wonder if I can trust you.' Does that sound familiar? For the record, coming home at this time is nothing new. You know I work late and go to the gym. If you do not trust me, just say so right now. If you know something I don't know, you need to speak up because I do not have time to play any games. If you got some sort of 'he said, she said' stuff going on with some of your friends, we can take care of this right here and now."

"Well uh, it's, it's nothing I heard or anything anyone said to me. I just thought that when men start coming home late, sometimes that could mean something is going on."

"What in the hell! What were you doing today? I cannot believe you could think of even saying something like that. I cannot believe you were able to fix your mouth to utter such words. We've been married for three years, and I always go to the gym. You know where I am the majority of the time. If you want to know where I am, you can call me."

"I know, but you could have called me to tell me you were going to be late coming home."

"Like I said before, this is not new; this is no different from any other time I have come home late. You're aware that three days out of the week I go the gym and come home late. Besides sitting there looking at me with that blank look on your face, is there anything you want to say?"

"No, there is nothing I want to say."

"Hey, if you have some unresolved issues from your past relationships, and you're allowing those issues to resurface and enter our marriage, Donna, this marriage is not going to last. If you need to go to counseling, you should go."

"If I decide to go, would you be willing to go with me?"

"Let me put it this way, Donna. The issues are not about me or us; these are issues about your past. Besides there may be some things you do not want me to hear right now. I believe you need to start this by yourself, and if the counselor requests or recommends I come with you, I will join you then. I do not want to start off making this look like this is strictly about us. I do not see any issues with us that we cannot address without counseling. There are some deep-rooted issues within you that are starting to surface, Issues I never experienced and you never talked about. Do this for you and us as a family. This is something I cannot force you to do, but I'm willing to support any way possible, if you choose to go. I will go and wait in the waiting room. I will be right there in case I'm needed."

"Okay, Derek, I'll make an appointment."

"Now, I got to get me something to eat. I had a hard work out. I'm very hungry. I had a long day, just as you have. Then I come home to argue with you, which, is another workout that makes me extra hungry."

"You're not funny."

"I'm not trying to be."

After eating and watching television, I went to bed. I lay in bed and had a talk with God about what has taken place this evening and prayed. "God, I hope that at some point and time, something will start to take some sort of shape or form. I'm not looking for much to happen, just enough to let me know that Donna is serious. I don't want to feel like I'm doing all the work. I'm already feeling burned-out from my job. I do not want to feel like a candle being burned on both ends. Something has to give, Amen."

Donna entered the room, "I know we all have some selfishness in us, Donna, and some of us have more than others. It makes me wonder, could you really please anybody by being you? Will it take some sort of materialistic item to please someone in order to keep the peace? Is it really necessary that we go out and purchase items to make a wrong a right or to repair an honest mistake? Doing it this way we're only applying a bandage to a wound, that requires more attention and care, than just applying a bandage?"

"What is that supposed to mean, Derek? Are you saying that you must buy me things in order for me to be cooperative or do what you want me to do?"

"See, it is not about what I want you to do. It's about what I want us to do as a couple and team. I apologize for bringing this up and offending you. If I did offend you, it's because I love you. I want us to have the best. I want to enjoy a part of life you or I did not have the opportunity to enjoy because we had other responsibilities and made sacrifices."

"Of course, Derek, I know you want the best for us. I'm really trying, and this all new for me, as well. I want to enjoy this new road we are traveling together and watch it blossom into a new life of beauty. Good night, Derek."

"Good night." *God, I wonder if she gets it.*

I was driving very slowly so Donna and I could get home safe. The roads were covered in snow and ice. I saw the light up ahead turn red, so I started slowing down. While slowing down, the car started sliding out of control. There was nothing I could do to regain control. The car slid right through the intersection, hitting a pole and deploying the airbags. Looking at Donna, I asked, "Are you all right?"

Pushing the airbag out of her face, she looked over at me angrily and sarcastically said, "Do I look like I'm all right?"

"Damn, you make a car accident look pleasant."

"What is that supposed to mean, Derek?"

"We were in a car accident. The both of us could have been seriously hurt. I asked about your well-being, but I get this angry sarcastic attitude and ..." Before I could finish my thought, a gentleman was knocking on the car window.

"Hey, hey, are you okay in there? Is anybody hurt?"

155

I opened the door, "No, we are fine; just a little shaken up." I've noticed a few good Samaritans offering support and comfort. There was this woman on the passenger side of the car, assisting Donna.

The woman said, "This is a bad intersection; when it snows there are always accidents."

I turn towards the man and woman and said, "Thanks for your assistance. It's greatly appreciated."

Still with an attitude and look of anger, Donna said, "Yes, thank you."

"Why don't the two of you come inside my restaurant to keep warm until the police arrive?" said the gentleman.

"Thank you, sir. We greatly appreciate your kindness." We went into the restaurant to keep warm and drank a cup of tea until the police arrived.

When the police officer arrived, he asked, "Are you alright, and do either one of you need any medical attention?"

The both of us looked at the officer, "No, we're fine."

The police officer turned, looking out the window and said, "Every winter there's always several accidents at this intersection. I don't know what it is with this section of the road, but when it snows, it becomes a danger zone. The town just needs to repave this area or post detour signs during inclement weather. If it keeps snowing, I will probably be back down here for another accident later today." The officer called a tow truck to have our vehicle towed and informed us of where it was being towed. A taxi was called for us to get home. Donna still had a look of anger on her face. I did not know why, and I was not in the mood to entertain her attitude. On the ride home, neither Donna nor I said a word to one another.

Eventually, I had to say something, "I'm going to have my car serviced. We could share my car to get back and forth to work until we get another car."

With an attitude Donna said, "What about me?"

"What do you mean?"

"Well, I don't have a car because you totaled my car."

Feeling the anger rising up within me, I responded with a firm tone, "I'm sorry about the car it was an accident. The roads were icy and slippery. There was nothing I could do. Even the people who assisted us commented on the horrible road conditions of that intersection when it snows."

"You know it happened because you were driving too fast."

"What are you talking about? I was driving under the speed limit." I was furious and said, "Don't worry! Like I said, we will get another car." I walked away to make a call to schedule an appointment to have my car serviced. I still had the thought in the back of my mind that after all that has taken place, she was worried about that damn car and what she's going to drive. She is so selfish.

The next morning, Donna and I were riding to work together and I said, "Do you want to go and look at cars?" She did not respond and I continued, "If you're still upset about the accident, you have to let it go."

"It's just that there are things I want to do and I cannot because we only have one car."

"I apologize; it's not like I planned for this to happen. You have to work with me. I have been very patient. I'm doing the best I can with what we have. Don't take this the wrong way, Donna, when I was trying to get you to take responsibility for your debt, you kept avoiding it. Now that we need a car, it falls on my shoulders. If this is how it is going to be, realistically, this marriage is going to crumble slowly or quickly."

"Don't worry about my debt; I will take care of it myself." With steam coming out of my head, I sat quietly. Then it came to the point that Donna and I were communicating very little. She decided to take the bus to work to avoid riding with me. I was perfectly fine with her decision. In my heart I knew I was not going to continue to let her keep catching the bus to work.

157

One day while driving to work, I decided I was going to stop at a few car dealerships. I would look at cars myself, and it would be a surprise for her. I was not planning on spending a lot of money on a car. My plan was to walk into a dealership, find the car I think she would like, make an offer, keeping it simple and to the point. I visited a few dealerships. I knew the dealerships I was most interested in visiting would have what I want. I know that Donna liked the Nissan Maxima. After visiting a few dealerships, I found the car I wanted at the dealership I liked the best. I knew this was the car even before I test-drove it. The car drove nice and smooth. The engine was quiet, and there were no signs of leaks. The car had low mileage, which was good for its year. It was clean inside and out, including the engine. I asked the salesman, "How much is the car being sold for?"

"This vehicle is being sold for $17,599."

"I will give you $14,000.00, and we can take care of the deal right here and now."

"Let me go talk to my manager."

"If that's who we need to talk with, then bring him or her out because my offer will not change."

He went to talk with the manager and came back two minutes later and asked, "Do you want to finance it with us?"

"No, I have the financial end all in order." I went home that evening and never said anything to Donna about purchasing the car. I had scheduled to pick the car up in a couple of days. She would get to see it then. Donna was in a better mood, and we were having conversations again, which made me feel good.

"Don't take the bus today. Let me drop you off and pick you up."

"Sure, that will be fine, Derek."

After dropping Donna off at work. I went to my office. I had appointments scheduled with a few clients. I planned to pick up the car during my lunch. I'm sure one of my co-workers would not mind taking me. "Hey Rene, could you take me to the dealership to pick up a car I purchased?"

"Sure, I need to get out of the office and get some fresh air."

"Thanks."

"You bought a new car?"

"Yes, but it's really for Donna."

"Oh excuse me, Mr. Derek, so you got it like that?"

"No, I had a few dollars saved, and besides we need another car. Donna blames me for the other car being totaled."

"Seriously, she blames you? I would not buy her anything if she's still blaming you for an accident. Unfortunately, we do not live in a perfect world, and accidents happen every day."

"I know what you mean, Rene; I just let go and let God."

"Amen!" Rene shouted.

We pulled in the dealership parking lot. "There is the car."

"Which car is it?"

"It's the Maxima."

"Did she pick out the car?"

"No, I picked out the car. I'm going to pick her up from work in it."

"Wow, she should be happy when she sees the car."

"I think she will be pleased, at least I hope so." After picking up the car I had to return back to the office and complete some paperwork before it was time to pick up Donna.

The time flew by, and it was time to go pick up Donna from work. I grabbed my jacket and rushed out the door. I wanted to get there before she got out of work. I jumped on the highway and since I was in a bit of a rush, I decided to see how the Max handled. Oh yeah, this car had a very nice pick-up and speed, and handled nicely. I started thinking maybe I need to keep this for myself, but I couldn't. This is for Donna and besides, this is not the type of car I want for myself. I arrived at Donna's job before she got out. I parked in the same parking space as usual, right across from the main entrance from where she exits the building. She came out of her office building. I sat in the car, watching her look around to see if I was in the area. I knew she was looking for the other car, so I hit the horn. She stared, than I stuck my head out the car window. I could tell she was happy. She had a big smile on her face. She got in the car, "When did you get the car?"

"Two days ago, but I was not able to pick it up until today. Do you like it?"

"I like it a lot."

"Good, because I got it for you."

"Thank you, Derek."

"You're welcome, and you deserve it. I know we went some months without a car. I know sometime there are things we do together. I want you to be able to do what you need to without us having to bump heads with our schedules. Like I always said, it's all about being effective, and most importantly, it's all about love."

Different Directions

D onna requested space to manage her finance and other responsibilities, so I respected her space. I did not want her to feel as
if I'm always looking over her shoulder, as if she's not responsible and
I don't trust her. Donna invested time working on her business projects
that she enjoyed. Her commitment to the business was questionable and
definitely not helping with her financial situation. She showed interest in
one thing, but before you knew it, she jumped into something else. No
matter what she was doing, it did not benefit us as a family. One day I
asked, "Do you have ADD (Attention Deficit Disorder), Donna?"

"She looked at me with a smirk on her face and said, "No I don't, and
I do not claim that."

"Some things you don't have to claim. In this case you do not have
to claim it because you are living it."

"If you are so concerned and want to know how I feel, you should ask.
Maybe I would be doing better in the things I'm trying to accomplish if
you would show me more support and interest."

"I show interest and support by listening to you, allowing you to do
those things, knowing that you're not taking care of the things that are
most important to this family. You know it's been over two years, and you
have not even attempted to take care of your debt. You have not given me

one nickel to put towards the house. You have not given me the $30.00 a month you agreed to do."

In an angry and loud tone, Donna said, "If I agreed to it, why are you worrying about it? I'll handle things the way I want, and when I'm ready you will know."

"First of all, you do not have to talk to me in that tone. I'm just communicating, being open and honest. So if there is a problem, let me know so we can work it out together. This is about us being responsible and accountable towards one another. The debts that you have, you don't care about."

"What are you talking about? That's ridiculous."

"You don't care about repairing your credit. It seems as if you want someone to take care of it for you as though somebody owes you something."

"Like I said, you don't have to worry about my debt. I will take care of it when I'm good and ready, my way."

I walked into the other room, sat down in front of the television. I started talking with God, asking him to continue to give me guidance, patience, and understanding to get us through this and that I don't lose my mind. I put my head back and closed my eyes, "God I'm willing to do what I can to support Donna to have her take responsibility, so we could move to the next step in our relationship and as a family. I refuse to burn myself out. Carry all the weight, especially when there is no support for me mentally or emotionally. If this requires me to do nothing, then so be it."

One afternoon a co-worker of mine, Rene and I went out to lunch and were having a casual conversation, "I've been struggling with something, Derek."

"What are you struggling with, if you don't mind me asking?"

"I've been having some problems with getting my credit back in order."

"What are you doing about it?"

"I was at a loss and then I was told by a member of my church about a financial management counseling program the church offers."

"I've hear those programs are very helpful, and I have heard some amazing stories from people who have completed the program."

"Funny you say that because I heard great things as well about the program. To be honest, I thought it would be another one of those typical programs about debt consolidation."

"Well then, what were your thoughts about the program?"

"I went to the orientation. It was very informative, beneficial, and with biblical guidance on how we should manage our finances. So I enrolled into the program, and it's working very well for me. In a matter of six months, I could see my debt going down."

I became excited, "Rene! God is definitely an on-time God."

"He sure is."

"You have any information about the program with you?"

"No I don't, but you could call the church I attend and sign up. It's open to everyone; you don't have to be a member of the church. You could also go online to get additional information. It's called Trust and Faith Financial.com."

"Thanks; I'm going to look into this today." I was so excited that as soon as I returned to my office, I went online and looked up Trust and Faith Financial. It appears to be a well-structured, organized, and beneficial program. I printed out some information; feeling so excited that I could not wait to share this information with Donna.

I walked in the house. "Hello, Derek. How was your day?"

"My day went well; it was an extraordinary day."

"Wow, what happened that may your day such an extraordinary day."

"I was talking with Rene, and out of the blue, she started sharing with me about her finances and debt problem."

"This is what made your day such a good day?"

"It's not that she just shared with me about her financial problems. She shared with me important information on how she is resolving her financial problem. Rene gave me the name of this finance program that is offered through her church."

"And, what does this has to do with us?"

"Listen, Donna, you remember the conversation we had the other night about our finances."

"Yes, I remember."

"I prayed asking for a way to assist and support you without being directly involved with your finances."

"So you're saying that God answered your prayer through Rene's financial problems."

"Yes, we were given information to assist us with the financial matter we've been discussing. I took the liberty of going online and printing out the information for the Trust and Faith Financial program. Honestly, I'm being very compassionate and sincere about this. Besides, you cannot keep holding on to this unnecessary baggage. All I ask of you, Donna, is that you read the information and consider enrolling in the program. We could go together."

"Okay, I see that you're very passionate about this, and you want us to start moving forward. Since you're being so sincere, yes, I will read the information. If I like it, I will give it some consideration."

"Great, thank you for listening and showing interest. I don't think you will be disappointed."

A few days had gone by since we discussed the financial program. One day as I was entering the house and about to hang up my jacket, Donna approached me. "This sounds like a very good program. I read the litera-ture you gave me. I requested additional information, and I received it in the mail. I like what the program offers." She walked over to me, giving me a big hug and kiss, "Thank you and I love you."

"You're welcome, it's all about love. I felt it was important that we found something that worked for us and most importantly that it met our needs."

"Tomorrow I'm going to sign up for the program."

"I would like us to attend together."

"No, I will ask one of my girlfriends to go, who is also having prob-lems with her finances. This would be great for the both of us."

"Okay, I will respect your decision, Donna. I'm excited, I truly believe this program will make a significant difference in our life together."

"You know something, Derek?"

"What would you like me to know?"

"I believe the same thing. I believe I could pay my debt off in less than a year. My goal is to truly have my debt paid off in a year."

"That sounds fair, and anyway I can be of support, let me know."

"Thanks for the offer, but for the moment you have done enough for now. Realistically, I do need to take care of this debt. I've been carrying this debt around for too long. It's not like it is going to vanish on its own."

Two months has gone by, and Donna had not mentioned the Trust and Faith Financial program. I did say to her that I would respect her space and allow her to manage this without intervening. One day I was sitting at the computer and Donna was reading a book, so, I had to ask, "How's the financial program?"

She put the book down, "I decided not to enroll in the program."

"What! Please tell me why!"

165

"I wanted to make sure that this was in my best interest. So, I talked with some of my friends, and they said that it's not a good thing to get into because it could make your credit look bad."

I could have fainted. I took a deep breath. I looked away and then back at Donna, "Who in the hell do your friends think they are? Your friends do not live in this house! What I'm really angry about is that you were not even going to tell me if I did not ask."

"I'm sorry. I was going to tell you."

"You know how this makes me feel. I feel as if you do not have any respect for me as a man, husband, or for our marriage. I could do badly by myself. I do not need this bull if this is how you want to live."

"I respect my friends and value their opinion."

"This is not an opinion; this is a fact. If you keep consulting and listening to those friends, you're going to be in the same situation they're in. Then you could ask them if you could live with them. Then you will see how much they're your friends and how much you value their opinion."

I walked out the room in total disgust as I shouted, "Do it your damn way, you don't need me!"

After some time reflecting on our relationship, I saw where it was really going, and it definitely was going south. We were not a team and were definitely not being effective in any way that was going to move us along as a healthy family unit. "Can I talk with you, Derek?"

"I'm listening."

"I do want more from our relationship."

"You know, Donna, I believe you. I also believe you don't want to put the work in to achieve it."

"I really do; there's just times when I have a difficult time concentrating and putting things together."

"I'm not the type of person to give you what you want. I believe this is supposed to be a team effort. When you're married, this does not mean you're entitled to sit back on your butt and expect your partner to do all the work."

"That's not my expectation at all, Derek. I really do want to get this right."

"What's funny about this is that you meet some women who want to be independent when it's convenient for them. Then they want to be traditional when they want a man to do for them. I say put up or shut up. It's time to be that authentic woman. I can't talk about this right now. I need to get some air."

The next morning Donna and I were sitting in the kitchen. She was putting the dishes away. I was pretending to be reading the paper and debating with myself about whether to ask the question: do I have the energy to continue our discussion? So here I go again, "So tell me, what is it that you want to do to manage things better?"

"Sorry, I do not feel like having this conversation now."

"Whether you want to or not, we have to talk about it. How do you expect us to grow if you're not willing to address anything? You have to give this debt in your life some serious attention for the following reasons. First of all we're married, second, why you still have this debt is because you refuse to talk about it, and third this must be dealt with if you want our family to grow and prosper. Most importantly, you will have more opportunities in your life. You must deal with your problems regardless of what they are."

""I do deal with my problems."

"You can't pick and choose because some are easier to manage than others. God is not going to give you any major responsibility when you cannot and refuse to handle the minor tasks. I'm going to suggest something in order to assist you with taking care of this debt."

"What do I have to do this time?"

"It's those kinds of remarks that annoys and frustrates me. You know something, Donna? Never mind, as I was saying, this is what I propose; you pay the rent for a year. I will pay the utilities and a few other things. I will have your debt paid off within that time frame."

"I do not feel comfortable doing that."

"What is wrong with you? I want to do this in order to help us. I do not know what else I could do, and I'm running out of ideas. If you come up with any, let me know. Other than that, you are on your own. I'm trying very hard to be of help because this is not just about you anymore. If I cannot assist you and you are not willing to let me help, ask yourself this question: how will we ever be able to help one another?"

"Why do you keep pressuring me?"

"Pressuring you! Pressuring you! All I asked is that you help me help you, so we can help us. If this is a comfortable place in your life so be it, but expect me to do only what is necessary and required until you want to handle this financial matter." I was burning up inside. I kept saying to myself, *she is a straight-up bonehead.* I kept getting unpleasant feelings, and we were definitely going in different directions.

I conducted a group for men who were experiencing emotional and verbal abuse from relationships. The topics discussed and stories that were shared made me self-evaluate my own personal relationship within my own marriage. Then it hit me, I have been facilitating these groups for approximately four years, and now I can actually feel what these men are going through. I am not just the group facilitator, but also a victim of verbal, mental, and emotional abuse. The thought never entered my mind that I was not just the group leader, but also a member. My eyes have been opened to how Donna speaks to me and manipulates our relationship to benefit her more than us as a family. The abuse she was inflicting was starting to escalate, causing emotional and mental stress and depression in my life. I would teach that we should not have to live in a hostile environment. I guess I should look in the mirror. I guess you could say that I'm living in that environment myself. Everything that I teach and speak about was taking place in my own life.

So, I decided that I would spend more time listening to Donna and stop debating with her. As the days and weeks went by I would listen and tune in more to what was coming out her mouth. Wow, she's verbally abusive. She's critical of my attributes and personality. As a man with spiritual, emotional, and physical strength, working hard to keep peace and balance, ooh, my patience was wearing thin. One evening I decided we should talk.

"We have to talk about us and what we are doing to one another, Donna."

"Okay let's talk, Derek."

"First let me start by asking, Donna, did you notice over the past few weeks I have not spoken much? I only talk with you about the things that pertain to us directly as a family and very little idle or casual conversation. I do not know about you, but I'm not happy or comfortable with us living this way."

"So, what are you saying, that you want us to separate or that you want a divorce?"

"No, I'm not saying any of those things. What put that in your mind? Have I given you the impression that is what I want?"

"No."

"By my saying, that I am not happy with us living this way, I'm saying that we have to do something different so we are happier, our relationship could grow more, and our family could be stronger and closer. What I'm saying is that we should go to a counselor, and not just any counselor, but a Christian counselor."

"I guess if you want, I will give it a try."

"Okay, I will call and schedule us an appointment."

"Honestly, Derek, I do not think that we need counseling. I believe you and I could manage things ourselves."

"I'm sure we could, Donna; I just feel that if we go to someone who is neutral, it will take the pressure and stress off of us. We'll be able to say or admit to things without worrying about how the other will respond or react."

Donna and I arrived on time to our counseling appointment. We were sitting in the waiting room to meet with the counselor. "Hello. My name is Nancy."

"Hello, Nancy. I'm Derek, and this is my wife Donna."

"Nice to meet you, Derek and Donna; welcome. Let's go into my office."

"Sure," I said.

"Have a seat and may I ask what brings the two of you here today?" I waited to respond to see if Donna would be willing to take the lead, but Donna just sat there as if she was waiting for me to answer.

"What brings us here today is that we are having difficulty communicating effectively with each other.

Donna interrupted, "No Derek! You are the one having a problem communicating. I communicate just fine."

"The both of you came here for something, so let us start by spending some time together and see if there is really a communication problem or not. There are situations where it's not so much a communication problem, but how we communicate to one another."

Donna stood up and said, "Yeah, talk with her Derek, and see if you have a communication problem or not. I do not have a problem; I do not even know why I wasted my day coming here. Derek, if you have problems, you need to deal with them, but don't drag me into them." Donna grabbed her purse and walked out the office.

"I'm so embarrassed, and I apologize for wasting your time."

"No, you have not wasted my time, Derek." The counselor put one hand on Derek's shoulder, "Give me a call if things change. Your wife may want to come back. Sometimes people need time to accept and admit to themselves that going to counseling does not mean something is wrong with you. Counseling is a way for people to make sense of certain life circumstances and situations, and it helps them see the bigger picture. Before you go, do you mind me asking you one more question?"

"Sure, I don't mind at all."

"You said, your reason for wanting to come to counseling was that you and your wife had difficulty communicating effectively; exactly what about communicating."

"Donna is verbally abusive a lot of the times and not just with me. There are times she makes comments towards others that are harmful. The expression on people faces shows of embarrassment, pain, or just a look of feeling uncomfortable. I talked with her about the words that come out of her mouth and shared with her there are times that some of her words cause scars and wounds, hurting people. That no matter how many times you say, 'I'm sorry' to a person, the wound is still there. She never takes responsibility for her actions. She blames me constantly, even for her own abusive conduct and behavior. When I confront her, she has an excuse to justify her actions. I did not know what to expect any more from day to day. I mean, I was subjected to insults, put downs, threats, shouting, and a lot of sarcastic comments. I've been criticized, called names, humiliated, and even embarrassed out in public. It came to the point that Donna's subtlest comment would hurt me just as much as her stronger, louder, and obvious deprecating remarks. She would end her verbal assaults by accusing me of provoking her or telling me I deserved it. Yes, its Derek's fault. She tells me that I need to pay more attention to what I say and how I say it. The funny thing is that she would attempt to disguise her snide or insinuating cutting comments as humor."

"Was there anything else that made you feel nervous or uncomfortable about Donna?"

"Yes, the different ways she communicates."

"What do you mean by the different ways?"

"I mean her body language sometimes says more than the words that come from her mouth."

"Can you give me an example?"

"Well, Nancy, for example, when Donna and I go out in public together, she walks in front of me, instead of beside me. To me this is a clear message that she does not care about me as if she is better than me or doesn't want to be seen with me. Then the one time I asked her if she would mind walking next to me, her response was. "What for? We know we are married." At that moment I felt as if I was hit with another dagger."

"Derek has there been any time that your wife made you feel deserving."

"Yes, when she wanted something from me. Don't get me wrong, Nancy. Donna has a good heart; I think she struggles with being open and honest as if she is afraid of being hurt. Yes, she rarely has anything nice to say to me or about me. She makes me feel unwanted and show very little appreciation and support. The other thing I don't understand is that she can present to be honest, but also dishonest."

"Tell me what you mean by your statement."

"She was forthcoming and honest with me about her financial situation, which I appreciated and respected. We even invested time together in developing a plan to resolve her financial situation. We started by sitting down, discussing ways of paying off some of her debt. We even came to an agreement on a strategy. This was nothing she was pressured or manipulated into agreeing to; it was an option for her. Then it seemed as if she became secretive, and my input did not matter anymore."

"What made you feel this way?"

"I shared with her financial information to assist with her debt. She shared with me that she was going to take advantage of this debt by participating in a financial management program. So, I gave her some space to get organized and settled in the program. After a month I asked her how were things going with the financial program. She told me that she decided not to participate in the program because her friends told her it was a bad idea and that the program would hurt her credit rather than help. I asked her how paying your debt would hurt you. At that very moment, I had to take a very deep and long breath because I was about to come out of character. I felt she lied and withheld information about an important matter that has an impact on our family. This made me wonder what other plans or commitments she would make without sharing with me. Mentally, I was becoming exhausted, frustrated, and confused. Trying to think what was going on with her and not getting anything from her was tearing me apart because she would not answer some of my questions. One day I was reading the Bible in First Corinthians. I was feeling mentally and emotionally exhausted, but I continued reading, and there it was in the second chapter, verses eleven and twelve: 'No one can know what anyone else is really thinking except that person alone, and no one can know what God's thought except God's own spirit. And God has actually given us his spirit (not the world's spirit) so we can know the wonderful things God has freely given us.' At that moment and time, I felt the Spirit of God come down upon me and lift that burden off my shoulder."

"What burden are you referring to, Derek?"

173

"I was no longer trying to think what Donna was thinking and started to feel good about myself once again."

"Wow, what version of the Bible did that scripture come from?"

"It came from the New Living Translation. Why do you ask?"

"That is a powerful scripture, Derek, from what I am hearing and what you shared with me. It does sound as if the lack of effective communication is having a strong impact on what could be a beautiful relationship."

"The times when I try to communicate with her she would barely listen to me. She showed very little tolerance of my opinions that differ from hers. It just came to the point that I no longer felt like an equal partner in the relationship, but rather an unequal partner. I guess some of us go through life learning some things the hard way, Nancy."

"Why do you say this?"

"I say this because living under a cloud of emotional abuse has a tremendous impact on a person's health and life. I understand communication in any relationship is important in order to make progress. It's important that the communication be done in love. When partners communicate, you should be able to discuss any matter in a way that the words being shared and the actions being displayed are not intimidating, causing discomfort to the person."

"Let me ask you this, Derek. Have you ever made an attempt to talk with Donna about how she communicates to you and how this make you feel?"

"Have I! Many times, and the conversations always seem to go south. She would ignore me, basically rejecting and being dismissive to what I have to say as if I did not matter. Then she would try to flip the script and say that I have a problem communicating. As time went on, I just saw that she was in denial about her behaviors. She would blame me for her inability to relate in a healthy way her love for me. I look at it this way, sometimes in life when a person has been kicked down. They don't know how to do anything, but kick people down themselves. Nancy, I am sorry for wasting your time and truly appreciate the time you have spent with me. I thought by coming here today that Donna and I were making progress. Now after today's episode in how she responded and reacted in our two-minute counseling session, I know I cannot do this alone. She has to be a willing participant. I feel that if she does not want to work together at salvaging our marriage, I guess I will have to implement my options of breaking free. Thanks for listening and allowing me to share, Nancy."

"You do not have to thank me, and if the two of you decide to give counseling another try, please do not hesitate to call me."

"Yes I will, without hesitation."

"Derek, I deal with all types and kinds of situations. A person can be verbally abused to the point they do not know what is true anymore. They can no longer make clear and good decisions. When a person is being abused and in this confused state, the abuser throws in lies as truth until the person being abused does not know what to believe anymore. The unfortunate thing about this is when the person being abused does not know what to believe anymore. They may go as far as embracing the lies and disregard the real truth. Do you mind me sharing my honest and professional opinion with you, Derek?"

"Of course not, I welcome any thought of wisdom, so please share."

"In this short period of time I listened to all that you have shared with me. You share as a Christian person. You have a strong and healthy mind whether you know it or not"

"Excuse me, Nancy, not Christian person; it's Christian man—you mean Christian man."

Nancy smiled, "Then excuse me, Christian man, and it's good to see that you are still capable of displaying a healthy attitude with humor."

"That is one thing about me: I do not hold grudges. It takes a lot to really get me angry. Besides, I cannot allow unfortunate situations or circumstance to bring me out of character, especially, to take it out on others who have no part in what is taking place in my life."

"You have a great way of thinking, Derek. I am going to share this one last thing with you before you go. This something I once read by an unknown author, "A godly person who you could trust is like a life saved to a person being abused or having trials and tribulations in their life." Proverbs 10:11 says that "The mouth of the righteous is a well of life."

While lying in bed I realized the opportunity to get the support we need was right in front of us. How could she refuse help? For some reason, Donna was persistent in wanting to argue and debate with me. There is only so much more of this I can take. I had to separate myself from her in the house. I spent time in the spare room, making it my office. "Can I talk to you for a moment, Derek?"

"Yes, what's going on?"

"The car needs to be serviced."

"Could you make an appointment for next week so we could drop the car off before going into work?"

"I don't have time to call and make the appointment, Derek."

"You don't have time. Go and pick up the phone and make the call, please. Huh! You don't have time while sitting and watching television, and you don't have time?" She continued taking blows at me with the words from her mouth. Most of the words did not make any sense. For my own sanity, I tried tuning her out. Her mouth forced me into the bedroom. I sat on the bed as I buried my head in my hands. I prayed and stayed in that position until I did not hear her voice anymore. When I finally did look up, she was out of the room. Then I came to the realization I could no longer live this way. I could no longer tolerate the change in mood and attitude.

"One evening while I was reading the Bible, Derek, I came to the realization that when a man and woman are married birth control should not be utilized. We should be fruitful and multiply."

"What are you talking about?"

"I want to let you know that I had stopped taking birth control." I did not like the sound of this. I became very silent. "Are you feeling well, Derek?"

"Okay, I heard why you have decided to stop taking birth control. My question is when did you stop?"

"Let me put it this way, I gave it a lot of thought and I do not believe spiritually, this is something that should be part of a marriage."

"I ask you again: when did you stop?"

"I think it was about two or three months ago, not sure exactly when, and yes, I am pregnant."

I know I had this look on my face as if I wanted to strangle Donna. "Unbelievable! You know what the mature, responsible, and respectful thing to do before you decided to make this decision without me?"

"What, discuss it with you?"

"You're impossible. You're a manipulative and deceitful woman. Yes, if you respect me as your husband and care for me as a person, you would have discussed this with me. It's obvious that you made up your mind about what you want! You only want to do when it comes to us—no, I mean what *you* want! Your decisions and plans only include you. You do not care about anyone but yourself. The growth and development of our marriage and family does not mean anything to you. We cannot communicate without something being taken out of context, resulting into an argument. You refuse to go to counseling, and then you expect me to say this is fine, no problem; don't worry about it. I'm sorry. I'm not one for playing these games. You just don't know how tired I am emotionally, physically, and mentally."

"Are you okay? Why are you sitting there with your head down?"

I looked at Donna and spoke slowly giving each word I spoke deep thought and consideration. "Let me ask you something, do you remember that long conversation we had about having kids before we got married and during marriage counseling."

"Yes, I remember the discussion, but Derek."

"No buts; just let me finish. You also stated that you were not ready to have more kids. Did you or did you not share this with me."

"Yes, I did say that when we were talking about kids."

"Then what in the hell is going on here? Do you really remember what we agreed to? If you don't, let me refresh your memory: we agreed to delay having children. This would not be a good idea because you have a son and I have a daughter. There is still a lot of work that has to be done with the development and nurturing of this relationship as a family. We are a blended family, and this is a challenge in itself. There is still so much to be done for us to be a family of one."

"Like what? I do not see anything we have to establish in our relationship."

"Okay, your son, Jeff, you must take into consideration."

"Jeff is fine; what is there to worry about?"

"Jeff's concerns and feelings should be taken into consideration. His needs and desires should not go unnoticed. He sees his father sporadically and wants a relationship with him. For him to get over this hurdle, he needs us and especially you. Don't take what I'm sharing with you the wrong way. There is nothing wrong with having children. In our current situation having a child takes away additional time from our son. Jeff is at an emotional stage. This could be a devastating and difficult situation for him. He's becoming more comfortable with me, and adjusting to this new phase of his life takes time. This could take months or even years depending on how receptive he is going to be. To be honest there are some kids who never adapt and adjust to the new family they have become a part of."

"If you do not want to have a child with me just say so; you don't have to use Jeff as your excuse. I know what I want as an adult and parent."

"Listen to what I am about to share with you, Donna. There are some parents who only think of themselves and what they want. I learned over the years that when kids are involved, most parents do not take in consideration the happiness of the child. Some parents are so selfish, they will give birth to a child not wanting the child, but want the person who is attached to the child. Then there are parents who are separated and barely spend time with their child or do not even acknowledge they have a child. Donna, I'm sharing my heart with you, and you have this look on your face as if I'm wasting your time. Honestly, I am struggling. I am having a very hard time coping with all of this. I have to take some time to myself and examine this whole situation."

Weeks went by since Donna and I talked, or should I say, had a meaningful conversation. The closeness and intimacy no longer existed. We were just going through the motions. One evening I was in the living room, listening to music and reading a book. Donna walked in the room sat on the sofa. "Are you feeling well, Donna?"

"I'm feeling fine; why do you ask?"

"Just checking, do you feel like talking?"

"Sure, go ahead and talk. I'm listening."

"When you told me you were pregnant. I felt as if I was hit with a low blow. I'm hurt, lost, confused, skeptical, and do not feel respected as a man, husband, or even a person. I am struggling with our marriage and us as a family. I do not know what to expect anymore or what you're going to tell me next. This is not how we treat people, especially our relationship if you truly, love, respect, care, and appreciate it. I feel betrayed, deceived, and hurt in a way I never been hurt before."

"You will get over this, and our relationship will grow stronger. You just need to get used to my way of doing things, Derek."

"What! So now you expect us to do things your way? Nothing I do seems to matter, and whenever I try to help, I feel like I'm in the way or being a nuisance. Your way is taking matters in your own hands without consulting me, regardless of the consequences. I do not know what to expect or believe anymore."

"I felt I have handled this situation very well, Derek. I mean I came forth. I did not have to say anything at all."

"Have you taken a good look at how you handled this situation and the way you approached me, Donna? How do you think I feel about you or us?"

"I do not know, but I do know I did not do this to trap you."

"What! Do you think before you speak? 'I did not do this to trap you?' Why would you even think of something like that to say unless that was your intention? First of all you're married to someone who cares for you and loves you. So, with that being said, there is no need to be setting any kind of traps. Honestly, that comment continues to ring in my head."

Donna blurted out, "I do not care about what's ringing in your head. You could leave if you do not want to be here."

"Unfortunately, Donna, that's already been established. You continue to make degrading, rude, disrespectful comments and remarks that tell me we are going in different directions. You do not want to work together to reconstruct our marriage. You're willing to take, but you're not a giving, caring and considerate partner."

"Really, Derek, do you think that I planned this whole pregnancy out?"

Dropping my head then lifting it up, I looked at Donna. "I lost trust in you and respect for you as a woman. Some things you just don't do in life to keep somebody, and adding another life into the picture is not fair to the other person and especially to the child. If you open your eyes to the situation and listen to me, this is not just about you being pregnant. This is deeper than you being pregnant. As a matter of fact, it goes further back than you care to know. I hate to be rude, but right now I do not care about much of anything, Donna."

"Why do you say this?"

"I keep repeating the same things over and over and over. You do not care or appreciate me. The reality is no matter what I say or do, you will never understand. The end result is my being disappointed and hurt. Just thinking about this whole situation is making me exhausted."

"Anyway, Derek, have you told anyone about me being pregnant?"

"Wow! You're unbelievable, and after all I shared with you, this is what you ask? Yes, I have told my mother. Why you asked?"

"No reason; just asking."

Monday night football is the one night out of the week when my mind becomes totally free from my difficult and challenging life. I decided to stop at my favorite sports bar to watch the game and eat wings. My friend, Kevin, walked up to me from out of nowhere and said, "Excuse me, sir; you're sitting here as if you're in a daze."

"Let me put it this way, Kevin, in a short period of time a lot has happened in my life."

"What are you talking about?"

"Donna's pregnant, and I'm not dealing with it well. Don't get me wrong having a child is beautiful and wonderful blessing."

"So, what is it that has you feeling as if your life is over?"

"I know my life is not over, and I will bounce back. I do not know what direction my marriage is going."

"Have the two of you discussed having a child?"

181

"Yes, we talked about having more children on more than one occasion. We agreed that having a child would not be in our best interest. We cannot even work through minor issues in our relationship without an argument or a negative inappropriate remark being tossed at me. When I'm being optimistic, she is either speaking or thinking negative. To make a long story short, she stopped taking birth control without consulting with me."

"Ooh, wow; I'm sorry, man. It sounds as if you're not so angry about the pregnancy but angry with Donna for not communicating to you about the decision she made."

"Yes, exactly. I feel betrayed and disrespected as a man and a husband. I do not feel as if I'm thinking straight at times, and this is affecting my performance at work. There are days I would sit in my office, isolated and talking with God to get me through this. When you been through some challenges and struggles in life, why would someone want to keep struggling? I don't know, Kevin; maybe I'm over thinking and shouldn't feel this way."

"I'm listening. I cannot even say I understand or relate with all you're going through. I can say I'm proud of you for being able to talk about all of this."

"Thanks, I really appreciate that. It means a lot to me. Honestly, I needed to hear something positive and healthy to make me feel as if I'm doing something right. Right now, things are at the point that I hate her and do not even want to be in the same room with her. I'm not even comfortable with touching her or even looking at her because it brings about so much pain and unhappiness. Even though I feel this way and hold in this discomfort, I feel the noble and respectful thing to do is continue to support her and assist her through this process of being pregnant. This feels like the hardest thing I ever had to do in my life."

"Come on, you and I know you been through challenges that have been very difficult, Derek. I know if I was to think back, I'm sure I could easily come up with a few."

"This is different because I'm married, and I never had anyone treat me this way. I'm at a loss on how to be supportive of someone that you are not happy with. Now having to attempt to work with someone who is selfish and invests a minimum amount of time in the life of her own child."

"Can I ask you a question, Derek?"

"Sure, nothing can be said or done at this moment that could make me feel any more worthless."

"First of all, don't talk that way. What I want to ask is whether Donna justifies this as being okay, and if so, how?"

"In her sight, things were always okay when they were not, even when the situation did not turn out in her favor. Then I would have to absorb all the anger and attitude from her. Right now, she is acting happy as if this is the best thing that ever happened to her. She brags about being pregnant as if she does not have any problems. I was so devastated that it took me awhile to share this with anyone."

"From the sounds of it, you are managing all of this very well, and God will get the two of you through it all. It's not about your will but His will, you know."

It was a quiet evening. I was sitting in the living room watching television. Then Donna entered the room. "May I speak with you, Derek?"

"Yes, what's going on?"

"Well, you do not want to have kids or stay married to me because you prefer to be single and have your freedom."

"I don't know where all of this is coming from. If my heart's desire was to remain free and single, I would not have married you. My choice to be married was to share life with someone I care for and love and to be able to enjoy all that God has given us. Whether you choose to believe me or not, that someone was you. I believe you wanted the same, but you showed me that you wanted something different in life and even in a marriage. We discussed in great detail that delaying to have a child was in our best interest just for the simple fact that other areas of our marriage needed attention."

"I know we discussed a lot of things."

"Let me finish; we discussed working on our financial problems, developing and shaping areas of your son's life, seeing that my daughter was comfortable, strengthening us as a family unit, and investing time in our marriage. We must take responsibility for our lives because no one will go to work in our place and no one will pay our bills for us. I'm trying very hard to be responsible with doing my part. All I ask is that you be responsible in doing yours. The decisions you demonstrated showed me irresponsibility on your part. Wow!"

"What's wrong; are you okay, Derek?"

"It's just that I'm exhausted from repeating myself, having the same conversations and going nowhere. Help me understand how we can reach out to each other."

"By communicating and doing what should be done so we don't have these disagreements."

I must have had an expression of anger and pain on my face in a calm and soothing tone, I said, "I don't believe in getting along by going along with what is wrong just to please someone. I am not a people pleaser, and yes, I do want to support and please my wife. I like to be able to support the growth and development of our relationship but not to please my wife by supporting selfishness, poor decisions, and lack of consideration." Donna had a blank look on her face as if not to care. I sat on the sofa with my head back, looking up towards the ceiling. "I'm out of words. Is there anything you want to say, Donna?"

"I believe if we just accept and deal with situations as they arise, we will be fine. You just get so worked up over nothing."

Derek quickly dropped his head turning his eyes on Donna and angrily said, "The decisions and choices you make are not for us; they're for Donna, and my input does not have any value. It's as if you do not acknowledge the problems we have, and as if it's okay that our relationship is disturbingly out of order. We cannot continue to live this way; it's not healthy. If you had been truly honest with me about what it is that you really want, I would have reconsidered getting married."

"Hey, I know we agreed to wait to have children and other things we agreed to, as well. You know, Derek, sometimes things happen that are just totally out of our control. This is one of those times we must learn to just deal with it."

"Seriously, do you listen to the things that come out of your mouth? I'm sorry, some things I don't believe in just dealing with. Having a child is a blessing and wonderful thing when both parties are in agreement, not something you just deal with. Being a single parent for a good number of years, I thought you of all people would understand. Since you think we should just deal with things, do you remember telling me you did not want more kids because there were areas of your life you had to work on?"

"Yes, I remember our discussion."

"Honestly, I respected you for sharing that with me. Why would you tell your friends you didn't want more kids, when in reality you did? My stance is that I'm going to assist and be there; just remember you decided you want to be a mother. Now it's time for you to be a mom—meaning you must be willing to make sacrifices. So as of this day, you better start learning how to make sacrifices, sit still, and get your priorities in order. For the record, I struggle with respecting and trusting you. A caring, loving, and genuine woman would not do something like this." I got up off the sofa, and before exiting the room I looked backed at Donna as she sat quietly and said, "If you have not realized it, Donna, I'm a realist, not an idealist. If you choose to live life in a haphazardly fashion and live a chaotic lifestyle, go right ahead. I don't need any help because I can do badly by myself."

"I'm sorry that you feel this way, Derek. I mean there is nothing we can do now. We cannot go back and change time."

"You're so right; we cannot change time, but we can change what is taking place currently in our lives."

"All I can say is that God is going to take care of you, and I hope he has mercy on you, Derek."

"You know God is going to take care of all of us. I'm only concerned how He judges me, not your judgment or anyone else. One other thing, Donna, you need to really listen to yourself and take responsibility for the things you do. Think about how you have contributed to our problems: the manipulation and your deceptive ways. Now you have what you want, you just want me to go along as if everything is fine. I'm sorry. I have feelings, and I cannot pretend this is okay when it's not."

While walking through the grocery store, I ran into Donna's friend, Mary. "Hello Derek."

"Hi, Mary. How are you doing?"

"I'm doing well, Derek. The question is how are you doing?"

"What are you talking about?"

"Donna told me that she is pregnant, and you are blaming her. You know it takes two to make a baby."

Looking at Mary with anger and frustration, I said, "You know there are three sides to every story, his, hers, and the truth. You only know one side, and yes it does take two to make a baby. Usually it takes two responsible adults to be in agreement."

"What is that supposed to mean, Derek? So, you're saying, you did not know she was trying to get pregnant?"

As I was walking away I replied, "You seem to know everything about my marriage; take that up with Donna." Man, I walked away very upset. I don't need this bull. I was angry and hungry. I went to get me something to eat. If I'm going to be angry and stressed, it might as well be on a full stomach. I stopped at this bistro to order me a sandwich. While sitting at the table, life was becoming cloudy. I was losing focus of my life and its purpose. All sorts of things were running through my mind, such as thoughts of when Donna and I first met and thoughts about God and how God puts people together, and if I was some sort of test or experiment of His. In my entire life, I never felt so disconnected and miserable with someone. I finished my meal, paid the check, and left the waitress a tip. I went to my car and sat there for a few minutes trying to figure out how I could relieve myself of this hurt and pain. I felt drained, abused, taken advantage of, and emotionally exhausted. I grabbed the steering wheel tight and cried. I couldn't think of the last time I cried. I felt stupid. This will never ever happen to me again. I know people are people, and by any means necessary they will do whatever it takes to get what they want at the expense of others. The thought of the conversation I had with Mary in the store felt like salt being poured onto an open wound. If Donna wants to tell people the story, she should tell the whole story from beginning to end. It seems as most women side with their friend even if their friend is wrong. True friends are honest and straight forward because they care. Proverbs says, "Wounds from your friends are better than kisses from your enemy." The truth of it all is that the thoughts and perceptions of others are not important. People will think what they want, and what they think they know. In the sight of some women, it's the man who disrupts the relationship as if men do not experience emotional pain by some of the decisions women make. Some do not realize how certain decisions could have a traumatic impact on a man life. Men are seen as tough and should not cry. Whoever believes that a man should not cry is dead wrong; even Jesus wept. As I reflected about my pain, my hurt, and the tears I shed, even though I was at a point in my life where I was not pleased with myself, my trust for Donna had changed significantly. I'm not afraid to man up about my feelings. This is what makes me a genuine man.

I walked in the house. Donna was sitting in the living room reading. "Hello, Donna, how are you?" She had the nerve to look at me with a look of disgust on her face. I'm thinking to myself, I do not feel guilty about anything I might have said or done. I continued into the kitchen, put away the groceries, and took a shower. After my shower, I walked in the bedroom. Donna was in the room on her laptop. "Do you know what it means to have JOY, Donna?"

"What are you talking about?" "I am talking about JOY. To have JOY means putting *J*esus first, *O*thers second, and *Y*ourself third to have an effective relationship and life."

"So, what does any of this have to do with me?"

"You put yourself first and said to hell with the rest of us. You expect everyone to be happy as if everything is all right, as if this is the way things are supposed to be. However, this is not alright, and this is not the way things are supposed to be. Let me share something with you, Donna. My success and moment to exhale was taken away when you decided to change our relationship to your standards, and by how you treat me as a man and as your husband."

"So, this is what you see and believe, Derek? This is what the enemy wants you to see and believe."

"Stop it, Donna! You spend more time going to church, different church functions, talking about being in agreement and submissive to your husband, putting your family first, and wearing the armor of God at all times to protect yourself from the enemy because we are always under attack. I hate to say it, unfortunately, you are not under attack. There are times you are your own worst enemy. You should try, or should I say, learn how to be sensitive to the needs of others."

"First of all, Derek, I'm real and sincere. I am also a caring, sharing, and respectful person. So, your perception of me is totally wrong."

"It's not my perception of you; it's what you do and say. Okay, Donna, you say you're a respectful person. There are two ways we could show respect and trust for people. Do you know what those two ways are?"

Sarcastically, Donna says, "No I don't, but I'm sure you're going to tell me."

I took a deep breath, and looked at her for a few seconds before I responded, "One way involves avoiding ulterior motives," I then went and grabbed the dictionary and looked up the definition and read it, "according to the *American Heritage Dictionary*, the word *ulterior* means 'lying beyond what is evident, revealed, or avowed, especially being concealed intentionally so as to deceive: *an ulterior motive*, Lying beyond or outside the area of immediate interest.' What's unfortunate is that some people will show more honor to their employer or even the pastor of their church than to their own family. As if they're looking to receive some sort of special benefits or treatment. Some people spend so much time and energy honoring wealthy people, hoping they can influence the wealthy to contribute to them or make a donation to a cause they're supporting. Then we have some people who will honor people they feel have power or are in a high-level position, hoping they will not use their authority against them, but for them. The second way is God's way; this involves love. When we honor God's love, we respect people and we respect one another because we have been created in God's image, and we respect the peace within our soul. With all the time you spend in church, Donna, you must know that we have a major responsibility to contribute to the people that we come into contact with by allowing God to love on them. Believe it or not this is done through us, people like you and I. Does God's way of honoring others sound too difficult for our competitive and selfish natures, Donna?" Donna looked down as to give the question some thought. "While you're still giving the question some attention, let me continue. Even though we shared our hearts' desires and life goals before we got married, were you serious about what you shared with me and where we were going?"

She slowly lifted her head up. In a low soft tone, she said, "I did not plan for things to turn out this way."

"I know you didn't. The problem is that we did not plan at all. Realistically and honestly you had this fairytale image in your head that only you knew about. The way I see it, is that you were not true or real from the beginning of this marriage, and neither was I. This marriage and the vows were just words because our hearts were somewhere else. There are days I sit back and wonder if we entered this marriage under false pretenses. I don't even feel as if I know you. What I mean is that I see and feel a totally different person than the one I married. I know longer know how you really feel about me or what you really want. I showed you how caring and giving I am by trying to assist you in areas of your life, especially when things seemed to be getting tough."

"Yes you did; you tried to help me in various ways. I could have done things differently to make life less difficult for all us, especially me."

"I don't know if you noticed, Donna, but from the time we started dating, I revealed this side of me. When you tell someone that you care, you're expressing a feeling of concern, attending to a person's needs or desires as well as showing an interest in that person's well-being. Caring requires you to have an emotional reaction, to minister to others, and to have affection and love for that person, in the same manner the way God loves us. I can say I truly cared for you before I loved you. From the time we spent together getting to know one another, I was caring and compassionate in the way I talked with you most of the time. Even more importantly I care how you feel."

"Why do you care so much about how I feel?"

"Let me put it this way, how you feel tells how we feel. I was always concerned about your well-being. To be perfectly honest, Donna, there were days I might have not said much to you because you were more caught up in meeting your own needs. The things I did were not just about me. It was about all of us—for our happiness as a family."

"I guess I allowed my mind to drift on the things that were irrelevant instead of things that were."

"It did not appear as if you were caring for yourself, in the way we should care for ourselves. You know what I mean?"

"I'm not quite sure what you mean."

"Sometimes we must ask ourselves tough questions that we don't want to answer. You're a talented, intelligent, and beautiful woman with a beautiful heart. In this life you can work hard, run all over the place, attend all the church functions you want, and at the same time you may be failing at taking care of home. That has resulted in your failing to have a happy family, happiness in the relationships you establish, and most importantly, a complete and happy soul."

Man Talk

O ne day, while at the gym, I ran into my good friend, John. John
knew all about what I was going through. John was a talented
and gifted man who owned his own business. He had a kind and generous
heart for helping others. He is one of the most dedicated and hard-work-
ingman I know. He was married for fifteen years that resulted in a divorce.
He says that it was a painful experience, and he has been enjoying the
time to himself and reestablishing his life. "Hey Derek, how's life treating
you these days?"

"I couldn't tell you if I tried or maybe I do not know how to articulate
and express what is going on. I can tell you that the connection is gone
between Donna and I. I don't know what to expect anymore. I feel as if
she's constantly trying to manipulate me. Life is definitely emotionally
and mentally exhausting these days. There are some days when I walk
through the door of our home, John, I'm overtaken by depression. I'm
lost; I do not know how to connect with her anymore."

"You've done a very good job expressing yourself for being uncertain.
I'm sorry to hear that you and Donna are going through such a difficult
time. Have the two of you been communicating?"

"We are at the point that we don't communicate about anything. I
hate to admit this, but it's even a struggle for me to look her in the face."

"This sounds as if you're in a very lonely place. If you are, it is not a healthy place for anyone to spend time, Derek."

"I'm not familiar with being in a state of loneliness or depression, but I bet you I'm close to it."

"Why would you say something like that?" asked John.

"There are days that the majority of the time I did not know why I was having certain thoughts, then shortly after, I could not remember what I had been thinking about."

"You may endure for the night, but joy will come in the morning. There were times, Derek, I would reflect about the hurt and pain I endured when I listened to the news some days and heard of people taking things in a relationship to the extreme, such as hurting or killing their partner. For example, yesterday this man killed his spouse and himself."

"Now that is something I do not even understand, John. Why in the world would someone go that far? Don't worry; I'm not going there."

"I hope not, my friend."

"Seriously, why do people kill their spouse, partner, significant other, or even commit suicide?"

"You know, Derek, this is something I don't think I will ever understand. My ex-wife and I had our share of problems, but I never thought about killing her. There were times she would make me want to kill her. I couldn't kill anyone, especially myself, no matter how bad things got between the two of us."

"Neither could I, John, because I love me some me."

John laughed and continued, "Same here, but for anyone to fathom the thought of killing another human being, you have some serious issues that require special care. Realistically, nothing gets that bad, and if you are that unhappy, leave, separate, or get a divorce, but don't go killing anybody. Have I ever told you the story, Derek, about this man I worked with who killed his wife, children, and himself?"

"Are you serious?"

"Very serious; I was working in this office. This gentleman I worked with was a very nice guy. He presented as being happily married and had three nice kids. One day we were informed at the office that this gentleman killed his entire family and himself. They were in some serious financial debt, and he embezzled money from the company. I sat and thought about this, but all I could say was wow. I tried to put myself in this man's position in trying to figure out what would trigger this man to go to the extreme of killing his family and then taking his own life. To take one's own life, something serious has to be going on, but what could be so serious as to take one's life?"

"One thing I can say is that I may feel hurt and confused, but I'm not crazy, John."

"I know you're not crazy, Derek. My question is, why is it that when some people go through disappointing life circumstances, they will go to great lengths to bring a permanent solution to a temporary problem instead of trying to find peaceful methods for dealing with the challenges and adversity they encounter? It's sad when people commit suicide; to me that person is a coward."

"I must agree with you, John. I know and you know that suicide is a cowardly way to avoid your life circumstances. Like you said, suicide is nothing more than a permanent solution to a temporary problem, and this is only if you are successful at committing suicide. There are people who attempt to commit suicide and are not successful, resulting in living with the memory of how they ended up in their current condition for the rest of their life."

"This is true. Also, anyone who considers committing suicide is only demonstrating how selfish they are. I see it this way, Derek: I believe that anyone who commits suicide or even considers it as an option has weak hope and faith in God or they don't know Him. They do not see or believe there is any hope that the future will be different from any pain of the past or present circumstances they have encountered. So, why entertain ending your life because of burdens, problems, or unresolved issues that are most likely something that could be resolved, even if it's over a period of time."

"I agree, John, and what makes this even more disappointing is that some people fail to realize that some problems remedy themselves. The problem is not that anyone really wants to die or take another person life; it's that they forgot how to live as they once lived and no longer have a healthy and productive life."

"Amen," replied John.

"Hey John, thanks for the conversation. I really appreciate it, and I appreciate you."

"No problem Derek; that is what friends are for."

"Through good times, bad times and ugly times that's what friends are for."

"Yes, sir."

"Suicide, how did we get on this topic?" asked Derek.

"You were talking in code about hurting yourself, Derek."

"Sorry man, that is not my style; besides, you're the crazy one. Seriously, John, we do have to end this conversation. I don't want to get one of those gym reputations you have."

"What reputation are you talking about?"

"The gym socializer—don't act like you don't know, people who have gym memberships to sit on machines and talk to people. I should probably open a gym call the Socializer Health Club and get specially made furniture that looks like gym equipment. John, you wouldn't have to join. I would give you a free membership and a key. I know you would get the customers flowing in, and I would even let you be the director for the training department. You could train all the new employees."

"You're not funny, but it is nice to see that you still have your sense of humor. If you don't have plans Sunday, football games are being watched at my house."

"Will there be anyone else there watching the game?"

"I invited Don, Al, and Kevin."

"It sounds like a plan. I'm there."

"Kickoff is at 1:00 p.m."

"Thanks again John, talking and laughing with you helped me to realize how good it is to have good friends."

"You're like a brother to me, Derek, and besides you were always there for me. Times like this are when we need someone the most, and I love you."

Later that evening I was at home reading my Bible, and I came across this scripture "Uphold me according to your word, that I may live; And do not let me be ashamed of my hope" (Ps. 119:116). I sat back in my soft leather chair and put my feet up. I closed my eyes and had a talk with God. "Why is it that some people fail to realize the decisions and choices they make could have a traumatic impact on another person's life, especially when the other party is not aware of what is taking place? It is very disappointing in life when someone lets you down and then you have to let them down. It truly hurts."

It was Sunday, and I went to church. The funny thing about today's service was that the pastor made the statement that he knows he could not preach too long because there were some men in there who wanted to get home and watch the football games—but that would depend on how good our offering looked. Some of the people in the church started laughing. We know our pastor has a good sense of humor. After service I went home to change before I went over to John's house to watch the football games with the other guys. I was the first to arrive. John and I were sitting down, eating appetizers. "You remember the other day in the gym when you and I were talking, Derek?"

"Yes, why are you thinking about taking me up on my offer about opening up the Socializer Health Club?"

John laughed, "No, but about working hard and appreciating the things we work hard for."

"Yes what about it?"

"The only thing you have to be careful of is that sometimes people can become more in love with the things they have than the people who are in their lives."

"Okay, and where are you going with this, John?"

"I'm sharing this with you because this was how I felt about my marriage. I was truly in love with my wife, but what was disappointing was that she was more in love with herself and materialistic items. I worked hard for us as a family. Through her eyes it did not seem that way because she would buy things she did not need and nothing she bought benefited us as a family. She would even buy things and hide them from me."

"Yes, I can relate; Donna used to do the same thing."

"Derek, when my wife and I first met, she had debt. I accepted her knowing her situation. By accepting her with the debt, I assisted her with cleaning it up." "

How much debt did she have if you don't mind me asking?"

"Of course not; she had approximately $17,121.54."

I laughed and said, "You still know it down to the dollars and cents."

"Yes sir, because I was the one who paid that tab, hoping it would assist us with having a healthy and a lifelong marriage, especially being that we had three kids between us. Even when I thought it was safe to come up for air, somehow more weight was thrown on me, keeping me under water. I never spent so much time on my job trying to pay so many bills in my life. I guess that saying is true depending how you want to look at it."

"What saying, John?"

"You know, people will take your kindness for your weakness and try to step all over you."

"Oh yeah, and the other saying: if you give some one inch they will take a yard."

"Actually, Derek, let me rephrase that in my case, if you tell her to take $50.00 out my wallet, she will take the credit cards and debit card, too."

"You're crazy."

"No I'm for real, man I put up with that for fifteen years, and I'm just starting to clear up some other financial mess she got us in after being divorced from her for four years. The straw that broke the camel's back was that we were out looking at RVs. We liked to travel by car when we went on vacation. My wife started to complain that she wanted to get an RV so we could enjoy the sights more when we traveled. I figured a RV would be a great investment, and it would get a lot of use. I was also starting to get tired of my wife's motor mouth." I laughed, and John said, "No man, I'm serious. Living with someone who likes to debate was starting to wear on my nerves. Every time we would travel somewhere I would hear it in the car about getting a RV. I'm stuck and can't run or hide. I can hear her right now with that high-pitched, squeaky voice, "If we had a RV, we would not have to stay in hotels and eat out all the time. "There were times I wanted to pull to the side of the road and tell her go ahead without me. I will hitch hike."

"You're crazy."

"Now we're RV shopping, and she wanted this special-edition RV. We went to several dealerships before we finally agreed on the RV to purchase. One evening, when we were at home discussing our finances,

I said to my wife that before I agree to sign for this RV, payments will have to be made for the next four years. Then I asked, do you have any credit or debt I need to know about? Her response was no, and I respected and believed her, so we signed for the RV. Okay, now we have this RV, and one day five months later, I decided to come home early from work. I went to get the mail. While flipping through the mail I saw this billing statement from some creditor with my name on it, so I opened it. Surprise, surprise, surprise, Derek, I saw this bill for $12,700.00. My heart fell in my stomach, and I felt nauseous. At this point I was no longer angry. I was hurt and felt betrayed because my wife and I met to talk about our finances before purchasing the RV. She told me she did not have any credit or debt we had to be concerned about. Knowing that she did, she still allowed me to sign for the RV."

"Why didn't you know about the bills coming into your house?"

"Why I never knew about this one particular bill? Because she usually gets home before me and when we were car-pooling she would get the mail. Anyway when she came home, I approached her in a calm, but hurt way.

She looked at me and said, "You looked as if you lost your best friend."

I replied, "I think I did."

She looked at me and said, "What happened?"

I pulled out the statement and said, "Can you tell me about this?" Her mouth fell open, and she stood there in silence.

The first thing that came out of her mouth was, "I'm so sorry."

I looked her straight in the face and asked, "You had this when we bought the RV."

She looked down at the floor and said, "Yes, but the bill didn't get that high until after we got the RV."

I replied, "And that is supposed to make it alright? I should feel better knowing that you waited until after buying the RV to spend $12,700.00. The truth of the matter is that you withheld important information from me. Yes, you lied. You know all the financial struggles we had. I thought we were at a point of being comfortable so we could breathe easy."

"What happened, John?"

"I told her we needed some time apart because the trust and respect in our relationship did not seem to exist. I never felt so hurt in my life. I thought we were a team. We even went to marriage counseling. To be honest, it helped us to be true about a lot of things, and one thing that was revealed was that we were no longer happy together. While we were in counseling, she had the nerve to say that she was entitled to have certain things. I looked at her as if she was crazy. I said to her, 'So you have certain expectations of me; well, let me tell you about your expectations.' You do not have the right to expect anything from anyone or expect anyone to do anything for you because you will be disappointed and unhappy. All we have is just the additives and preservatives that people have in a marriage to help cultivate happiness into their lives. There are some married couples who do not own a car, house, jewelry, money, and all the latest and fancy household items, but they're happy. So don't try to run this entitlement garbage with me. Just to let you know, you can have everything; this is how much materialistic possessions mean to me. If these things we have are what make you happy, then keep them. I don't need them. I will even pay off your car for you."

"So, did counseling work?"

"Counseling was a combination of success and a lack of success."

"What do you mean that it was a combination of success?"

"What I mean, Derek, is that it was successful in the sense that we were able to be honest and share our true feelings about one another and our relationship. It was unsuccessful because it did not pull our marriage together, which resulted in us separating. After fifteen years of marriage, we decided to divorce. This was the hardest thing I ever had to do in my entire life. I thought signing that marriage license was hard. Signing that divorce paper was even harder because I loved her, but I could not live in an idealistic world that was about materialistic objects to impress people. I'm a realist, and you know me: I couldn't care less of what others think. One big important lesson I learned is that you cannot live for other people, even if the other person is your spouse. You have to live for God and allow him to lead your heart. Sometimes even God Himself will try to pull you from the things that you are trying so hard to hold onto. Being with someone who wants what they want when they want it and does not care how it affects you as a family is being totally selfish. This is why I believe, Derek, that some married men die at an early age because of living a life of hard labor."

"I hear you because you go to your job and have to deal with people, your employer, your co-workers and the politics. You deal with the pressure and stress of trying to perform at your highest level on your job, so you can get a paycheck to take home. Then you have to go home and deal with additional pressure and stress, which makes you feel lousy. Your home is to be a safe haven, a place of comfort where there is peace and happiness. I have come to realize, John, that many men who work hard to make their marriage work, usually do not get the acknowledgment and recognition they so greatly deserve."

"It's different in our society for men. As men we have a lot more challenges and adversity to face today, and the list continues to grow."

"This is true, Derek, as men we struggle with dealing with our feelings and remain in the relationship as long as possible. For me, things were unfortunate because there were no positive response or action in the efforts that were put forth, resulting in me becoming emotionally torn, feeling as if I failed myself, the person who I thought was supposed to be my life partner, and most importantly God."

"You know, John, it's just as disappointing for men who stay the course and do not get a positive response and reaction or any acknowledgement, consideration, or recognition that they deserve. They do not feel the love and appreciation they desire."

"I can relate; these are the forgotten men or the underrated men, Derek. Women are not the only ones who need emotional support, have stressful and frustrating times, and have to face the struggles and adversity of life. Men also have those moments in life when there does not seem to be any relief, but they must stay focused and have faith in God, believing that He will make a way when we think there is no way. It's tough for men and women, but when it's all said and done, men get less support."

"When the divorce was finalized, how did you approach life?" asked Derek.

"Well, let me put it this way, Derek, it was a process. First of all, I was not planning on dating right away. I have taken my time with restructuring and rebuilding my life, getting comfortable with getting to know me and enjoying time to myself, but most importantly, I had to refine my soul to have peace. As time went on, the person I thought I would spend the rest of my life with suddenly drifted out of the picture. If you are a true, respectful, and responsible person, you know not to dive into another relationship before you have dealt with your emotions. If those emotions are not dealt with, you're setting yourself up for failure. I quickly learned that the world as you once knew it has changed and even the people."

"It's funny that you mention dealing with your emotions before putting yourself out there again because when Donna and I were together, there would be things I would do or say that were healthy, and she would treat me like someone from her past relationships. I think this affected her self-esteem because she would not trust me for any apparent reason.

Honestly, I never gave her any reason to doubt or question the trust in our relationship. What made this challenging for me is that I did not know how to be myself around her anymore. I was too afraid of doing or saying something that would make her feel uncomfortable. It felt as if anything that I gestured, would remind her of a past relationship."

"What I've found to be an important aspect of life after any painful event is, knowing how to proceed with life, Derek."

"That's exactly it, John."

"I took a year to myself before I started to meet women. This was to bring closure, and my intentions were not to develop any serious relationships. This was an opportunity to build new relationships as friends. Most importantly I did not want to force something that is not of God. Not too many women I came across lived a healthy spiritual life."

"Wow, John, acclimating to a single life had to be a challenge for you, especially after being married for fifteen years."

"It really was not easy for me; it took work to be at the point in my life where I'm no longer reliving the events of my marriage. I was no longer angry with my ex-wife. Most of all, I understood my part in what went wrong."

Derek moved closer to John, put his hand on John's shoulder, and said, "I completely understand what you're saying. I appreciate you and what you have shared with me. You're a strong and amazing man. You're still in good spirits about life and able to talk about it."

"Honestly, it took some work with the help of God and having good friends such as you."

"Thanks because I feel the same about you, John. You have been there for me in more ways than you could imagine, and you continue to still be here for me. There is one thing I want out of a relationship."

"What's that, Derek?"

"Real love, not conditional, then again what is real love?"

"Excellent question, Derek. I'm glad you asked, and my answer to your question is that the only real love we will ever have is the love of God."

"Yes I know and what about ..." the doorbell rang. "Hold that thought, Derek."

It was Don, Al, and Kevin. We greeted one another with a handshake and hug to show our expression of love for one another. Don was a nice and respectful guy, but he did not date much or he kept his relationships private. Don had a bad experience in a relationship that resulted in his questioning a woman's trust and honesty. "What's up with the game?" asked Al.

"Derek and I were just having a moment of man talk," replied John.

"So, what is this man-talk discussion we are having, Derek?" asked Don.

"Well, if you really want to know it was about relationships."

Kevin then put in his two cents and said, "Don this is something you do not know anything about. Maybe we should continue the conversation so Don can take some notes."

John interrupted and said; "before you clowns rang the doorbell we were talking about real love."

Al said, "Real love is when you're with a person you're looking forward to spending the rest of your life with. I guess the kind of love we all long for, that special love, when you care about the happiness of someone else without thinking about what's in it for yourself or what can you get away with without telling him or her. This kind of real love brings about true happiness. It's genuine, with a sense of peace that satisfies and edifies the soul."

"Now wouldn't that be something special," said Derek.

Kevin replied, "You know something? You see these movies and plays about men taking advantage of women and mistreating them, but when will someone actually come out with a movie that truly talks about men's pain and what they endure in a relationship?"

Al said, "Yeah, just like the things we're sharing. We're supposed to be the man and all the weight usually falls on us, no matter what happens. The only time that a man might get a little sympathy is if the woman dies. Even if a woman cheats on you, you may get a pat on the back and hear, don't worry, you will be all right. She was not the one for you anyway, as if they know who the one for you is."

Don said, "I hear ya partner, but that one is out there; you have to have an open heart and allow yourself to feel the heart of that person. You know something else, gentlemen? You have to close your eyes to color because you hear women that talk about being with their own kind, staying within their own race. Either they stereotype or are too concerned about what their family and friends think and because of this, they sacrifice happiness."

"It's that kind of attitude that turns me off from some women, especially when they say they're a Christian."

"Yes, I know what you mean, Al," said Don.

Don replied, "Let me finish, you also have some men that feel the way as some of these women feel. Let me tell you something, I left that race, color and nationality thing alone when I established a heartfelt, understanding relationship with God, because God does not see color. God sees the heart because love does not see color. When Jesus died on the cross for our sins; it was the blood of Jesus that washed away the color barrier."

"That is so true, Don," replied Kevin.

Don continued to share, "Life is too short to worry about what others have to say. They're going to talk no matter what."

"This is true," said Derek.

Before he could get another word out, John jumped in, "I see it this way; love comes in all shapes and forms. Why I say this is because I felt that the love relationship I experienced was selfish love. Selfish love causes destruction in a relationship, and why some people break up or friendships are ruined is because the other person is more concerned with their own needs."

Kevin jumped in with this look of relief on his face and said, "You know something, gentlemen, this conversation we are having is all right. I mean you just don't see or hear about men getting together, sharing their thoughts and feelings about life, and especially about relationships. What we're truly sharing here is love."

"Yeah, yeah, yeah; I can feel the love. Hey, John, can you feel the love?" Derek replied.

We laughed for a moment, but then Kevin interrupted, "Seriously we are truly sharing the love, respect, trust, and care we have for one another."

"I agree with you, Kevin," said John.

"Love does not discriminate; we cannot help who our heart is drawn and connected to," said Don.

Looking at John, Derek said, "You know this is good and healthy for us to talk among ourselves like this. I mean, it helps us as individuals and also shows that we are here for one another, as well. Eleanor Roosevelt said it best; and this may not be her exact words, "You should do what you feel in your heart to be right for you will be criticized anyway." If you feel you're connected to someone who is outside of your race, a different color, or whatever the case maybe, to being happy, ultimately love is the key to a happy life."

Don said, "Yes that quote by Mrs. Roosevelt assisted me with the decision I made with Lori. You guys remember that bad experience I had with Lori?"

"Do we remember you were dating Lori for over a year?" said John.

"What are you talking about? Who is Lori?" asked Al.

"Al, you were living in Texas when this took place. That situation was so bad that it was too uncomfortable to talk about for months. Our man here, Don, was devastated and broken," said John.

"Since Don is talking about it now it cannot be painful anymore. Okay, so who is going to fill me in?" asked Al.

"I will," said Don. "Since I brought it up, let me share with you what happened. It's not painful to talk about; I have a better grasped of my life since that occurred. Now I view it as a learning experience, a life lesson that helped me mature."

"Well then, share with me and stop procrastinating."

"Okay, I was dating this beautiful woman named Lori for over a year. We were very much connected and in love. We spent a lot of quality time together. Time was invested in our future to be together. We discussed marriage and kids."

"You did not tell us all this was going on," said Kevin.

"Anyway, the day after Thanksgiving we went to the mall to do some Christmas shopping. We walked into this one particular store looking around, when a friend of Lori's approached her. I continued to look around while they talked.

Then I overheard her friend ask Lori," "How are things going between you and Rich?"

Lori said, "We're still separated and looking at getting a divorce."

"Well whatever you decide to do I'm here for you. You deserve to be happy and to be with someone who will love and respect you."

"Now as I overheard this conversation I was very much disappointed and hurt. I'm thinking how I can approach this because I feel as if I'm with a woman I do not even know. So, on the way home while in the car I came right out and asked, are you married?"

207

She said, "Don let me explain to you."

"I looked at her and said; explain what, being with me for over a year and you never told me you're married."

She says, "I'm separated and looking at getting a divorce."

"With a look of anger and disappointment I said, Lori you're still married and we could never be together a hundred percent or have a life together as one. I'm here as your cushion to get you over that hump, right? How long have you been married? Now listen to this, she tells me.

"I've been married for ten years and you're not here to get me over any hump. You're here as my friend, partner, and someone I care for deeply. Don, I want to be with you and want to be part of your life."

"Man, she was lucky I didn't curse or allow myself to come totally out of character. Anyway, I looked at her in the eyes and said, if you really felt that way about me. We would not be having this conversation, now would we? I told her that we couldn't accomplish anything at this stage. This is wasted time and you probably want to be with your husband."

Now she wants to defend herself by saying, "My husband and I are two different people and have nothing in common. We have grown apart and I spent many years dealing with mental and emotional abuse from him that made me a nervous wreck. There was a time I went to live with my mother because I was losing weight and he was starting to scare me."

"My response was, I do not know your husband, but from what you are sharing with me, it sounds as if you were willing to tolerate the relationship. You dealt with it for ten years. There are woman that are physically, mentally, and emotionally abused by their husbands or significant others, but they will continue to stay with that person until the day they die. They would leave temporarily and once they get that second wind, they go back and do it all over again. I think they get some sort of satisfaction out of it or they're just that insecure. The bottom line is that you were not honest with me about your marriage. You shared that you lived alone, not dating anyone, but failed to mention that you're married. I looked her straight in the face and said, Lori I have to go because I'm very angry, and not in a very good place to talk about this any further. We probably can talk once I feel focused."

"So did you ever talked to her again?" asked Al.

"Yeah, a few weeks later, I called Lori after I cleared my head. I asked her if we could get together and talk about this situation. We met and I shared with her that it appears that you're faced with some challenges, obstacles, and dilemmas that are difficult for you to manage. I pray that you have a breakthrough in your life, so you can enjoy life the way a woman deserves to enjoy life and a healthy relationship. I feel that you're being pulled in many directions. You're trying to avoid conflict and disappointing anyone. I do not want to become another challenge or dilemma in your life. I feel it will be best for me to remove myself from this relationship, so you can have less to focus on. Maybe in time, depending on where we are in our lives, maybe we will be able to revisit what we have. We can be friends, but not close friends, because we build this unique pyramid. Our relationship started out as acquaintances, to friends, then to a true and respectable loving relationship that made us a genuine couple. Lori, use this time however you need, so you can make sure that you do the right thing. I do want to thank you for the time we spent together. In all that you do, have faith; faith will eliminates the pride of our effort, and it exalts what God has already done. It's not about what we do. It's being able to admit and knowing that we cannot measure up to God's standard and we need help, and it's based on our relationship with God. It has nothing to do with our performance for God. I gave her a hug and kiss and walked away."

"Wow, that's deep. How did you feel putting it all out like that knowing how you felt for this woman?"

209

"To be honest, Al, this was the hardest thing that I ever had to do. I really loved that woman. I know she really loved me, but it was the right thing to do. This made me realize that people go through life with someone for years feeling unhappy and stuck in a relationship. I guess some of us are fortunate and meet that special person early in life, and for others that person comes later, or not at all because they miss that special moment."

"Did you ever hear from Lori again or did you guys ever try to reconnect?"

"Yes, Al, I heard from her through an email one day."

"Did she want to get back together and try to work things out?"

"Actually, she was thanking me for being honest with her, and for being a respectable man. She said, I have been the brightest spot in her life and that she has not felt more complete or more at one with anyone as she had with me. She appreciates that I was looking out for her, which is what two people do when they truly love one another. Her dilemma was to go back to her husband and try to make things right or just move on with her life. They were two different people, with different ideas, different ideologies, different in every way two people can possibly be. She felt in her heart that the relationship didn't and could never work, not because she and her husband did not care about one another, but because of who they were. That it's intrinsic and unchangeable."

"Well, I have to ask this silly question, Don."

"What is it? Spit it out, John."

"Now riddle me this, why in the world would someone want to go back to someone that for years was making them miserable, scares, and abuses them?"

"It's funny you say that because when she talked about her dilemma of going back to her husband, I thought the same thing because she already knows what to expect. She knows how she's going to be treated. I just pray that things don't get so bad that she ends up dead or he ends up dead, if they get back together. Anyway, one thing I probably should not have said to Lori that day was that we could revisit the relationship at a later time."

Al, with a confused look on his face, said, "Why would you say that?"

"My reason is because she mentioned it in the email. She said, I hope you're right. I do hope we can revisit this decision because the last thing in the world I want is not to have you in my life. I was not going to reply, but I did not want her to think I was ignoring her or trying to avoid her."

"Really, seriously, she's withholding important information from you is not a good enough reason? You should have not responded to anything she had to say. You just don't play with people's emotions like that," said Kevin.

"Don, you're lucky I was away because if I was here ..."

"Yeah, yeah, yeah, if you were here, you would have done what, Al?"

"I would have given you my shoulder to cry on. Since I was not here and you're talking about it now, I figure I could joke about it. So, out of curiosity what did you say in the email?"

"Hey, I just told her to do whatever it is that she needs to, in order to release the happiness that is within her. I shared with her that God will always be happy with our failures and faults. This is why he sent his son Jesus to die on the cross for our sins. God knows we'll never be able to keep up with his standards. That this is why I love God—because of all he has done for me and continues to do for me."

The Bookstore

One afternoon I was coming out of the bank, and I heard someone shouting my name, "Hey Derek! Derek! Over here across the street." I looked, and it was Sheryl. I walked across the street, and we greeted each other with a big hug. "Wow, Derek, it's been a long time since we have seen each other or even talked. How are you doing, Derek?"

"I can't complain, I'm doing a lot better than I was a few months ago. How are you doing, Sheryl?"

"I'm doing well, you know; hanging in there."

"So, are you married or dating?"

"Unfortunately no, too many knuckleheads and some men are not ready to be real mature men."

"Let me rephrase the question, are you still being hard on men when they approach you?"

"What are you talking about?"

"Come on; you know what I mean."

Sheryl laughed, "I do not know what you're talking about."

"Now do I need to refresh your memory?"

"Yes, please refresh my memory." I looked at Sheryl with this smile on my face because she knew where I was going.

"Do you remember the first time I met you? We were at church, and you were assisting with serving lunch. You dropped a tray, and I assisted you in cleaning up the floor. You did not even say thank you or anything. You just went about your business, leaving me there to finish cleaning up, as if this was my job."

Sheryl with a smirk on her face, "You know that is not even true."

"Honestly Sheryl, you're not an easy person to approach. You're an attractive, beautiful, caring, and giving person, but when I first met you, I thought you were the intimidator. However, I found that it's all good."

"At that time I was going through some things, rebuilding my life and relationship with God."

"I hear you. The good thing was that you acknowledged what it was you needed to do to have a peaceful soul and meaningful life. So, what are you doing later this evening about 7:00 p.m.?"

"I don't have any plans."

"I will be at the bookstore, and if you have time stop by, and I will let you treat me to a beverage."

Sheryl tilted her head to one side and said in an aggressive tone, "What do you mean you will let me treat *you*, to a beverage? If anyone going to be doing any treating, it is going to be you."

I laughed, "Relax Sheryl, I'm only kidding. I will treat because it does not cost anything to drink from the water fountain."

"Yeah whatever. If I meet you at the bookstore later you are going to buy me a coffee latte."

"Now how do I look buying you something you cannot even pronounce or spell?" Before she could get another word out I said, "Just kidding and just come out later, so we can finish talking. I can share with you where I am in my life now."

"That sounds good; I will be there. What bookstore?"

"The new store called Books and More next door to the mall."

I arrived at the bookstore about 6:30 p.m. As I was setting up my laptop, Sheryl walked up to me and said, "What's with the laptop? Are you planning on interviewing or writing a report on me? If you are, you will have to talk with my agent. If this is business, I get paid for my time."

"I laughed, "You're still crazy."

"Thank you, at least I know I still can make you laugh. It's good to see you, Derek. I mean I always enjoyed sitting down with you and talking."

"Yes, this is nice since we have not spoken to one another for a few years. The conversations we had were real and meaningful. I respect that we did not jeopardize that part of our relationship."

"We had boundaries, Derek, and we made a great team working to build an awesome ministry for the kids to enjoy. I would never risk destroying what God put together."

"That is true; I matured knowing that there are some relationships that are meant to be, what they are meant to be, even if that means friends no more or less."

"Thinking back I respected you for being you, Derck, because some people would manipulate and jeopardize the friendship we had. You know what I mean, by venturing off and engaging into other extracurricular activities complicating the true root and foundation of the relationship.

Then the relationship deteriorates. The two people drift apart because they went somewhere in the relationship they should not have gone because they allowed their feelings to be confused with what they may perceive to be love, when it was only infatuation."

"Yes, I know Sheryl, but it helps if people know the meaning of the words they are using instead of just using them."

"What do you mean?"

"For example, infatuation: having a strong, but often short-lived liking for another person. This is when you allow yourself to be inspired by your desires and there is no true attachment. You're only setting your-self up for a major disappointment."

"Yes, I know what you mean, and this is because too many people are too busy trying to play games."

"Huh, playing games or thinking they got game. There is not many who even know the meaning of the game."

"Hey Derek, there is a vacant table over there; let's sit there."

"Sure as long as I can plug in my laptop."

"So, you never told me."

"Tell you what, Sheryl?"

"What's up with the laptop?"

"Well, I find that the best way to feel good about something and bring peace into your heart and soul is by writing it on paper. So what I'm doing is writing another book."

"Wait a minute, what do you mean another book? I did not know you had written a first book."

"The first book is in the process of being published, but once it becomes available I will let you know, so you can go and buy a copy."

"What do mean buy it? I do not get a special signed copy from the author?"

"Sorry, like you said, this is business. You have to buy it. I need to make money, but once you buy it, let me know and then I will sign it." Sheryl had this puzzled look on her face.

"One thing about you, Derek, is that you speak to people with a serious tone and look on your face. It's those moments I do not know if I should take you serious or not."

"I'm not serious, I will hook you up. For you I will charge you half price and initial it." Quickly I said, "Only kidding."

"Huh. I thought so, because I know I was not buying your book. You're going to give me a signed copy."

"Yeah. I guess some things never change."

"What are you talking about?"

"You still got that mouth."

"Never mind my mouth; tell me about this writing you have been doing."

"Let me share this with you. I have been through a lot over the past several years. I experienced some challenges, adversity, and obstacles. I started to notice anger growing within me. I was at a point where I was starting not to like myself. I lost focus of the path I was traveling. I felt lost, and nothing I was doing made sense. Even work was becoming a burden, because I lost confidence in helping my clients. There were times I felt as if I could not even help myself. I was feeling burned out. I came to the realization that I had to consider a career change with a different role and responsibilities. I felt like the prodigal son as if I had turned my back on God my Father. Sheryl, do you remember how happy and joyful I was when I was actively involved in ministry, how diligent I was in reading and studying, developing my spiritual life? I mean I never felt so happy and at peace in my entire life. I knew without a doubt where I was with my relationship with God. Then gradually, I felt I was being pulled in so many directions and not getting any support. My marriage started off great, but then it started to gradually crumble. I will admit that I know I had contributed in many ways by being stubborn, demanding, argumentative, selfish, having high expectations, and probably a host of other things. I also know that there were some minor issues. I had no problem working on them; unfortunately, nothing can be done when your partner refuses to work with you on the minors. If you cannot work on the minors, how are you going to work on the majors together? I felt alone, and the job became a lot harder. I was not asking much from Donna, which made this so unfortunate. I just wanted us to be effective as a team. I was not looking for her, myself, or even us together to be right about the things we could have accomplished. I wanted us to be effective as well as being able to say and see that we were making progress. It's progress that leads to success. I could not do it all by myself. The pressure and stress was gradually building on me. I knew it when I started having chest pains. This is when I knew something was definitely wrong. I had to make some decisions. I did not feel that Donna was looking out for me or us as a family."

Sheryl had a look of sadness on her face, as if she was going to cry. "Have you ever gone to the doctor about your chest pain?"

"Yes."

"Well, what was the problem?"

"The doctor did a routine examination and said I was in good health. My chest pain was from acid reflux, and he gave me a prescription. He said that if the pain persisted, I should come and see him immediately. He would admit me into the hospital for further evaluation. When I heard those words, I never felt so scared in my life. The first thing came to my mind was that I had family members who had a heart attack. One survived his; the other two died, and they were all young. One was my age and he died. I never shared my health condition with my family."

"Why didn't you share your health condition?"

"I did not want anyone to worry about me. My family knew I was going through a lot. The last person I wanted to worry about me was my mother. One day I had decided I needed to take some time to myself and examine my life. I had to see what it was that I've been missing."

"Were you able to figure out what was missing?"

"I sure did; it was my relationship with God, and so like the prodigal son I had to go back and asked for his forgiveness. I asked God to come back into my life and assist me with having a peaceful soul and placing me where He wants me to be so that I could better serve him, in order for me to know the purpose he has for my life. I needed to get to that place whatever He wanted me to do, I would do, and wherever He led me, I would follow. I had to look at things of my past, those things I started and had not completed, which were all healthy and positive, such as finishing my doctorate degree and having my book published. Those were the things I was doing before I got married. I was focused and lived a balanced, happy, joyful, and peaceful life. Now I'm getting back to where I need to be, thanks to the grace of God."

"Wow, you have been through a lot. I'm sorry you had to go through all of that, but everything happens for a reason."

"This is true."

"Well, are you still married or separated?"

"Neither, I'm divorced." Sheryl became silent as if she did not know what to say. "Hey, it's okay because Donna and I were going in different directions. The direction she was going was not about us as husband and wife or as a family. I noticed she was not even attempting to make any adjustments so we could be a family. I'm not proud about the divorce. This was not something I was looking forward to when I got married. I believe that when you have gone through certain experiences in your life, you learn from those experiences so that you can build onto your life. Then on top of this she manipulated this whole situation in order to get pregnant. She decided to stop using her birth control without my knowledge."

"You're not serious; she did not do that?"

"Yes, she did."

"Are you serious?"

"I'm as serious as a heart attack. This definitely confirmed our relationship was one sided."

"So, I take it that you have another child?"

"No."

"I don't understand Derek, how do you not have another child if Donna was pregnant?"

"She had a miscarriage that made the relationship more uncomfortable. I shared with Donna that if she needs anything at any time that I could be of assistance with feel free to call me. In a joking way one time I told her that she has ADD (Attention Deficit Disorder). After witnessing other behaviors she displayed at times, I think she may even be bipolar."

"Can I tell you something, Derek?"

"Sure, there is nothing that could be said or done that could top what I have experienced."

"Well, there were a lot of people saying that you shouldn't get married, that you should wait because other people saw something in Donna that was not being displayed when you were around. Most of all, people saw you making some great strides in your life with all the work you have been doing in the community."

"Unfortunately, I cannot go back and change any of this. To be honest, I really loved Donna and wanted us to share in so much together."

"Now, if you and Donna could work this out, would you go back?" I looked at Sheryl for a few seconds, which felt like twenty minutes before I even answered her question.

"No."

"Why?"

"I would make it personal for the simple fact that I had been deceived, lied to, and hurt. I could not look at her the same. The same trust and respect will not be there as when I first met her. I would always feel as if I need to be cautious in everything I do with her. I do not want to live with anyone under those conditions. The relationship was at a point that I felt I had to walk on eggshells. Mentally and emotionally I was exhausted and physically beaten. I even had to be careful in how I communicated with her; it was a challenge to share something simple. It would be taken out of context. Then, when I would attempt to bring some sort of understanding to resolve the miscommunication and establish a sense of peace,

I would get this cold and distant treatment. For example, we were to meet at the mall on a Wednesday. Something came up at work that delayed me. I called Donna and left her a voice message saying, I will meet you at the mall today, which was the Wednesday we were to meet, but I will be there at 6:15 p.m. instead of 6:00 p.m. Then I get a voice message on my phone saying, I got your message today that you will meet me at the mall at 6:15 p.m. instead of 6:00 p.m. Is this for today or next week? I did not call her back. I was curious to see if she was going to show up or not. When I arrived, she said to me I was not sure if you meant today or another day. Calm and relaxed, I looked at her and said, what did I say in the message? She replayed the message on her phone for me as we listen and the message said, Hello, Donna, this is Derek I will meet you at the mall today, but I will be there at 6:15 p.m. instead of 6:00 p.m. I looked at her and said what didn't you understand? So she gets an attitude with me because I had her take time to not just listen, but hear what I said, but she had nothing to say. She stormed away from me with an attitude and left the mall."

"She probably felt you were treating her like a child."

"Well, I never thought that I was treating her like a child. This was not done with the intent to belittle her or make her feel incompetent. I would share with her. I respond the way I do at times because I want her to have patience in all that she does because sometimes we rush to do things without getting all the information. We all make mistakes because we are listening, not hearing, and we are not patient."

"Have you ever considered doing a little extra to make things a little easier for her, especially since you were aware of her weakness?"

"I shared with her that I could manage things myself, but we were put together for a particular reason—so I can build her where she is weak and strengthen her where she is torn and so that she could do the same for me. The relationship was definitely spiraling out of control, Sheryl.

It was at the point where the best way for me to communicate to her was by writing her letters so that she could see it on paper. Then if she had any questions she could refer back to the paper as a reference guide. If I made a mistake then she could show it to me. In this way, she could not question or debate what I said."

"So you were playing it safe, Derek?"

"I was trying to keep the peace and ease all the unnecessary tension."

"From my perspective, Derek, it sounds as if you were on the right track. You appeared to be handling things very well."

"It's not me; it's from having a strong spiritual life, staying in the word and reaching my soul. If it was not for my spiritual life, wonderful family and friends, I do not know where I would be today."

"Isn't it just awesome knowing He is always in your corner no matter what you're going through?" said Sheryl.

"Let me tell you, it is something special that words cannot describe."

"If you do not mind me asking, are you dating?"

"No. That is not in the plan, and it is not a priority. I do not feel I need somebody in my life now. I want to get back on track on to where I should be and continue to enhance my spiritual life. After being married, dating right away would not be healthy, and it would not be in my best interest. That is one of the problems most people have with relationships, Sheryl."

"What do you mean?"

"People who go through an unpleasant break up or any relational issue are hurt, confused, and lonely. Instead of spending time to themselves, attempting to strengthen and develop their life, they deprive themselves of the opportunity. Most people's answer is to search for someone and start a new relationship, in order to avoid dealing with themselves to become complete and whole again. Besides, relocating has been on my mind, and I'm seriously considering it. I have not mentioned this to anyone, but I'm

221

looking to move to the South or Midwest. I have had a couple of offers, but nothing worth relocating for."

"Wow, relocating that would be a big move and what about your daughter?"

"My daughter would move with me, which would be a good experience for her. I'm not going to jump right into this. I gave this some serious thought and realistically the timing is off. My daughter is close to completing high school and to uproot her to relocate would be very selfish of me. She deserves to remain among her friends and classmates, so she could enjoy her high school years with people she already knows."

"Good point, Derek. Besides, her senior year of high school should be memories of people that she has solid relationships with already."

"Relocating was something I had planned to do for several years. I think about this area, which is great, but I'm due for a change. I would like to be somewhere that the taxes are not as high, and you get more for your money when buying a house. One other important thing, I do not want to be working to pay bills. Having extra money for me would be nice. Another reason for relocating is that I have land in North Carolina I want to build a house on."

"Then you should build the house and then move."

"I'm not trying to force anything. I will know in my heart when it's the right time to move; some things require patience."

"Well, Derek, I'm going to miss this time we spend getting together."

"Now wait a minute, Sheryl, I'm still here and what are you talking about? I'm going to miss the time we spend getting together. You sound as if I'm leaving tomorrow. We will always be friends. When and if that time comes, I will keep in touch."

Sheryl looked down at her watch and then at me, "Oh, I have to go, but I will talk to you later."

"Is everything all right?"

"Yes, I just have to go and meet with Barbara."

One afternoon I received a call from Sheryl. "Hello."

"Hi, Derek. It's me, Sheryl; how are you doing on this beautiful day?"

"Hello, Sheryl, I'm doing better than I deserve. Sooooo, what do I owe for the pleasure of this call?"

"Since you put it that way, meet me at the bookstore this evening at 7:00 p.m. I was thinking about our conversation the other day, and there is something I want to discuss with you."

"Sounds like a plan; I was planning to go to the bookstore this evening, anyway. I will see you at 7:00 p.m." I had not spoken to Sheryl in a couple of weeks, so I was very curious of what she wanted to talk about.

"Hey, Sheryl; how are you doing?"

"I'm doing well. I had a good and uneventful day."

"Could I get you a tea or coffee, Sheryl?"

"Sure, let me see what I want."

"Now don't go ordering something you cannot pronounce."

"I'm not paying you any attention. I would like a hazelnut latte."

Jokingly, "it's not latty; it's latte. You still want things you cannot pronounce."

"Will you just go and get my latte." I went to purchase Sheryl latte and for me tea. I returned and sat down.

"So, what is going on? I'm very curious why you asked to meet with me."

"The reason I wanted to meet with you, Derek, is that the short amount of time we spent together the last time we were here. A lot has been on my mind, and I wanted to share my thoughts with you."

In my mind I was thinking, *"Oh boy, here we go, this does not sound good."*

"Well Derek, as you know, we talked about a lot of things during the short amount of time we spent together. You shared with me that you were thinking about relocation. If that's what you really want to do, you have to do what is best for you. The problem that I see is that you're ready to walk away from people who care about you and people who need you."

Now I was thinking, "*I do not like the sound of this at all.*"

"What I want may no longer be an issue since you decided that the first chance you get to leave you will take it. I feel sad not only for those who need you here, but also for us."

"What are you talking about? Us? Am I missing something?"

"You have made it clear that we are only friends. I feel the time we spent together and working together in the past had a purpose. Now we're brought together again for a reason. This is special and could be the beginning of a beautiful relationship. I have heard you say to your other friends that you were not seeing anyone. That kind of hurts because you have been seeing someone for a while now, it's just that you have not made a commitment and hide what we are as friends. As far as a commitment, I think you probably will not make one. At least not with me anyway, since you're ready to make a new start with your life. To be honest you want to relocate hurt. You and I have had a very special relationship, even before you got married. The issue of committing to me is something you do not want to do because you do not want to hurt Donna's feelings. That is the real reason you do not want to date me. This is ironic because she hurt you. Now you want to preserve her feelings, but at the same time, I'm here to help in any way that I can. In all honesty my feelings are the ones being hurt. How many times have I heard you say, that is not where I am at right now? Usually the excuse you gave me was that you needed to accomplish certain things. You're heading in a certain direction, but since then, you have accomplished a lot of the things you wanted to accomplish. In your own words, you were healing from your divorce, yet you still want to run.

I know I'm not perfect, and I will probably do some goofy things, but the one thing I do know is that I'm a good woman. Some of the things I do are for you, and I share the things I share with you because I know I have a good heart. I have no agendas, no ulterior motives, and nothing up my sleeve. I may not have it all together on the outside, which is still a work in progress, but on the inside I'm okay. I can honestly say that what you see is what it is. I would never hurt you or betray your trust. The hardest thing about talking about this is that, I still think back to when we first met, getting to know each other while working together. I found you to be very special because you were so compassionate in what you were doing. This is a rare quality in a man. I know I said we were okay as friends. I know it would be easier for you if we remained friends, without the commitment. When we would talk or spend time together, a little piece of me stays with you and it hurts. It hurts because you have not and will probably never be able to give me those parts of you. I have loved you for a long time, Derek, but now I think it is time for me to collect those pieces, pick them up, and move on myself just as you had to spend time with God to get the healing process started from all you have endure. Now I have to spend time with God to get my own healing process started." As I look at Sheryl, I can see the wells of her eyes filled with water as she continued talking, "I finally came to the conclusion that if we were meant to be together then we would have been. I do not want to be friends with you anymore because I see and feel your heart when we talk, and that is where I want to be. I'm aware you have a lot going on in your life, and you're working through it, as well. I do not want to be in the way of the rebuilding process of your life, especially, your spiritual life."

"Wow! Sheryl I did not see this coming, and I feel miserable. I never knew you felt this way. Let me rephrase that; I never knew you felt this strongly about me or I should say us, especially after all these years. I'm sorry, and I'm not ready to go there with you or anyone at this time. My divorce had a devastating impact on me, and I'm just starting to make sense of my life once again."

As the wells of her eyes filled with water, a tear rolled down her face, and she said, "I shared my heart with you. I thought the feelings I had for you were not there anymore, but obviously there are still strong feelings. I feel the way I do, not because you're a nice guy, but because you're sincere, compassionate, and a patient man who loves and cares for people and is not quick to judge others." As a tear rolled down, Sheryl took a napkin and wiped her cheek and said, "I think it would be best that we do not call each other anymore and that we go on with our lives individually."

I grabbed her hand and said, "I'm truly just starting to adapt and adjust to living a peaceful life. I'm comfortable knowing that I do not have to worry about walking on eggshells when I come home from work. I no longer have to worry about the mind games or the emotional and verbal abuse. It took great strength for me to remove myself from an unpleasant, unhealthy, and hostile environment. I'm sorry, and yes, I enjoy our conversations. I do have to respect you, your feelings, and your decision. I will miss talking with you. You may call me any time when you're comfortable. I must admit that I'm still under construction. I hope you can understand and our friendship does not have to end this way."

Sheryl got up out of her chair, leaned over, gave me a hug and kiss, and put her hand on my shoulder and said, "Good-bye, Derek."

I grabbed her hand as it was on my shoulder. I stood up, looking at Sheryl as another tear rolled down her face and said, "Before you leave I would like to say, I feel crushed because you're a special person and we are good friends. Yes, we made a great team, but I know I'm not ready to entertain a serious relationship. Even after sharing this with you I thought you would understand."

"I do understand. I want to have a relationship of my own, Derek."

"This is a difficult situation for you and me, having to make a decision between friendship and having a committed relationship. With all I have endured over the past few years, can't a man get a chance to come up for air? I feel no matter how honest I am with you, I have managed to hurt your feelings and our friendship, which was not my attention. My purpose for sharing with you was that, I see you as a supportive and caring friend. One friend to another, Sheryl, entering in a serious relationship would not have been healthy for either one of us."

"Good bye-Derek."

Time to Man Up

D on, Kevin, John, Al, and I met for an early dinner Saturday. "Excuse me gentlemen, I would like to share something with you. When you think of the phrase *man up*, what do you feel?"

"Here goes Derek the philosopher," said John.

Kevin chimed in and said, "Nope, he is Mr. Philosopher."

I repeated my question in a serious tone, "Come on, I'm being serious. When any one of you think of the phrase *man up*, how does that feel to you? What does it look like?"

"Well, to me it's about being a responsible man."

"Right, Al," I said.

Don started to speak as if he was not sure what to say, "Well, I never really thought much about it, personally. I mean, I would hear people say to man up, but in a joking way. I don't know. I guess if I had to say, it means it's about caring for people."

"You're right, Don."

"Derek, where are you going with this? You said Al was right, too," said Don."

Yes I know, so what about you, Kevin?"

"I don't know, Derek."

"You have to have something you want to share. Kevin, just take a moment and allow the words that are in your heart to be shared. Don't think about it; feel it."

"Well, I guess I would say being open and honest."

"You're right."

"Well gentlemen, I think we can say that Derek is officially losing it, and he is stressed out," said Kevin.

"Hey, gentlemen, I'm feeling extraordinary. You will see where I'm going," said Derek.

John interrupted, "No, Derek is right. All of you are right."

Don asked, "If all of us are right, John, what do you think it is?"

"What I feel when I hear the phrase *man up* is being real," replied John.

"You're right, too! Now, Derek, tell the man what he has won," replied Al.

We laughed and I continued, "You all are right. There is no wrong answer. Gentlemen, let me share something with you. When you man up, you allow your heart to share openness, honesty, caring for people, being responsible, and being real just like all of you shared."

"Then let us ask you the question, Derek, what do you feel when you hear the phrase *man up*?"

"I'm glad you asked John. As you all know I've been through some difficult and challenging times. This required me investing time in myself. During this time I read this book, I don't remember the name or writer, but it assisted me with putting that part of my life back into its rightful place. I will share with you my thoughts and paraphrase some of the things I read, and how it relates to the phrase *man up*."

"Then stop with all the additional side talk and get to the meat and potatoes of things."

"Let me start off by saying, Kevin, that being able to man up is a rare quality in men today. It requires a man to be real and true to himself, viewing himself and the world around him as being stable with the reality and honesty of life. This is a time for a man to express his feelings. He may not know what his emotions mean, but he must be alert to experience them honestly. As men, we should not ignore your emotions, as most men do. Those who are in touch with their emotions are real men. A real man is very much aware of his feelings because he knows who he is and does confuse it with what he does. When those emotions develop in a real man, he will not back down from them. When you man up, you are accepting other roles and responsibilities as a real man. You quickly respond to what you're feeling and what is taking place around you. This feeling becomes a feeling of spontaneity; this allows you to respond freely. When it's time to man up, it is handled in a mature, responsible, and controlled manner. You process what you're feeling and assess it; then you release your feelings and respond to them in a responsible manner. When it's time to man up, you remember that you respond and not react. You have the understanding that your feelings are a part of being a man. Therefore, when you man up, you're an authentic man, a real man, making you the genuine thing."

Kevin looked at Derek with a smile and said, "You are the Man. You are the Real Deal."

Derek continued, "As men we should be willing to bond with one another."

"We do bond, Derek; for example like now we are having dinner together as men. We hang out, play pool, and go to the gym," replied Don.

"What I mean, is having an emotional and intimate relationship."

"Hey Derek, I do not know what you're talking about, but that sounds like something freaky. It also sounds like something that I am definitely not into, if you know what I mean," says John.

Don and Kevin laughed at John's remark. Looking at John, Derek respond, "Real funny, but what I'm talking about is being able to develop trust and respect, where we are able to communicate what truly hurts us or is hurting us. All of us at some point in our life have had a bad experience that scarred a part of us. We vowed to ourselves never to revisit that area of our life again, but this is what causes us to distance ourselves from one another."

Don interrupted, "Personally speaking, Derek, many men find it difficult to share that side of them because this makes them transparent to other men. I know it is a challenge for me. Besides, it's our nature as men to be competitive, and if we were to open ourselves up, it would be like walking around with a bulls eye on your back, making yourself more vulnerable than you could handle."

"That is what I'm exactly talking about, Don: the unknown, the uncertainty, appearing weak, and the fear of being misunderstood."

John chimed in, "And don't forget the thrill of victory and the agony of defeat," as Kevin, Al, and Don laughed.

"Hey, John, I didn't know you were thinking about making a career change to become a comedian," replied Derek.

"I'm not."

"And don't." Derek continued, "On a serious note, so many men have high blood pressure and heart attacks because of this kind of fear. We keep to ourselves; some of us are wearing a mask or putting on a good act when we are out in public. As men, we keep our deepest, scariest feelings, fears, and concerns bottled up inside until we explode." "Come on, Derek. Do you truly believe men should engage or entertain this style of relationship?"

"Yes I do, Don. Why not? We're all very much aware that men today struggle with a lot. The adversity and challenges we are faced with on the job, in our homes, in relationships, and the list goes on. Gentlemen, God forbid that anyone knows we as men don't have it all together."

"This is what I believe, Derek."

231

"What do you believe, Don?"

"That most men are not capable of sharing with another man their struggles, grief, family issues, personal issues, or even relational issues. As men we are always trying to protect our emotional well-being from any further damage. Real men do not talk about feelings or relationships; real men do not share their heart. Most men feel weak when they share that deep emotional side of themselves."

"News flash," said Derek, "For a man to not be able to share his heart does not make him a real man. A man who is capable of sharing his heart is a genuine and authentic man. He is connected with his soul. Genuine and authentic men are confident and know who they are and do not dare to confuse this with what they are. They have an emotional and special relationship with God that keeps them balanced in life. Genuine and authentic men know they are not alone in whatever they're going through. They have a special connection developed with other men. Gentlemen, as genuine and authentic men, we strengthen and build one another and care for one another in a special way without putting them down or making them feel less than they truly are. We would encourage, sacrifice, teach, mentor, edify, and demonstrate God's love on them, as God did for us. 'For God so loved the world that he gave his only Son, so that everyone who believes in him will not perish but have eternal life."

As Kevin was getting ready to speak, the waitress came to our table and asked if we were ready to order. Kevin looked at the waitress and said, "Excuse me, before we order I would like to introduce you to Mr. Philosopher."

The waitress said, "Hello, Mr. Philosopher. You must be a profound and intellectual man. May I take your order?" I smiled and gave the waitress my order.

After having dinner with the guys while driving home, I started to reflect about the last conversation I had with Donna. The conversation was not terrible, but uncomfortable and difficult. It was a different expression of love being shared between two people. Believe me this was not easy for me to do, because I was self-conscious and unsure how Donna might react. I still felt at times that I had to walk on eggshells when I was around her so that I would not feel as if I was doing something wrong. This was not my style, and it took me out of my comfort zone. I learned that taking the right actions assisted me with being able to have the right feelings within myself to be able to speak to Donna. This allowed me to set boundaries relating to the change with our relationship since we were no longer married.

"I told her that since we are divorced and she is no longer my wife, I'm no longer her husband and I'm not responsible for her, the things that she does with her life, or how she wants to live her life, but I'm willing to assist her as a friend if she wants me to."

She gave me this sarcastic response, "You do not have to worry about me and my life because my life is none of your business."

I said, "Okay. I just want to let you know that I'm still here for you regardless of our indifference. I know having conversations like this with people is not easy, especially when it's with someone you have had a close relationship with."

As I was driving my phone rang, "Hello."

"Hi, Derek, this is Donna."

"Hi, is everything alright?"

"Yes and no, I'm having some car trouble and wanted to know if you could take a look at my car?"

"Sure, I will stop by before I go home."

"I hope it's not too late and I'm not taking you from anything?"

"I just left from having dinner with the guys. It's only 6:00 p.m.— early enough for me to stop by. See you soon."

"Thanks, I really appreciate you doing this, bye."

See what happens? When you start thinking about something, you speak life into it. I hope this does not become an unpleasant visit. I guess we'll see when I arrive.

When I arrived, Donna was sitting outside in front of her house. I got out the car and started walking towards the house. "Hello, Donna." She looked at me with a happy, but not-so-happy look on her face.

"Hi, how are you doing, Derek?"

"I can't complain, I'm making progress and taking each day one day at a time." As I was leaning against the stair railing, a question came to mind. Now I'm contemplating in my mind should I or shouldn't I ask. Well, why not, "So, may I ask you a question, Donna?"

"Sure; of course you may."

"I was wondering if the things that occurred in your life are because of your relationship with God. Not to say that you have a bad relationship with God. Subconsciously, we put ourselves in a position when we have people on one side, and then God on another. Then it becomes people versus God. As people, we're quick to say that we have a relationship with God. We are quick to say we have faith, and stand on His word and He will get you through. There is nothing wrong with having friends and family for moral support, but do not replace God with these people. This is something that we can allow to happen without even realizing it."

"What are you trying to say Derek? I don't follow; where is all this coming from?"

"What I mean is that we all go through some sort of challenging time in our lives. Then we have this void in our life. We fill this void subconsciously with people, which is easy. In reality, God should fill this void. I see it this way, Donna. People are not perfect, and there are no guarantees of what you're going to get from people. By allowing another person to fill the void in your life, you're giving them control of opening up that void again, causing you more hurt and pain. This is why we need to allow God to fill our voids because He is not going to do anything to open it up, and He will definitely not use it against you to cause you more hurt and pain. This is why I believe that people should never fill the voids in our lives, only God. Then you have to ask yourself: am I putting my faith in God or people to bring the true happiness that God wants me to have."

Donna had this intense look on her face and said, "Why are you sharing this with me? Are you trying to tell me something?"

"Why I'm sharing this with you is because I acknowledge that I do it myself, and it is not healthy. I had to dig deep down inside, and examine my heart because God knows my heart. I feel that it is important that I know my heart and be true to my heart, so I can make my soul whole. In order to accomplish this it requires, self-discipline, dedication, and being real to oneself. I'm talking from experience because when I examined myself and the challenging life I was having, I had to spend time away once or twice a week at some quiet area to give all my attention to God. This was time for me to regain and balance my spiritual life. This assists me with keeping people or things from coming into my circle that is not healthy for me. My mission was to know that it was God rebuilding and healing my soul. When the time is right, then I can allow people and things into my circle with an open mind. This time also allowed me to be a better model for others that I come in contact with. I even found myself being more humble. You can say I'm at a point in my life where I can look at you and talk to you. I also would like to apologize to you, and anyone else who has been affected by my actions. I accept the anger, disgust, hatred, and whatever else that came my way because of my actions, and I'm able to say, I forgive and all I do is in love. I'm able to share this with you now where before I could not." I smiled at Donna and gave her a little wink just to let her know that things are good. Before Donna could get a word out of her mouth, I quickly said, "So what is the problem with your car?"

While handing me the keys to her car, Donna continued, "I was about to say before you interrupted is that loves never fails, Derek."

"You're so right; love never fails, but people do. We must realize that love is the key that opens our life. We must be able to love ourselves and know how to love others, by being truthful and honest in the most difficult times, and understand that love never fails, because God is love." As I was walking towards the driver side of the car, there was an awkward moment of silence that seems as if it was an hour of silence. Donna started walking away. "Where are you going?"

"I forgot I have something cooking in the oven."

"Okay." I started the car and noticed that there was a slight hesitation in it starting. I got out of the car, opened the hood and noticed the battery terminals were filled with corrosion. I cleaned off the terminals and started the car again, and it started up without any hesitation.

Donna returned, "How did you get it started? What was the problem?" Asked Donna.

"I don't think anything is wrong. Your battery terminals had to be cleaned. After cleaning them, the car started just fine. If the problem continues, you may need a new battery because this is the original battery from when the car was purchased."

"Thank you; I really appreciate you taking the time to stop by and assist me."

"Not a problem. I will talk with you later." I walked back to my car got in and drove off. As I was driving, I started to think about how I do not feel the way I once did for Donna in my heart. I did not have much trust or respect for her as a woman. I understood what she would do and was capable of doing to get her way. I was able to get myself to the point where I was able to forgive Donna. I would like to say that the forgiveness was a process and took time for me to develop. To be truly honest, forgiving someone that hurts you requires you to have space and to put things in perspective. It was a self-evaluation and cleansing process: you know, out with the bad and in with the new strengthening for your soul. Just the thought of thinking how difficult it was to communicate to Donna at times slightly irritated me. Sometimes just talking with her could ignite an argument or some sort of hostility. She still would take things totally out of context or say things without thinking. So, I had to find a way to demonstrate some sort of action of forgiveness. I had to limit what I would say to her or what was being said. You know, sort of like staying a step ahead of her, which was not hard to do. I would gradually speak to her about certain things that I felt were safe to discuss with her.

It was still early in the evening, so I decided to stop at The Jazz Place. The Jazz Place is a place where people go and wind down after work, to read a book, relax, or socialize with friends.

Jazz music is a form of art that expresses a person's mood and emotions. Jazz is not just music you listen to with your ears but feel with your heart, as well. When I walked in, I saw Don sitting at a table by himself. I walked over to his table, "You look like you're out for an evening of peace and relaxation."

"Yes, sir. Have a seat unless you are here with someone."

"As a matter of fact I am."

"Who are you with?" Asked Don.

"Me, myself, and I," replied Derek.

"Have a seat, Derek, and I will get the waitress to take your order."

"You know, Don, it's refreshing to openly talk about some of the challenges and difficulties we face. The Sunday we were at John's house, everyone was relaxed, put their guards down, and shared without worrying about being judged."

"I'm glad you brought that up. Can I share something with you, Derek?"

"Sure, go right ahead. I'm listening."

"You know something, Derek; it is not that I do not want to get married someday. I just don't want to be with a woman who feels that once you're married, they own you or something. I've been looking at all that being submissive stuff you read in the Bible."

"What about being submissive?" Asked Derek.

"I think it assists with developing the foundation of marriage. I'm also aware that this goes right out the window with some women once you're hitched."

Derek laughs, "Hitched—interesting. I can understand where you're coming from, but like you said that day at John's house, love does not discriminate. If you feel you have met someone that you truly love, care for, and the feelings are mutual; and the two of you can put everything on the table and communicate openly and honestly; you will be fine. Fortunately, all women are not terrible, and some do not intend to be, well let's just say, difficult. Some women just like some men; they have a lot of things that went on in their lives. The reality of it is that they just have not taken the right steps to free themselves from the things of their pasts, so they're not at peace. Unfortunately, when those past issues are not dealt with, they come out in the relationship, creating hardship in the relationship. Some people have a habit or habits they cannot control, or should I say, choose not to control."

Don hesitated before speaking, "I clearly understand what you're saying, but it just seems that when something goes wrong in some relationships, the woman is usually the victim. The man cannot be the victim because he is the man. He is the one that is supposed to uphold the household and family. The man is the one who is supposed to keep it all together no matter how hard times get. It's the man that is expected to carry the load and get you through it, but who is there for the man once he gets you through it all?" Asked Don. The waitress had delivered our drinks to our table. I took a sip of my glass of wine and looked at Don.

"Hey, you know who is going to get you through it all," said Derek.

"Who?"

"God. He is going to get you and your significant other or wife through it all. If it's meant to be, it will be. We must be real at times and take notice that God Himself may be trying to pull us from the things we are holding onto. Not all things are in God's will."

"You know, Derek, some things just don't seem fair, the way I see it."

"What do mean, things don't seem fair?"

"What I'm talking about is that everyone else goes on about their daily business reaping the benefits of a man's hard labor, not taking in consideration the stressful moments, long days of confusion, and emotional ups and downs that some men have to face. My question is, what is it that a man should do when he has a heavy heart or just has a vision of what he wants to happen but without support?"

"He should pray, Don, and spend time with God. He should refine his soul to put himself at ease and to develop some peace within his life—or he could go out and listen to some jazz."

"Okay seriously, times can get so hard when you have to deal with the many sides of adversity in today's society."

"Well, you know my situation. What I have been through is no secret. I always thought of home as a safe haven, a place for peace, comfort, love, acceptance, moral support, and happiness. However, manipulation and deception adds fuel to the fire. Donna would say, 'I cannot stand someone who would sit in my face and lie to me.' I would look at her and say, 'You've been lying to me since the beginning.' Understand that we lie in so many ways or we have people justify a lie by saying that a little white lie will not hurt. A lie is a lie whether it is blue, black, green, brown, purple, orange, or even white. The bottom line is that no lie is pretty, and every lie has an impact on somebody, especially when you lie just to get what you want. What's funny about this is that the teller of any lie, even if the lie is of manipulation or deception, usually ends up being viewed as the victim." Derek paused.

"Are you okay, Derek? Why are you smiling?" Asked Don.

"Just a quick thought came to mind, unfortunately, the woman probably will always be thought of as the victim."

"I clearly hear what you're saying. I believe that some women will lie by any means necessary to get what they want and still be the victim."

"Yes, Don, but keep in mind that there are some legitimate circumstances where women are the victims. I once read that the crucial element of lying is in deception, it is not in what you say. That means lies are told in many ways such as silence, avoidance, and by making explicit statements. That the worst form of lying is with the use of the eye; this style of lying is known to be worse than someone verbally lying to you, at least when someone verbally lies to you. You could at least see it or hear it coming and prepare yourself for how you need to address what was said to you. There are other types of lies that catch you off guard; they're secretive and do not allow you enough time to put up your protective defense mechanism."

"Wow, Derek, I feel like I'm in a counseling session with you."

"I'm only keeping it real, Don, just keeping it real."

"You know, this sounds like something I have heard other people experience," said Don.

"What do you mean it sounds like something other people experience? We all experience some sort of emotional or internal abuse. It may not have been as severe as others. Besides Don, why do you think you started up this conversation with me?"

"Hey, I was just making conversation about something that was on my mind."

"It's all right, Don; this is what friends are for. Let me give you a deeper insight about what I experienced. I felt like running away from the problems I encountered. I did not isolate myself even though there were times I did not want to be bothered with work, friends, or family. I felt I needed to start life from the ground floor in order to get where I needed to be."

"I know, Derek; you started investing time in your spiritual life."

"Yes, and I took it a step further. I started to open up to people more about my problems and the challenges I was dealing with. I would spend time whenever I could in prayer and developing healthy relationships. I realized that I had to stay clear of addictive behaviors, unhealthy relationships, and especially, not allow myself to be sensitive to what other people think about me. The last thing I wanted was to end up in a deepened depressed state. I had to look back at when I was the happiest in my life. Some people do not believe in going back, Don."

"Personally, I believe that sometimes you have to go back to know where you are going. There's nothing wrong with going back to visit; you just don't want to visit too long."

"Bingo, Don. Donna would say she never goes back. I would look at her and say, there are times we need to go back to see where we got off course in order to put the pieces back together in our life or to complete certain tasks. I also believe she was afraid of going back because there were some unresolved issues that she left dangling and that needed closure. This was her way of running and avoiding."

"You know something, Derek?"

"What?"

"Ahh, forget it."

"Go ahead spit it out, Don. We're having good conversation, right?"

"Yes, I was thinking about the story I shared at John's."

"Oh, the relationship you had with Lori."

"Yes."

"What about it; did something trigger?"

"I was a victim getting hit from the blind side. This is the worst way for anyone to be emotionally hurt. This is not even something a doctor could even heal or even give you a prescription for because the medication would just be a temporary solution. I do have a question to ask you, Derek, if you don't mind."

"Sure!"

"Your divorce: how did you cope with it so well?"

"I will be the first to admit that it has been a hard and long struggle for me to cope with. First of all, I did not want to just cope or deal with it. I was also trying to find where I belong, find myself again, and most importantly put my soul back together. I could look back and see the things that God has done in my life, including the path I was on. However, my biggest challenge was being able to go back and pick up the pieces and complete what I had begun without feeling angry or guilty. I felt as if I had turned my back on God with all I was doing."

"Man, you sound as if you were not in a happy place," replied Don.

"I was not, but I learned about the place I was. I learned enough to know that I will not be revisiting that place ever again. It's easy to fall into the trap of ignoring the past, because no one wants to revisit and take that drive down the painful memory lane. In order to really move forward, you have to step back. You do not want to start developing bad patterns, setting yourself up for disappointment. I realized that any present mistakes I make must be new mistakes, not old mistakes." Don took a sip of his drink and remained silent as if he was in another place.

So I gave him a moment to himself to see how long he would remain in that state. Then, after several seconds that seemed like minutes, I said, "Are you okay, Don?"

"Yes, I'm fine, and I know what I have to do now. Thanks, man."

"What are you talking about? What is it that you have to do?" Asked Derek.

"I have to start the rehabilitation process for myself to get where I should be in my spiritual life. I must admit that a part of my life has been a journey. I admit I was not being fair to myself and to the people who could have been a special part of my life. Most importantly, I failed to put God first, not allowing His patience, peace, and promises to guide me. I feared what others might have thought, or how they might view me. I want to be in a healthy relationship and get married someday, Derek."

"What are you talking about? Your spiritual life is intact. We're not perfect and, besides, all of our spiritual lives needs work—some more than others. Don't try to become perfect; you'll end up disappointing yourself because we're not perfect." With a smile on my face, looking at Don, I said, "You know what it is you really need to do, Don?"

"Well, by the look of that smile on your face it is probably something silly. So what is it I need to do?"

"You sure you really want to know?"

"All right come on, Derek, stop playing and tell me."

"You need to *man up*! I sat here and listened to you. It's not that you don't know what you should be doing with your relationships. You're not putting what you know to practice. Trust yourself and trust your heart; just man up and stop avoiding the promises of God. Don't take this personal. I'm not trying to hurt you. I'm just sharing and keeping it real as friends." Then there was a moment of silence between Don and I. During that moment we just took in the jazz that was playing and drank our wine.

Then Don said, "These guys are good."

"Yeah, the music is a nice style of jazz with a nice flow to it." I started to give some more thought to what Don was sharing with me. "Hey, Don."

"Yeah, what's up?"

"You're not one for talking about the women you are dating or bringing them around family or friends. I'm starting to get this feeling that there is more to this. You know that feeling. The one that says, this does not add up. So I must ask, and I'm going to ask you this once, and keep it real with me."

"Now, what are you talking about?"

"Come on, Don, like the Marvin Gaye song, "What's Going On?" I want to know what's going on."

Don looked at me with this confused look on his face, "What are you talking about? Nothing is going on here."

"Come on, you're sitting here talking about relationships and wanting to get married someday. So I want to know—what's going on?"

Don got quiet for a moment, "All right; I'm going to be real about what's going on." I started laughing, and Don said, "What's so funny?"

"Yeah, Don, the jig is up."

Don laughed and then went onto say, "All right. Do you want know or not?"

"All right I'm going to be serious; I'm listening."

"Of course, you know that dating is very challenging. We work so hard to date people of our type, such as social class, race, spiritual foundation, and with similar interests."

"Yes, we do work hard on trying to make and find that match that fits us."

"Now, let me stop you for a moment. When you look around this room what do you see, Derek?"

I obeyed Don, did a brief scan of the place, and said, "I see people, couples sitting around eating, drinking, reading, enjoying the music and having a relaxing evening."

"No, dig deeper than that."

"Well if you want to get deeper ..." So, I took another sip of my wine, and surveyed the room again, "You probably have couples here from different backgrounds, social class, different sides of the track, and different lifestyles. See that couple over there? The woman is dressed like a professional, while the guy is dressed in his baggy attire. There are several interracial couples in here; you have black and white, Latino and black, Asian and white, and several others."

"That is it."

"What's it, Don?"

"There are mixed couples out there, and they all appear to be happy and comfortable in their relationships."

"What's so bad about that?" Asked Derek.

"Nothing is bad or wrong with it. This is what is going on with me. A couple of months ago, I was sitting in here having a glass of wine and reading a book. It was a crowded evening, and I was sitting alone at a table for two. Then this Asian woman came over to me and asked if the other seat was taken. I said no, and she asked would be okay for her to sit there."

"What did you say?'

"Of course I said yes, she may sit there. Then the waitress came over and asked us if we wanted to order anything. We both ordered a glass of wine; we introduced ourselves to one another and conversed for at least two hours. We shared a lot, and I felt a connection with her that I have not felt with anyone else. I sat, talked, and dated many women and never felt like this about anyone one of them as I do with this woman. I always imagined that the type of woman I wanted to be with was the type I met in business school who were business-like, ambitious, and focused. That is pretty much the kind of women I dated through my twenties and the early part of my thirties, but nothing clicked like the way things clicked between Sharon and I."

"Wow, I got a name—Sharon. I guess you're in the sharing moment for Sharon," said Derek.

"I'm being serious."

"Okay, why is Sharon not ambitious, smart, and focused?"

"Yes, she is and then some, but she is not in the business field."

"Well, what does she do for work?"

"She works as a chef, enjoys art, photography, hiking, and biking. Before we left, I asked her for her phone number and asked if she would like to get together for lunch. She was comfortable with this and ever since then, we have been spending time together. Sharon is a sweet and beautiful person inside and out. She is very different from a lot of the women I have dated. She would compliment me, plans romantic dates, and she is open with me about us. She's not materialistic, lives a basic simple and beautiful life. I love this woman, and struggle with telling her."

"Why? Because she is an Asian chef, and you think others would look at you as if you lowered your standards? Let me tell you something. You or I cannot control whom our heart connects with. Besides, you need to open the eyes of your heart and be open, to meeting all different kinds of people and not depend on your initial view of a person. It sounds like you're meant to be with the person you met. The two of you are probably meant for one another. Relationships like you're describing are rare. Some people meet that special person early in life. Some later in life, after they went through a few bad relationships or even a divorce, and some people continue to repeat the same patterns. Then there are some that never meet anyone and grow old and alone."

"Okay, let me share something else with you, Derek. Do you remember that Sunday we were at John's house having that conversation about love, friendship, and relationships with people of different races or nationalities?"

"Yes, I remember the conversation."

"When I brought all this up that day, I was dating Sharon at the time."

"Well, how does she feel about you?"

"I know she feels the same because when we're together it's like we always knew each other."

"Hey, Don, listen up. All you had shared that day at John's house, you need to put into practice. Don't wait because when you wait for the perfect condition you will never get anything done. You will experience more special moments than perfect conditions. Like I said, man up, and step to the plate. The fact that you want to define your relationship with this woman tells me that you view her as a woman who is worth investing time with and getting to know better. When I ask you this next question, I want you to be true to your heart."

"Okay," replied Don.

"Is it really worth it to you to say no to her because of what others may think?"

"No."

"What's even more important, are you going to allow others to decide what should or shouldn't make you happy?"

"No, I can't live my life that way, Derek."

"Usually, what other people believe is based on their own opinions and prejudices. To put it out on the table, they're bigots and small minded."

"Your happiness is based on you, Don. Besides, it sounds as if you would be giving a great gift to your friends, family, and most importantly yourself, showing them the confident and open-minded man that you truly are. If dating this woman feels right for you, please go for it. Man, just be true to yourself. Do you hear me? Just be true to you."

"You're right, I have to start opening up and expressing my happiness."

"Just remember, that God blesses us with special things, people, love, and happiness in the most unexpected places and at the most unexpected times."

"Sharon is a very special woman. I have never felt the qualities, love, and compassion in any other woman I've dated as I see and feel in her. She has this natural tranquility of love for other people. She has a strong and healthy spiritual life. She shares with me this level of intimacy in a caring and loving way with such honesty."

"What do you mean?" Asked Derek.

"What I mean, is when we talk the conversations are deep and intimate. It's as if I met a woman who has an intimate relationship with God that we all so desire." Derek looked at Don with this smile on his face.

"What are you smiling about?"

"When God comes through, He comes through. It sounds as if God has truly blessed you, Don."

"This is what I prayed for, and I do thank God for Sharon."

"May I share this one last thing with you?"

"Go right ahead, Derek. We shared so much already we might as well keep sharing."

"Well this is something that I never shared with anyone, and nobody has shared this with me. After my divorce I spent a lot of time to myself and with God. I always read the Bible, but it is funny how certain things stick out to you more when you read it a second, third and fourth time."

"I'm not following you."

"God shared with me a lot about relationships with men and women whether as friends, co-workers, spiritual friendships, and as couples. It is that a man should cherish a woman in a way that God wants a man to cherish a woman, especially if that woman is supportive and assists that man in being all he can inside, meaning, assisting that man with being able to see his heart as well as hers, embrace his true identity, and being one with his soul."

"Now, that was deep, Derek."

Derek continued, "You discover the man that God wants you to be and not what you think society wants you to be. You're now capable of opening your heart and allowing people to read what's been inscribed on your heart, defining the kind of man you are. Having a supportive partner in allowing you to venture off for self-exploration, and to discover God's true plan for your life is a wonderful feeling. In the first chapter of Jeremiah, God tells us that he knew us before we were formed in our mother's womb. God has a special plan for all or our lives."

"Okay Derek, I hear you saying; some of us must be faithful and obedient enough at some point in our life to do a little self-exploration and discover this plan. What does this all mean?"

"It means it's making you a new found man or woman. This is not easy; it's actually very challenging, but in the end this newfound man will benefit your partner and the people around you. Donna and I shared so much about our dreams, goals, and objectives and how we wanted God to work in our lives. Donna started to make changes and adjustments that I could no longer support. I started developing a lot of anger and resentment within me."

"So, Derek, what are you really saying?"

"I'm saying that I just want you to be happy and not go into something with your eyes closed."

"In my heart I feel that Sharon is an exceptional woman." Derek chuckled at Don's statement. "What do you find to be so funny?"

"That word makes me laugh."

249

"What word?" Asked Don.

"The word exceptional made me laugh."

"Why, did I miss something?"

"No you didn't miss anything, Don. It just reminds me of this person I met and her outlook on relationships."

"Tell me about it."

"You may find this comical."

"Well I like to have a good laugh just as you do."

"I once had the opportunity to meet this very confused woman."

"What do you mean she was confused?"

"Paula was coo coo for cocoa puffs. She had an interest in me, which I think was more physical than anything else. The first time we met, she had shared with me that she has been married three times before the age of thirty. She wanted kids and did not care to be married or in a serious relationship. She lived at home with her mother, and it was interesting how she and her mother entertained relationships—weird and very questionable."

"What was questionable about this?"

"She shared with me that they would meet guys over the Internet, then go out and meet them, and bring some of these guys to their house. When I attempted to have a conversation with her about how risky it was to meet people over the Internet, she did not want to hear anything I had to say. She started justifying what she was doing and why, as if this was typical and normal. I learned that she had a low self-esteem, was insecure, and had a negative attitude. She also experienced mood swings, identity issues, and had a history of abuse. I learned that she struggled with maturity and entertaining a respectful and healthy relationship."

"What do you mean?" Asked Don.

"What I mean is that she wanted to have a serious relationship and hold onto past relationships. According to her, those relationships were not platonic, if you know what I mean. This was her normal and typical way with relationships."

"Why would she expect somebody to take her seriously?"

"Hey, my point exactly. She wanted to know more about my personal life, including my relationships with friends and family. She wanted to meet my friends and family, which was not necessary because we were not serious like that. I told her that I couldn't take her seriously, and there was no spiritual connection. What came out of her mouth was that she was spiritual, but what I witnessed and heard told me she lacked spiritual readiness when it came to relationships."

"Did you ever have an actual conversation with her about that spiritual part of her life, relating to relationships?"

"Oh, did I, but she didn't get it. Now check this out, one day she shared with me that she does not feel as if she is the exception in our relationship."

"Wait a minute, she actually said this to you?"

"Yes, sir."

"She was exceptionally out of her mind for making that statement to you."

"Yes, I was thinking those exact words, but I did not want to go there. I believed that would have crushed her. I was trying to get her to understand that we do not have that kind of relationship."

"Did you really come out and tell her that the two of you were just friends?"

"I told her that in more ways than one. I asked her, 'How in the world you expect a mature and respectful man such as myself to take you seriously?"

"Why did you even bother to continue to have conversations with her, Derek?"

251

"I guess it's in my nature to assist people with life challenges and adversity, which is something we all have. Anyway, she asked me why I don't take her seriously."

"Did you tell her why?"

"Of course, I just put it out on the table even though it sounded ugly. I told her that I'm not the kind of man who is looking to spend time with a woman who periodically hangs out and gets drunk, enjoys using obscene language, and enjoys spending time at clubs and partying with young kids. This way of living is not attractive. I told her that she is at an age where she should be moving in a direction, doing new and different things in her life as a mature adult."

"How did she take it?"

"She took it well. Then she asked, 'Why don't I see the affectionate, romantic, caring and loving side of you?'"

"Wow, it really sounds like she didn't get it."

"You're right; she didn't get it and will not know how to embrace a healthy relationship. I just came out and told her that I'm not the kind of man to display those emotions and feelings with a woman that shows little respect for herself, relationships, and for me. The respect I expect, should be surpassing. I told her that as a woman, she ought to present herself in a fashion that men should be asking themselves whether they are worthy of her."

"It sounds like she is one of those women who want to have her cake and eat it, too."

"She can have somebody's cake and eat it, but it won't be mine, at least not on my watch."

Don laughs, "You're crazy."

Sometimes you have to laugh at things like this because it really makes you wonder what people are thinking. It's draining, trying to work with someone with a chaotic and unhealthy lifestyle, especially a grown woman, who is not growing. She was worse than any of my clients." Don started laughing as if he had a private joke. "What are you laughing at.

"I'm thinking about the story you just told me. What made me laugh is that she asked you why she is not being treated as the exception. Wow, she really missed the forest for the trees. It sounds as if she should be on medication."

"She is definitely unbalanced, lacks patience, and has anxiety."

"You sound like you were her therapist."

"I hate to admit it, but there were times I was really feeling that way. At least with some people you meet, you could at least say you're on the same chapter, but we're not even in the same book."

"Maybe she thought she was the exception with you."

"I will put it this way, Don, she was exceptionally different."

"So, what do you think makes a woman the exception, Derek?"

"Exceptional is in the eye of the beholder. For me, I find their spiritual foundation to be attractive, knowing what it means to be in a relationship being equals, willing to make sacrifices, working toward a common goal, and being capable of nurturing and cultivating a relationship for long-term growth. She would have class. She would pray for us. She would respect me and have the utmost respect for herself. She is a trustful confidant, has respectful morals and values, and is willing to share. I'm not talking about money or materialistic possessions. I mean communicating and being willing to share her heart with me. What makes a woman even more exceptional is knowing she's in the next room, and she's missed. Why do you ask?"

"I was thinking about my relationship with Sharon, and to be honest she is the exception in my life. We embrace one another with overwhelming love and spend a lot of quality time sharing."

"Well, my brother, I'm sharing this with you because I love you. I'm sharing something with you that nobody ever shared with me. This is what relationships are all about, Don: people being able to share with one another, and that person knowing they have someone to share with in return."

"Thanks, Derek. That word *sharing* is a strong word."

"Yes it is, because anyone can talk, but in order to share you have to care. One other thing about sharing that's important ..."

"What is that, Derek?"

"The moral of this sharing, if you see only with your eyes, is that you will be easy to fool."

Don put his glass of wine down. Put his hand on Derek's shoulder and said, "Thanks man, I appreciate you."

"Back at ya."

BLENDED FAMILIES

O ne day I was sitting on my front porch, thinking about the conversation Don and I had the other night. I watched couples walk by and some with their kids, and then it hit me. What Don and I were talking about is nothing new; mixed relationships go back in history. The only new thing about mixed relationships is that we never opened our heart or eyes to it. As a kid I could remember hearing people say, "Stick with your own kind because in the long run you will be better off." Still today, I do not know what that really is supposed to mean. Just thinking about the relationships I had, and the ones my friends talked about, concludes we were not all truly happy.

"Hey, Derek, over here!" I heard someone calling my name. I looked across the street and it was my neighbor Julie.

"Hello Julie."

"Derek, come here I want to talk with you." I stepped down from my porch to see what she was shouting about.

"Hey, what's going on Julie?"

"What's going on is that I'm having a little get together at my house this Saturday at 7:00 p.m., and I would like for you to stop by."

"Sure I will. I don't think I have anything planned."

"Don't worry about having to bring anything, just you."

"All right Julie, and thanks for the invitation."

"Make sure that you come by even if it is for a few minutes, but I think you will have a good time."

"All right, Julie, I will be there; see you Saturday."

"Okay, bye, Derek."

I returned to my house to prepare dinner for Kim and me. I walked into the house, and Kim was already cooking dinner and the table was set. "Hey, Kim; are you feeling okay?"

"You sound like you were her therapist."

"I'm feeling fine. Why do you ask?"

"First of all, you are cooking dinner. I thought I walked into the wrong house or someone traded daughter's with me."

"Funny Dad, ha, ha. Dinner is about ready; go wash your hands and have a seat." I went to wash up for dinner and returned to the kitchen to assist Kim, but she had everything under control. We sat down, and I blessed the food. "So Dad, I saw you talking with Julie. Is she trying to get you out on a date?"

"No, Julie and I are neighbors who happen to be good friends."

"Well, Dad, you know Julie is a beautiful black woman, but I also think she is mixed with something else; anyway she is an attractive woman."

"She invited me to a little get together she is having at her house on Saturday."

"Are you going?"

"Yes, I told her I would stop by."

"Dad,"

"Yes, Kim."

"I'm sure she wants to get together with you."

"Dinner is good."

"Don't try and change the subject, and thank you. So, are you going to ask Julie out on a date since we had this little talk?"

"No, and like I said, we're good friends. I do not see Julie as someone I would want to entertain a relationship with."

"Well Dad, you know that if you just..."

"Well, Kim, you know if you just fill your mouth up with food you will not be able to talk as much."

"But Dad ..."

"But Kim, your mouth needs a refill."

"All right Dad, I can take a hint. I'm going to leave this alone, for now!"

"Thank you and I love you."

"I love you, too, Dad."

Saturday evening arrived, and I was preparing myself to go over to Julie's house. "Feeling nervous, Dad? Yes? No? Maybe? It's okay if you're feeling nervous."

"It's not that serious, Kim. Besides, we already had this conversation, and I'm not going to entertain it."

"Well then can I have some money to go out with Nikki and her mother? They invited me to go to the mall and dinner with them."

"Sure, if it keeps you from harassing me." I finished getting dressed and went to Julie's house. I rang the doorbell, and Julie answered the door. We greeted one another with a hug and kiss as she invited me in.

"Can I get you anything thing, Derek?"

"A glass of wine would be nice."

"Would you like red or white?"

"I will have red."

"One glass of red wine coming up. Feel free to help yourself to something to eat." While Julie went to get the glass of wine, I scanned the room and noticed that Julie had a mix of friends, which was cool and this also let me know that she is an open-minded woman. As I was making my way to the living room, I saw a couple of our other neighbors, Michael and Emily. Michael approached me, and we started talking about sports. Michael was an Eagles fan, and I was a Cowboys fan, so we always had some words for one another. While Michael and I were talking, a gentleman walked over and handed each of us a glass of wine.

We both said, "thank you."

"Gentlemen, you're welcome. Let me introduce myself to you: I'm Ted, Julie's significant other."

With a look of surprise, "Hello, my name is Derek, Julie's neighbor."

"Nice to meet you, Derek, and enjoy yourself. I'm sure we will talk before you leave."

"Sure, Ted, I look forward to talking with you."

As Ted walked away, Michael said, "Why did you look so surprised when he said he was Julie's significant other?"

"To be honest Michael, I did not think Julie would be dating a white man."

"Today, people, let me rephrase that and say, some people follow their heart because our heart does not discriminate; it is us as people that discriminate."

"You're right, but did I look that obvious?"

"You almost choked on your wine."

"Maybe I should go and apologize to Ted for my reaction."

"I'm sure that he's fine and did not make anything of you choking on your wine in his face when he told you he was Julie's significant other. Of course, he didn't make anything of it."

"Oh, you have jokes. I just embarrassed myself and probably made him feel uncomfortable. I'm going to walk over and talk with Ted."

"All right, I will talk with you later to see how you made out. If I hear someone choking, I know you're not doing so well."

"Let me go before I choke you." I walked over toward Ted and tapped him on the shoulder. Ted turned.

"Hello Derek, is everything all right?"

"Everything is fine; I would like to talk with you for a moment."

"Sure Derek, do you need something?"

"No, I just want to apologize for how I reacted when you told me that you're Julie's significant other."

"It's not a problem, Derek."

"No, I'm serious. I hope I didn't make you feel uncomfortable."

"Hey, man, like I said, it is not a problem, but let me ask you this question."

"Sure; go right ahead."

"When I shared with you that Julie and I are in a relationship, was your reaction because she is a black woman and I am a white man?"

"No, I mean, uh, uh, yeah."

"Don't worry; that's cool we live in a world that has become accustomed to a belief system that we should stick with our own kind and not blend families."

"What do you mean by blended families?"

"You know, blended families, mixed families; however you would like to phrase it. Actually, blended families have become the nuclear family of today. I do not just mean interracial couples. This includes couples that are from the same race, nationality, or ethnic background. Some of those relationships end up in divorce, and sometimes one or both partners end up remarrying, and there usually kids involved. So even if it is a white, black, Latino, Italian, or Asian man and woman remarrying for the second time and kids are involved, they are blending and mixing families. This is what I mean by blended families. See, Derek, I was married before to a very beautiful, educated, intelligent, professional woman. We loved one another, but we were not in love with one another. My heart was not drawn to my ex-wife as it is with Julie."

While we were talking Julie appeared out of nowhere and asked, "Is this a private conversation?"

Ted grabbed Julie by her hand and pulled her close to him, "No." Ted continued to say, "Derek was just taken back when I told him that we are a couple."

"Is this because you're a white man and I'm a gorgeous black woman?"

"Yes, I must admit I was taken by surprise, and I had to apologize to Ted for my reaction."

Julie continued to say, "When I was growing up, I grew up in a house with both of my biological parents present. Nobody in my family had ever been divorced. Derek, I was the first member in my family to get a divorce, so I guess you could say I'm the family rebel. Ted and I been together for about two years, and we're engaged to be married."

"That is great, and congratulations. It sounds as if the two of you are pacing yourselves."

"Both of us have been divorced, and I have been single for about two years since my divorce."

"I have been single for about four years since my divorce," said Ted."

I can understand where you guys are coming from because I have been divorced for three years myself." Julie put her arm around Ted's waist.

"Let us tell you a funny and intriguing story. Everyone we tell this story to finds it to be hilarious,"

"Sure, Julie."

"Since Ted and I were dating, the comments and questions were always being directed at us. Sometimes we would think that these comments and questions would be endless. There is this one question that sticks with Ted and me."

"What would this question be?"I asked.

"Well the church that Ted and I attend was having this youth rally. Ted and I volunteer to assist with the event. This teenage girl at the church saw Ted and me holding hands while walking into the building. Later that evening Pastor Charles, the youth pastor, came to us and said, may I share something with you? We said, 'Sure, Pastor.' He shared with us that a teenage girl was curious in knowing if God approved of people of a different color, race, and nationality to date and marry."

"Were you embarrassed by the question?" asked Derek.

Ted replied, "Of course not; we just laughed. Julie, Pastor Charles, and I realized that people are going to have differences of opinions about interracial dating and marriages, especially if they lack a strong sense of multicultural awareness."

Julie added, "Those, whose multicultural awareness is weak, think that children of interracial couples are usually cute and very attractive, and that this is God's blessing on interracial couples. Some people feel and even see that it's a compliment to tell Ted or me that he or I have found a good catch."

"What do you mean?"

"What I mean, Derek, is that being a woman willing to date Ted without any concerns or worries about what others think, or Ted worrying about what other thinks."

Derek looked at Ted, "Do you think this to be true for you as a white man dating a black woman?"

"Well the truth is that people choose to focus on the possible challenges of an interracial couple and think that any major problem we have come from our differences in race."

"Just sitting here listening to the both of you talk about interracial couples, I now understand that it's our society and culture that created these norms. I mean, some of the things we experience in relationships are rules made up by our society. Society has its own way of trying to protect people from loving and caring for others outside of their race and culture. It appears we live in a society that creates certain rules to make certain individuals and groups of people feel secure about themselves and their relationships. Unfortunately, society does not see this as a way from preventing relational happiness."

"I totally agree, when we're faced with adversity we must see this as a time for teaching and learning, so there is a beautiful side to all of this."

"What is this beautiful side, Ted?"

"Well, Derek, the beautiful side of this is that adversity, challenges, obstacles, and differences are beautiful gifts that in reality could open your eyes to the negative views of society."

"What do you mean? I'm not following you," I told him.

"What I mean is that this will assist us with focusing on our physical, mental, emotional, and spiritual side and not on society's view and perception, while establishing peaceful souls. When we allow our spiritual being to be more Christ-centered instead of self-centered, we develop a deeper and more meaningful understanding of what it means to be created in God's image, and at the same time becoming one with our soul. When God created us it was not by color, race, nationality, or ethnic groups. God created us by gender, male and female. God said that it is not good for man to be alone. God wanted us to have relationships with all people, without any special stipulations or rules to separate us. Like you said, Derek, we as a society separated ourselves, and when we separated ourselves, we separated ourselves from love and happiness because of the opinions of others."

Derek said, "It makes me think of Dr. Martin Luther King's speech, 'I Have A Dream' in which he said *that my four little children will one day live in a nation where they will not be judged by the color of their skin but by the content of their character.*"

"It appears that we have come a long way but still have a long way to go," said Julie.

"Yes we do, Julie, and maybe someday those that are embraced in an interracial or intercultural relationship will not be judged by their differences, but by the contentment of their love for one another."

"Oooh, now that was deep. I like that, Derek," said Ted. Julie nodded, showing she was in agreement with Ted.

"Thanks, it just felt right for the moment. I do have another question for you guys if you do not mind me asking."

"Sure, go ahead and ask away," said Ted.

"Do you two find yourselves in any disagreement, differences, or preferences because of your differences in color? Because I know as a black man, I'm accustomed to some things that black people like to do. I know that there are some things that white people like more than black."

Julie said, "One thing I must admit is that Ted and I being together has been interesting at times. The minor and minimal differences and preferences have forced us to examine the true realities about our relationship. For example, sometime I like to watch television shows, movies, and go to plays, art shows that have people of different color, race, and nationalities."

"Why do you say this, Julie?"

"I say this Derek, because the majorities of shows, movies, plays and art that I'm exposed to now and even as a child are not of different races or nationalities."

"What do you think about what Julie has shared Ted?"

"I think you're trying to cause trouble between my woman and me."

The three of them laughed as I responded, "Now, this is not my intention."

"I'm just kidding, but seriously, in reality white entertainment has a targeted audience and watching one of Julie's selected shows is not a regular event for me. As in all relationships there will be differences, which makes this a great time to embrace those special moments for growing, sharing, and establishing a complete soul as one. I hope you do not misunderstand what we're saying. The different kinds of entertainment is not the source of our problems."

"No, I completely hear and understand where you guys are coming from. It sounds as if the two of you invested a lot of time in the development of your relationship, allowing Christ to be the center and foundation as your relationship continues to grow. Wow, life is amazing. No, let me rephrase that—God is amazing." I looked down as if in a moment of deep thought.

"What, Derek? Are you okay?"

I looked up at Julie and Ted, "I'm fine, Ted. My, how times have changed."

"Changed how?" asked Julie.

"You know if you look back in history that interracial relationships were taking place hundreds of years ago, for example, Thomas Jefferson and Sally Hemings, John Rolfe and Pochahantas, and even Frederick Douglas and his second wife Helen Pitts, and back in that time, all of them were involved in an interracial relationship and guilty of breaking the forbidden law."

"What law was that?"

"You know the laws of marriage, Ted, cohabitating, sexual relationships between mixed races, and not staying with your own kind."

"Then I guess you could say, interracial relationships are nothing new, it's just more out in the open," said Ted.

"Yes, sir," said Derek.

Ted and Julie were still arm in arm as Ted asked, "So what are your thoughts on all of this honey?"

"Well, you know, gentlemen, if I was asked while growing up my opinion about dating outside of my race. I do not think I would have supported it or even suggested to anyone to entertain the idea. I must admit, as I have grown and matured, my thoughts and feelings have changed significantly. My spiritual life has assisted me with being more caring, sensitive, and compassionate about people, interracial relationships, and about a lot of other things. From a woman's point of view, I just want to see women in general loved and cared for whether that love comes from dating within or out of their race. I'm just glad to know that my friends are with men who adore them and they're happy. I wish it was realistic to say that every woman who wants to be loved and embraced by a man of their race would find that particular man of their race; unfortunately, this is not always possible. As I have matured over the years and continue to mature, I just say, date whoever you want and love whoever loves you back unconditionally, and keep moving on. I learned that falling in love with someone that is of your race and has a similar background does not keep you from being hurt or mistreated."

I looked down at the floor and said, "I know what you mean."

Ted put his hand on Derek's shoulder and say, "Real love takes work. Regardless of your race, whether the two of you are black, white, brown, green, red, or from different races, love is something that you have to work at by nurturing and cultivating it."

Julie interrupted, adding, "When you find that special person who fills that special space in your heart, you will know. Keep in mind that you have found a good thing, regardless of that person's color, race, nationality, or background. Did we talk your ears off or what, Derek?"

"Not at all, Julie. I respect the two of you and your relationship. I respect the conversation and sharing. What the two of you have shared has taught me that true love, or should I say real love, does not see color, race, or nationality, and most importantly does not judge nor discriminate.

We must learn to open the eyes of our heart. I just would like to say to the both of you, thank you, and thank you for inviting me Julie. You're a Godsend."

"Why do you say this?"

"I say this because a friend and I were just having a similar conversation. He is struggling with dating a woman of another race and because she's a chef. I basically told him that we cannot help whom we fall in love with or whom your heart connects with. We are human, and we have these sudden feelings of attachments that we cannot always explain. We love on the basis of the kind of person we are, and the kind of person we choose to be with. Just like you said Julie, date who you want, who you love, and who will love you back, and keep moving on. In 1 Samuel 16:7, we learn that God does not see man as man sees man, and God does not judge us by the color of our skin or appearance but by our inner appearance, which is our heart."

Ted reached over and put his hand over Derek's heart and said, "Amen." As we were talking we were interrupted by one of the party guests, Anthony.

"Excuse me, Julie and Ted, I don't mean to interrupt. I just want you to know that you are running out of ice."

Julie replied, "Don't worry; I have plenty in the freezer. Excuse me, guys, while I go and get more ice."

"I will go with you and help."

"That's okay, Anthony, stay and talk with Ted and Derek."

"Hello Anthony, this is Derek, Julie's next door neighbor," said Ted.

"Hello, Anthony," said Derek.

"So what are you guys up to?"

"Well Anthony, the three of us were having this conversation about interracial couples," replied Ted.

Anthony replied while looking at Derek, "What exactly about inter-racial relationships were you discussing?"

"Julie and I were just sharing with Derek that we have some challenges, but nothing that's really any different from couples of the same race."

Ted put a hand on Anthony's shoulder, "Since you're part of the conversation, and if you wouldn't mind, would you like to share with Derek and me a little about your relationship with your wife, Nicole."

"Of course I don't mind, especially if I'm able to share something that could potentially help somebody, I'm all for it. Well let me start by saying that I'm a black man and had never been married. I have a seven-year-old son. I was in this relationship for five years, but, unfortunately, the mother of my son and I did not cherish the same things in life. The both of us believed in God, attended church regularly, and were very active in the church. She did not respect me as a man and only loved me for what I could do for her or give her. The love was not genuine, and it was not unconditional love. Dealing with the adversity on my job, finances, trying to keep a roof over our heads, and pay the bills, I felt alone as if I was not getting any support."

"I can relate," I told him.

Anthony looked at Ted and then Derek as he sighed, "People are people, and they're going to like and dislike whatever meets or satisfies their own personal needs because it's about self. Not everyone is going to be accepting and compassionate about interracial couples because how we've been marked by history. As you can see Derek, I am a black man, and my wife Nicole is not of the same race. Nicole and I met two years after my son's mother and I went our separate ways. I was not out there trying to meet anyone. When I met Nicole, we dated for two years; then we were engaged for another year and a half before we decided to get married. Nicole has been through an ugly and bitter divorce. She has three children, five- and seven-year-old daughters and a nine-year-old son. Nicole was divorced for three years when we met. We dated for seven months before we decided we would meet one another's kids. We waited an additional two months before our children met one another and spent any time together. This is what Nicole and I agreed to while dating. Our children knew we were dating, but we agreed not to introduce our kids to one another and even ourselves to one another's kids, until we were sure and comfortable with the relationship and able to communicate that we were serious with one another. What really assisted Nicole and I with getting us through this relationship, and that lead us to marriage were our beliefs. Having a solid spiritual foundation. We've been through unpleasant relationships and understood what it meant to be happy, be at peace, and be loved. We both started to attend the same church as a family. What lead us to know that God was guiding us was that the church had a ministry for blended families that was just getting started. This ministry assisted us as a family, letting us knows that God loves us, regardless of our differences. When we did marry, we knew that everyone involved was suddenly thrown into a new and unknown environment, known as a blended family. We understood that this occurs even if the kids do not live in the same household. The children that are involved will spend weekends, holidays, vacations, and other days with both parents, meaning biological and stepparents. So, what is important is not about the adults, but the children, because they will need time and the opportunities that will assist them with feeling as if they belong. As adults whether we remarry or not, we go on with our lives; we forget that the children hurt and suffer the most because they truly do not understand anything that has taken place."

I stood looking and listening intensely, and before Anthony could say another word, I had to ask, "May I ask you a question, Anthony, relating to the children's situation?"

"Sure Derek."

"Well, Anthony, let me know if I'm being too personal, but my question is what about new children such as a newborn?"

"Funny you asked, because this was one of the things Nicole and I discussed in the early stages of our relationship. We agreed to commit to one another, investing more time with one another and the relationship. Nicole and I had decided that for us, it was more important to enjoy one another and focus on the four children we were bringing together, enriching their lives. We learned that adding a newborn into the family dynamics could add more to our plate, and we knew our plate was full. We had couples in the group that have been a part of blended families for years. Blended families are couples of the same and different race, but society does not acknowledge this or even many churches. I can remember this one couple attesting to the success of their blended family when they got involved in each other lives. They strongly emphasized that it takes a special kind of involvement, and this involvement demonstrates a special bond and love. As a family they would pray together and take part in family activities or projects."

"That sounds great, Anthony. It appears as if you and Nicole have really benefited from the ministry in your church," replied Ted.

"It was definitely a blessing for us, as well as for others. When I say it was a blessing, I mean you learned to embrace the assistance and support from those that have gone through the challenges of being part of a blended family before you. All of this was very helpful for Nicole and me, but I do not want the two of you walking away from this thinking that this was easy. This was something that took time, and there were the good times along with the bad, as well as the ugly. Some of the things we struggled with were the things that other families struggled with, and it required a whole lot of patience, understanding, open and honest communication, and prayer."

269

"So, Anthony, if there was anything that you would share with anyone about your experience, what would that be?"

"I would like to say being a parent in a blended family is challenging at times, and it is extremely rewarding, Derek. You definitely should proceed with caution when it comes to taking suggestions or advice from someone that has no idea what they're talking about, because you may find out very quickly that advice is not free and could come with a hefty price you cannot afford. Your focus and goals as a parent in a blended family should be the same as being the biological parent. Yes, the process is different, but the goals and purpose are the same. Nicole's and my goals were to raise happy, healthy, respectful, caring, loving, spiritual, productive kids, who will, as they become adults, be productive members of society. We believe by setting a spiritual foundation and allowing our children to set their own goals as we give them guidance in other important areas of their life, such as honesty, self-respect, integrity, work ethics, communication, multicultural awareness, and peace. This will assist in their success as they choose what road they want to travel." Anthony raised his hands putting one hand on Ted shoulder and the other on Derek's shoulder.

Anthony looked at Ted and then at Derek, making sure to make eye contact and in a slow, firm, and compassionate tone said, "You don't want anyone to feel as if your taking sides. So gentlemen, what's most important is that you need to be honest with yourselves, your children, your spouse, and your spouse's children, letting them know you're there for them just as much as you're there for your own children and letting them know that you love them because they're part of the person you love and married. Oh and, gentlemen, one other thing I would like to share with you ..."

"What is this?" asked Ted.

"We don't use labels, such as saying blended, additional or extended families in our home. We do not refer to anyone as stepmother, stepfather, stepbrother, stepsister or step anything. I have a wife, two sons, and two daughters, and we are a family, nothing else."

"Thanks, Anthony."

"Why are you thanking me, Ted?"

"You shared a lot with Derek and me. Personally speaking what you shared gave me some new insight and spiritual guidance for Julie's and my relationship."

"Seriously, this is what really helped Nicole and I. I mean, talking and sharing with other couples and individuals. Come on, guys, nothing we're doing is new. This is about relationships: people willing to bridge gaps by communicating and sharing with care and compassion with a heart of love," said Anthony.

Ted checking on me said, "How are you doing over there, Derek?"

Smiling, I said, "I'm doing well over here. You know, Anthony, as I listen to you, it seems as if blended families can be challenging and scary for everyone involved. It sounds as if communicating and having the heart to accept everyone with love in the way you describe is hard work."

"This is true, but I look at it this way: whatever involves hard work in the beginning usually has great rewards and benefits in the end for all who are involved, and that's something special."

"Well, then how would you describe those great rewards and benefits at the end?"

"I see it this way, Derek, the end result is that you and your family will be one. You will know that you're survivors, a loving family, and your souls are at peace," said Anthony.

Julie walks back into the room with Anthony's wife, Nicole, and said, "You guys still talking? What are you guys talking about; is it man talk?"

"I was sharing with them our coming together as a family and how we're blessed as a family," said Anthony.

"Did you tell them that things were not always smooth sailing?"

"Well, I must admit that there are times that Nicole and I felt banged up, as if things were spiraling out of control, and I will admit that I beat myself up emotionally and mentally at times. There were times we started to believe that we were failing and struggling to make this work for us as a family, so we came together with the kids and pray. I read a scripture for all of us to meditate on, to encourage us, and give us strength. I told the kids that the devil is a liar, and the devil is out to kill, steal and destroy God's wonderful creations and the love that God wants us all to share as a family. I told them that we have the strength and the power to defeat the devil through prayer, reading the word of God, and trusting and believing that God is bigger than any challenge that they will ever face or encounter in their lives. Being a father to four children in a blended family can be very challenging at times, resulting in me doing some idiotic things myself."

Nicole interrupted, "It was not easy for me, either. I spent long hours and days praying for our family. I proudly and personally embraced Anthony's son when I got to know him. Yes, during this process, I have said or done some things that were unpleasant. I wish I could go back in time and undo those things. Unfortunately, life does not work that way, but we're given the gift of forgiveness, and our do-over starts the next day or even later in the day by apologizing and asking for forgiveness put us on the road to a fresh start, or as Anthony likes to put it, a new beginning."

Anthony continue, "That's right, every day is a new beginning for something new and special to take place in your life, or for you to have the opportunity to make something new happen in your life. We learned that our faith and belief had to be shared in all our relationships and with family because this was the foundation and rock. It's having a strong spiritual foundation that can develop a wonderful, special, fun-loving bond and unity with blended families. I believe that God allows and promises blended families to have a new beginning just like he promises us a new morning. This is why I would always tell Nicole to stop beating herself up because we may endure for the night, but joy will come in the morning. What we need to be capitalizing on is embracing interracial relationships, blended families, and how God made this beautiful mix of people to be together as one. In order for us to have true and meaningful conversations about blended families or interracial couples, we as Christians and as a society need to have more understanding and be more compassionate."

"Amen," said Ted.

"On that note, Julie, I'm going to get home and check on my daughter. I'm going to let you get back to the rest of your guests. I don't want them to think I'm being selfish by monopolizing all of the host's time by keeping you to myself."

"Thanks for coming, Derek."

"Thanks for inviting me. Tonight was a blessing for me."

Derek returned home, and Kim was watching television. Derek sat on the sofa next to Kim and helped himself to some of her popcorn. "How was your evening, Kim?"

Kim was quick to say, "Great! I had a very good evening." Kim, picked up the television remote and turned down the sound, "And how was your evening, Dad? So, when are you and Julie going out on a real date?"

"Slow down; slow down, and put your mind at a halt before anything else pops into it. Julie is engaged, and I met her fiancé at the party."

"Is he as nice as you, Dad?"

"I spent some time talking with him, and he appears to be a very nice gentleman. If Julie has been dating him for two years, he has to be a nice person."

"Wow, Julie has been dating someone for two years? I never knew."

"You never knew, Kim, because it is not your or my business to know. The one thing I found interesting when I first met him..."

"What is that, Dad?"

"He is a white man."

"What? Dad I do not see Julie as a woman that would date outside of her race."

"Then what does a person look like who dates outside of their race, Kim?"

"I did not mean it like that, Dad. So Kim, What do you think about mixed, or to be politically correct, interracial relationships?"

"Come on, Dad; there is nothing wrong with having jungle fever today."

"Well then Kim, I have a question for you."

"Yes, Dad. What is the question?"

"What do you think about interracial relationships?"

"Dad, I see it every day, and it does not mean much to me. I see it as two people being happy. When it comes to relationships, Dad, I don't think we can control who we're attracted to and how our heart leads us. Like you always told me, God created us all in his image, and he does not look at the person's outer appearance but the inner person, which is the heart."

"Well, I guess you do listen when I speak."

"You're right, Dad."

"No, Kim, God is right. You know in Galatians 3:28, tells us that Christ has destroyed the barriers that we as people built between ourselves. We can have real relationships with people who are not like us. There are many barriers that we allow to divide us from each other such as age, gender, background, appearance, intelligence, politics, social and economic status, and especially race and nationality. What we fail to realize is that because of Christ's death, we are all one."

"You're right, Dad, because in school we talk about multicultural diversity. We demonstrate this by seeking out and appreciating people that are not like us and our friends. We find out that we have a lot in common and learn something new."

Lost and Found

———————⧫———————

Kim graduated from high school and was accepted into the college of her choice. She talked about this day since she entered high school. Kim was one of those teenagers who wanted do what she wants when she wants. Oh yes, and there were those times Kim would want to act like an adult, when she wanted to have her way. Then there were those times she wanted to act like a child when she wanted or needed something. When I would talk to her about this sort of behavior, she would get an attitude. Then she wants to play the avoidance game and not talk. When we did talk, her response was, "I know, Dad." I would tell her she does not have a clue and does not know. So what I started doing was to taper off on what I would give her and how much, especially money. She had to get a job. When she asked for something I told her that if she came up with half the money, I would assist with the other half. There were certain items Kim wanted that I found to be a waste of money. I would tell Kim up front that I would not waste money and that she would have to earn things on her own.

One day Kim came to me and said, "Dad, why are you hard on me? You do not let me do anything or go anywhere. You have all these rules. I'm limited with time no matter what I'm doing."

"Well, let me start off by saying this: you're exaggerating. I allow you to do a lot of things. Besides, you have more freedom than you realize. I'm very fair and flexible. I have rules. I may be hard at times; that's because I love you. There are some kids who do not have anyone or any place to call home. There are hundreds of kids out there who would trade places with you at a drop of a dime. When you go away to college, you'll see the difference in home life and being independent. Then again you'll have it all together, and I will not probably hear from you, except maybe for an occasional phone call now and then just to say, 'Hello, Dad, could you send me some money?'"

Kim laughed, "Dad I don't mean to sound like I don't care; I do. I just want more freedom."

"Don't worry, Princess; you will have a lot of freedom when you leave for college."

"I have my driver's license, and that puts me in the adult category."

"Interesting. Do you really think so?"

"Yes, I do."

"Well then, Princess, be an adult and go buy your own car."

"Real funny, Dad. I can see that this conversation is not going anywhere."

"Believe me it's going somewhere; let me share something with you. All that you hear and see me do, you may view as me being difficult or hard on you. In all honesty Kim, all I do with and for you, is all about love."

The summer was coming to an end and it was time for Kim to get ready for college. I remember the day we packed the truck and drove to her new home. Kim was excited about the transition of going to college. This was a new phase of her life where she would start to develop and structure the beginning of her new life. "I want you to know that a new beginning is a wonderful opportunity. This is a time for defining you as a woman in other areas of your life, to enhance your identity."

"I'm feeling nervous and excited at the same time, Dad."

"That's a natural feeling when we're about to do something new or enter the unknown. They're called butterflies, and you will be fine." We arrived at the school, and there were parents dropping off their kids and unpacking their vehicles. Once we located Kim's dorm, her new home, we unloaded the vehicle of Kim's belongings. When we were done, Kim had this sad look on her face. A look as if she was being kicked out of the house. I walked towards Kim and put my arms around her, "Hey, Princess, home is still home. This is only temporary, and you're just a visitor. I love you. I'm proud of you. If there is a problem, do not be afraid to call regardless of what the problem is, and if I need to come here, I will in a heartbeat. Just stay focused, have fun, and do the right thing. God is always here no matter what. You can call, text or email me any time. Remember, no matter what, I love you."

"I love you too, Dad, and thank you." As we were in her room saying good-bye, Kim's roommate walked into the room.

"Hello, my name is Kim, and this is my father."

"Hello and welcome. My name is Charlotte." She appeared to be Asian. She was polite and respectful in her greeting. "I'm on my way to a social in the campus center; it's for new students. Why don't you come with me?"

"Yes, I will meet you over there after my dad leaves."

"Go ahead with Charlotte, so you guys can get to know each other. I will get back on the road. Just give me a call tonight."

"Okay, Dad, I will call."

"I'll see you again, Charlotte, and nice meeting you."

"Okay, nice to meet you and have a safe ride home."

"Hey, Charlotte, this semester flew by. The holidays are coming, and I'm looking forward to spending the holiday with my family. We have an awesome time together."

"So, what is it that you do with your family for the holidays that makes it so awesome?"

"First and most important, my dad makes this a priority. We go out and cut down a tree for Christmas. We get together later that evening, spend time decorating the tree, and listening to Christmas music. After decorating the tree, any gifts we have that are wrapped, we put under the tree. On Christmas Day, we spend time visiting family and friends. We would go to the home of one family member, play games, have dinner, exchange gifts, and spend time catching up on what is going on in each other's lives. It is a joyful and pleasant day for all of us."

"That sounds wonderful; it sounds like a pleasant and wonderful day."

"Well, how about you Charlotte, what are your plans when you go home? What is it that you and your family do for the holidays?"

"My family and I do not do anything, because I do not have a family."

"What do you mean that you do not have a family? Everyone has a family."

"Well, I do not, I spent most of my life in the system."

"What system are you talking about?"

"The child welfare system. I was one of those children who grew up not knowing my family. I never could say I had real friends because they all have come and gone."

"I'm sorry; I did not know."

"Don't be sorry. You should be happy for me because many kids in the system don't make it this far."

"If you do not mind me asking, but how did all of this happen?"

"Well, I went into care at ten years of age. I was put up for adoption, but I never was adopted. When you're up for adoption you're almost like a person in prison. They take your picture and assigned you a number in the photo listing. People go through the list and pick what kid they want to try out, and most of the time it does not work out for us. There are some of us that are so angry with our situation that we act in ways that sabotage any opportunity we could have with a family. It's not easy just going to live with someone you know nothing about, and having to trust them. There are a lot of us who miss our families even though we never had the opportunity to really get to know them. I know that sounds weird—missing people you never met or really built any kind of relationship with. I guess there is that part of us deep in our hearts that wants that connection just to feel normal. I do not have any pictures of my mother or father. I do know that my mother was Asian and my father was black. Other than that, I remember or know very little about the people who were the first of many losses in my life. When my parents died, my grandparents were given custody of me. I loved my grandparents and was very close to them. My grandparents would spend a lot of time with me. I think they felt sorry for me. They would take me to the park, movies, and shopping. We would go on vacations, and they were usually places close to home. After living with my grandparents for two years, my grandmother died from cancer. I was starting to feel like I was just losing the people I was close with and cared for. Then it was just my grandfather and me. I would go to bed at night, wondering whether he would leave me next. Then where would I go? I never felt so afraid in my entire young life. Playing with the neighbor's daughter helped keep my mind off of all the tragedy I experienced. This was also helping me feel connected to a family as if this is where I belonged. The Simons were very nice people, and they were very good to my grandfather and me. They would allow me to spend the night with them. They would offer to take me on trips. Sometimes I would go, and sometimes I would not. I think they felt sorry for me. I remember this one particular evening when I was sitting in my room doing my homework. I walked down stairs to ask my grandfather a question. When I walked into the living room, my grandfather and the Simons were meeting. It seemed as if they were having a very serious conversation. They called me into the room. The Simons asked me how I would feel about coming to live with them for a little while. I asked why. My grandfather told me that he had to go into the hospital to have some tests done, and he would be there for a few days. So, I went to live with the Simons and their daughter. They would take me to see my grandfather in the hospital every day after school. I remember on this one particular visit there were these two white women in my grandfather's room when we arrived. They said they were from DSS. I did not know what DSS stood for, so they explained to me that it meant the Department of Social Services. Anyway, I was still at a loss and did not have a clue of what was going on. I did not know what social service was, and I thought it was for my grandfather, but it was for me. I was told that my grandfather was dying. He wanted me to go and live with the Simons. My grandfather signed some papers for the Simons to have responsibility of me, but I also became custody of the state like a prisoner. My life at this point was going downhill, and I was so miserable. Then a week later my grandfather died, and there were no other family or relatives for me to live with. I ended up living with the Simons for a while, but this changed, too. I became very unhappy about my life at a young age. I was having difficulty in school. I did not care about anything or anyone. I wanted to die, so I tried to kill myself by cutting my arm and taking pills. I was then put into a hospital and put on all kinds of medication. The Simons continued to be there for me; they would continue to visit, being supportive and encouraging. However, instead of going back to live with the Simons, I was put into a group home. The family was asked if they wanted to adopt me, but so much was going on I don't think they were ready for this, especially since they had a daughter the same age. I now can understand why they probably didn't, but they still wanted to be part of my life and for me to be part of theirs."

"So were you adopted, Charlotte."

"One day this caseworker told me that I was up for adoption, which was also the weekend the Simons were coming to pick me up. When I was with the Simons, I told them that I was told I was up for adoption. I asked what that meant. They told me what it meant. I did not like any of this at all. A few months went by, and then I was told there was this pre-adoptive family who wanted to meet me and I would start spending time with them. I said, 'What about the Simons? I will still be able to visit with them, right?' I was told yes, but not that weekend. Then as the weekends would come, I noticed that I was spending less and less time with the Simons family. Then my caseworker told me that I would not see the Simons family anymore because I had to start building a new life with this new family. I was crushed again; the Simons were a family I loved and enjoyed being with. They felt like a real family to me. They were my family, and I was separated from them. I was happy being with the Simon family and happy with just the way things were. They did not have to adopt me, and I did not want to be adopted. Anyway going through this was a horrible, miserable, disappointing, and depressing experience for me, I was never adopted. I lost contact with the Simons family. I also found out that the Simons family was told that they needed to decide on adopting me, and if they were not interested, our ties needed to be severed. This was for my best interest, so I could have a fresh start with a pre-adoptive family. This so-called family, the State, wanted to make me a new family. They didn't realize that I was making a fresh start with the Simons. This was the family I was making it with, and the state ended it because they wanted me to be adopted. They wanted to get me out of their system that I did not ask to be a part of. This system that is supposed to protect kids like me has done more damage to us than they realize. There are so many of us that are kicked out of these program once we become eighteen years old with nowhere to go. Some of the other kids who struggled with academics did not receive their high school diploma or GED. Some left with no basic life skills to be self-sufficient, and some just ran away. Some kids would rather be dead than having to deal with the torture of having to go through our child welfare system. Some kids even tried to commit suicide, not because they had mental problems but because they were locked into an ugly system, a system they were unhappy with and were tired of being a part of. I spent time in many homes during this period, and I was becoming more and more depressed. I can remember being in this one group home for a few years, and I wrote this letter when I was fifteen years old. I kept the letter."

"What made you keep it?"

"I'm not sure. Maybe to remind myself that nothing else in life could ever get this bad or frightening and that I'm loved. I keep this letter in my Bible. This is what I wrote; while I remained in that group home they kept trying to give me all this medication."

"Charlotte, you don't have to read it. It sounds personal."

"I do not mind because I'm not that angry person anymore. This is what I wrote:

While I remain in this group home, they keep trying to give me all this medication. I don't know what some of these so-called social workers, counselors, therapists, psychologists, or psychiatrists are thinking, but medication is not the solution to heal a wounded heart. You know, I hate life sometimes. I wonder why I was put on this earth, and when will I be taken off of it. I wish I could go back to the life I lived when I lived with the Simons. I wish God didn't take the people I love. Why did God choose this life for me? Why was I taken from the Simons? These people don't care for me. I miss my mom and dad even though I don't have any good thoughts of them. I still miss them. I wish we could have shared some good things together, but we didn't and we never will. I miss my grandparents and the Simons. People look at my outer appearance and see this happy, cheerful girl laughing and joking at times. Yeah, I can put up a good front, but really the inner person is still hurt and in pain inside. I feel it will never go away because I'm still missing one thing in life, and that is my real family. I have learned to adapt and adjust to where I'm at in my present life, and even at this time things may seem to be easy, but they're not. I would talk a good game as some people would say, but right now that is all I know how to do. No matter what people do, it's not really about me, it's about them because everything is always done at the pace of others, not mine. So, I just go along with it like it's no problem. I would like to have real friends that will not be here today and gone tomorrow. I feel that I'm always messing up, and at my age life is hard. People who talk to me say I have not really learned about life yet and when I'm out there on my own trying to make it, I will then learn about life. Sometimes I just want to scream and yell, *hey you wake up!* Now come into my world—the real world. I have no family, I'm living in this pathetic system, and whether you want to believe it or not, I'm here on my own. You guys are only here to say you're providing me some service or support to earn you a paycheck. So when you go home to your family, I'm still by myself. So if you want to experience life, lose all the people in your life, and spend a part of your life under the care of the state. Right now and no matter how you look at it, the state is my family and I don't even know them. I know there are people who say they believe in me and my potential. This sounds nice, but it will feel better when I believe in myself, which will happen soon. Life is good for the time being, but until that part of my life is filled, life will never be good to me. I miss my family and the Simons. I would do anything to have them back. I wish I were not like this. I spent my life living in a messed-up place with messed-up people. It's this system's fault that I struggle in my education. I received a poor education for being in the care of the state, but I know I have to start to take matters in my own hands. What I need to do to get an education and to learn about life because there are too many people who have come and gone in and out of my life that I cannot count on. I'm only fifteen years old going on sixteen, meaning that I don't have a normal teenager's life because I have to undo some thing that others had done. I have to be my own parent and child. I know I'm messed up because of what you people have done to me. It took me a long time to realize what you people have done to me. Now I'm scared that I won't make it in life, but you people are not scared for me because you think you did your job, your duty, but you didn't do anything.

Now I have to pick myself up; yeah, me, myself, and I. All I want to say is thank you. Yeah, thank you for nothing. You gave me no other options to have any real opportunity, and your only purpose was to get this cute little girl adopted. She is adoptable; she should be easy to get rid of, but your plan didn't work and you never offered me anything else or gave me any other options. Yeah, so I would like to thank you again for what, *nothing*! Why am I doing this? Somebody please tell me, I need to know. I'm still scared that I'm still going to lose everybody I come in contact with. I can't stand to lose somebody else. When new people come into my life I'm scared to get close because I know sooner or later they are going to be gone. I'm just a problem for people, so I wish people would just stay away because when it is my time I'm going to get out of this messed-up system, and never come back.

"Wow Charlotte, if I have known this I would not brought up the holiday."

"How would you have known unless you were in the system with me? Like I said, I'm doing a lot better and I've grown a lot. Now the answer to your question, Christmas is not special, because I went through many Christmas holidays without spending it with family. To be honest, I do not know what it's really like to be a family. I have been through so much and met so many families and had to change so much about me to like each new place or lifestyle that it was like culture shock. When Christmas would come around, I used to get depressed. Most of my Christmases were spent in a group home with a group of other kids. None of us were related and, you see, kids come and go, so it was never anything special for me. I would see kids being picked up and dropped off, to go and spend time with their family for a few hours. I remember there was this girl name Julie who was my roommate. Julie would share with me that Christmas was a day of being alone for her. Every time the Christmas season was approaching. Julie would get too depressed to go to school. Julie would celebrate Christmas at the Department of Social Service in an old dirty empty room that she had seen six previous times to visit her mother, who showed up once. Julie would always say that she hated being in that building because it was always cold, depressing, and dark inside. The visiting room was empty except for two chairs, a desk, and a box of filthy, germ-spreading toys. The adults ignored her as if her being there was a waste of their time, but Julie would say it was all worth it because it gave her a chance to see her mother and the hope of possibly going to live with her again someday."

"If you don't mind me asking Charlotte, what are your feelings about Christmas now?"

"I have mixed feelings about Christmas, Kim. Now that I'm older, I'm able to appreciate and be grateful for what little I do have. I give thanks to God for allowing me to make it this far in my life. I know He will always be with me no matter what. I'm His child, in His family, and He will never leave me. I learned over the years how to cope with disappointment, and conflicting feelings of loss or betrayal, guilt, anger, and emotions that I do not understand at times. If I did not have God in my life, I would not have a life, and I would not be here telling you my story. I pray every day for kids in the system, and especially for those who are going through their first Christmas alone. Every holiday season, I feel the pain of those kids; and I'm sure for most of them, the holidays cannot be over soon enough. I learned to share this story with everyone because this is my testimony: to let people know that no matter how bad life seems to be, just turn your eyes towards the hill from which comes your help. This is not for anyone to cry about. I do not want anyone to feel as if they must feel sorry for me. This is to let people know that love never fails because God is love, but people can be very disappointing and people do fail." Charlotte noticed that Kim was crying. She went over to Kim and put her arms around her, "It's all right, Kim, because I'm where I need to be, and my soul is in its right place."

"I feel as if I was living a selfish life."

Kim lay down in her bed and started to think about Charlotte's life story. She also started to think about her own life, and how thankful and appreciative she should be. She realized that her life is not half as bad in comparison to what Charlotte and thousands of other kids had to go through. Kim prayed, "God, I would like to thank you for Charlotte. Charlotte is living proof that you will continue to take care of all those kids who have no home, family, or place to go. What Charlotte and the thousands of other kids go through is a traumatic experience. For them to be able to get through such a terrifying and lonely experience, they have to be special individuals with great and special strength. Please allow me to be just as strong. Open my heart, so I could be more caring and giving to those that are less fortune than I, Amen."

"Amen," replied Charlotte.

The next morning Kim jump out of bed, "Hey! Charlotte you awake?"

"I am now; you feeling okay?"

"I'm feeling great. You want to know something, Charlotte?"

"What?"

"I was crying because of your story and also because I do not know my mother. When I was eight years old, my mother left me with her mother. A few days had gone by and my grandmother and father knew she was not coming back. My father had me live with him and since living with him, we have had a great relationship. He was always there for me, and we spend a lot of quality time together. Still today, we have a great relationship and he makes a lot of sacrifices for me. He is my mother and father."

"Did you ever find out what happened to your mother?"

"My father said she had a drug problem. My grandmother told me that she ran away because she was not ready to take care of a child. My grandmother told me that my father told me that my mother was on drugs because he did not want me to be hurt, knowing that my mother did not want to be bothered with me. Charlotte, I must admit when I think about my mother leaving, I used to get very angry, but thanks to God, He showed me that he cares for us no matter what we're going through and no matter how we're treated by others."

"I can attest to that, Kim. I truly understand because He did so much for me."

"Hey, Charlotte."

"Yes, Kim."

"You're coming home with me for Christmas, not just because of what you shared with me last night, but because you helped me to see my life in a different light. I mean you helped me open my eyes to something new. I also feel in my heart that you and I being roommates is not by accident. It was for a purpose and a reason. I do believe that things don't just happen. I also believe that you and I are going to be close friends for a long time. I say this because my heart feels different. I had this strange feeling about you when we first met, but a good strange feeling. You know what I mean?"

"Yes, I do."

"I'm going to call my father today and share with him that you're coming home for Christmas with me."

289

"Thanks Kim, I really appreciate you and your compassion. I do have a place to go for the holidays, so I will be fine."

"I know you do, but I just want to share with you how I spend the holidays with my family. I want us to bond more during the holiday season outside of school and all. Someday, I will go to your home or wherever you like and bond with you."

"Okay, I like that and I will take you up on your offer. I will spend Christmas with you and your family."

"Hello, Kim. How are you doing today?"

"I'm doing well, Dad. Dad, I want to ask you something."

"Is this something I need to sit down for?"

"No, I just want to know if Charlotte can spend Christmas with us."

"Sure, but doesn't Charlotte want to spend Christmas with her family?"

"She does not have a biological family to spend Christmas with. She never really had a real family Christmas."

"Sure, she is welcome. It sounds like you and Charlotte are becoming very close friends."

"Dad, there is one other thing I want to share with you."

"Yes, I'm listening."

"Dad I know I never told you this, but I want you to know that you're a great father. You gave me the opportunity and freedom to be myself, explore and enjoy life, and most of all, you inspire me to always strive for doing my best. Dad, you deserve to be praised and loved more, for all the wonderful and great things you do. You're a wonderful Dad and father. I pray that many special and great things will enter your life because you deserve to be happy. I love you, Dad. You're the bestest."

"Thank you; that means a lot to me. I love you, Kim. Tell Charlotte I said hello. I will see the two of you soon."

"Okay. Bye, Dad."

New Beginnings

———◆———

Maria and I knew one another for about five years as colleagues, working in the same office building. When I would see her, she would always appear to be in a joyful and pleasant mood. One evening I was working late. I noticed Maria was still in her office working. "Knock, knock,"

"Hi, Derek, come in. Is there something I can do for you?"

"No Maria, I'm going out to grab something to eat, would you like anything?"

"Where are you going?"

"I'm going to take a walk to the deli next door."

"Yes, a salad would be great. Let me get you some money."

"Don't worry about it, this is on me."

"Thank you."

"You're welcome." I returned to the office with our food. We sat in the conference room, eating and having casual conversations. Out of nowhere I asked, "Are you dating anyone Maria?"

"Why do you ask?"

"I noticed that you spend a lot of your time in this office building. You also have been spending a lot of your weekends in here."

"Well, I'm just trying to catch up on some things; you know how it is."

"No, I don't know how it is, Maria, and I do not spend too many evenings in this office. I sure don't spend my weekends here."

"I'd like to share something with you to get a man's point of view."

"Sure, what is it?"

"Okay, I have been single for about two years because I was in an abusive relationship with a man that was addicted to drugs. He was emotionally, mentally abusive, and would throw things. Yes, you could say I'm a domestic violence victim. There was also the struggle of spending quality time together or anytime at all. I went through this for five years before I realized I had had enough. I noticed that the abuse in the relationship was starting to escalate. I was very much afraid and concerned this was going to lead to something more serious. I did not want to wait around to find out. You hear about the stories of women in these abusive relationships, and they keep going back to that abusive relationship—or they leave and go out, meeting someone new who is also abusive. I do not want that for myself. I want a meaningful and loving relationship. I know there will be good and bad times, but that person will be just as caring and willing to communicate through those good and bad times. Is it a terrible thing for a person to want to have as part of their life, two people wanting to share in a loving relationship?"

"Do you really want my honest opinion on this?" I asked

"Sure."

"It's not terrible and it's not asking for much. You know, sometimes people who are truly meant to be together are brought together in ways that do not require much effort to get the relationship started. We must also have a clear understanding that not all relationships are meant to be." I looked at the clock and saw that it was seven o'clock and time for me to go. "Maria, not to be rude, but I need to get to the gym so I can work out."

"Do you mind if I ask you a question before you go?"

"No, I don't mind. Go right ahead."

"What about your better half?" I sat in silence for a few seconds with a smile on my face. "Why are you smiling, did I say something funny?"

"Well, Maria, it's not that you said something funny, but intriguing. You asked me about my better half. First of all, I do not believe in having half of anything. When God created man and woman, He created us whole. So the answer to your question is that I do not believe, a whole man deserves a half woman or a whole woman deserves a half man. All relationships should be whole and of one sound. He wants us to have special relationships that blend together and balance in harmony."

"Wow. That is a deep and profound statement."

"God is a deep and profound God. Before I go, I have a question for you."

"Shoot."

"If you do not mind, would you like to go out and have dinner tomorrow evening and finish this conversation? I was listening and respect all that you were saying, and I believe that it's important to share what is heavy on our hearts at times."

"I guess we could go out for dinner."

"Don't worry, this will be good. Besides, what else are you going to do—sit in this office and start making up work to do?"

"You're very funny; go to the gym. I will talk with you tomorrow."

"This is a nice restaurant, Derek, and I really enjoy jazz music. I find it to be comforting, soothing, and peaceful."

"Yes, I agree with you, I feel the same about jazz myself. So, yesterday evening's conversation ..."

"Yes, what about it, Derek?"

"Question, what you think about people needing to be more caring and compassionate with a need to speak from the heart?"

"What do you mean?"

293

"I mean being able to speak from the heart is love; we tend to take what is placed on our heart and bring it upstairs. We want to change things in a way that is comfortable for us, but being able to speak from the heart, you must be a mature, compassionate, caring, giving, and loving person. I'm not perfect. I know I have flaws, but I try to share with people from the heart. I interpret this as being real and true."

"I understand what you're saying, Derek, but what if it's something that may hurt or make a person feel bad?"

"There are times you must pick your battles, and there is a time and place for everything. You must take in consideration the present state of the person. They may not be ready for what you have to share with them right then and there. Still, you should be able to express yourself in a loving and caring way, without the other person reading more into it. I am sure this could be challenging for some people, especially men, but then you must be clear and concise in what you mean so that there is no misunderstanding. Realistically if you look at society today, how love is displayed among adults, family, friends, and even for our children, there is usually some sort of sexual or intimate involvement, which leads to our mind being tainted."

"Yes, because our media plays a big role in this as well, such as the movies and television shows that are aired today. I could see how this could be confusing for some people today, even those who are in the Christian world. Derek, I have a nephew, and I was watching him play a video game that was supposedly age appropriate. In the video game, there were characters dressed provocatively in some sort of sexual manner. They showed the men, and especially the women, as revealing images, leaving almost nothing to the imagination."

"Yes, I know exactly what you are talking about Maria."

"Thank you, Derek."

"What are you thanking me for? I didn't pay for dinner yet."

"No silly, it's refreshing to sit here and talk with you about love in this fashion without it being taken out of context. I do find it hard just to say to someone 'I love you' without having to worry that it will be taken out of context. It's great knowing and hearing someone being able to share in this manner without getting flustered or feeling uncomfortable."

"Now I have something else to share with you."

"Okay, shoot again."

"Now look at this, Maria. You are a white woman, and I am a black man. We have a society that's still prejudice and racist. If you are not paired up with some one of the same race, nationality or even social status, this is viewed as a problem; and some of those individuals who make it a problem consider themselves Christians."

"Well, I believe that when two people are together and there is a connection, none of that should not matter. We should want to be with someone with a good heart, someone you connect with and feel good about. Their race or nationality should not be the focus, but with some people there are certain traditions that interfere. It shouldn't be such a big deal. What are your thoughts, Derek?"

"I agree, and we should allow ourselves to become blind to color and open the eyes of our heart, especially if you feel connected to a person who's different from you. Often we're too afraid to act on it because this person is not viewed as the same as you. Many people will not admit it, but the views of society control some of these people and their happiness. If you really look at life, Maria, and the way we function as a society realistically, it is our natural inclination to feel uncomfortable around people who are different from us, and to gravitate toward those who are similar to us."

"I truly believe that, Derek."

"Believe what?"

"The comment you just made, about people are more comfortable with people like them. Unfortunately, this concept takes place in corporate America just as much."

"Unfortunately Maria, when we allow our differences to separate us from other people, we disregard all that Jesus has endured for us. We need to be open in building relationships with other people, especially those we appreciate and even more so with people who are not like us and our friends that we easily identify with. We may be surprised, and come to the realization that we have a lot in common."

Maria sat back in her seat, "You know that is so true, it makes you wonder about people who call themselves Christians and also display racist behaviors. If you were to turn you and me inside out, people would not know our colors, and if people were just to look at the hearts of people, they would not see color."

"Hey, I like that analogy," replied Derek.

"It's people who see color, Derek, that makes life more challenging for those who do not see color."

"I agree with you one hundred percent because those who do not see color see the beauty of life that we were blessed with. He has blessed us with so much that another person's color should be the least of our concerns. If Jesus and his disciples discriminated and only helped particular people, how do think those who were in great need would have felt? They saw people's hearts, the goodness they displayed, and their needs. Unfortunately, we live in a society that even some people who call themselves Christians make it difficult to display love and affection to people within the same race."

"I can definitely testify to that, Derek. I have had encounters with a few Christians who were having a difficult time getting along with their own race and even people within the church. It's easy for some people to go around and pretend to love others, speak kindly, avoid hurting the feelings of others, and even pretend to like or show some interest in others. Sometimes the love of others is so fake that they would pretend to feel moved with compassion when they hear of people's needs. It's not the heart that sees color; it is people who see color. Sometimes I feel I need to be more cautious of some of the people who call themselves Christian, than of those who are not. I have friends who are not Christians who are more real and sincere than those who claim to be."

"Yes, this is so unfortunate, Maria, but on the other hand, this is the reality of life we have to go through. When we demonstrate any act of love, God wants us to be real and sincere and not to pretend. True, sincere love requires taking the time and effort to reconnect with your soul. You must be willing to put any prejudice or indifferences you have to the side, as well as any other barrier that prevents you from displaying this kind of love. There are so many barriers out there today that people feed into, allowing themselves to be divided from each other that we neglect the things that God intends for us to enjoy."

"What kind of things do you think divides us and creates barriers, Derek?"

"There are so many, but I will share a few, like politics, appearance, age, race, nationality, sex, intelligence, financial status, social class, titles, and even different interests. When people create barriers or divisions, they're suppressing Christ's love and damaging their souls, meaning they are only willing to be friendly with those people they consider to be like them. Jesus has knocked down these barriers and many others in order to make us one big, happy family."

"I know that's right; this is so amazing, Derek."

"What's so amazing?"

"It feels so refreshing just to hear another person be able to share in a sincere, loving, and realistic conversation. I know when we die and go to heaven, race, money, titles, economic class, and any other barriers are not going to matter. When we are in heaven, we will be at peace and truly be one big, happy family."

I slowly lifted my head up and said, "This is so true, and I am ready for when it is my time." Bringing my head down and making eye contact with Maria, I said, "You know, when Jesus died on the cross, He destroyed those barriers people build between themselves, and we all are in the same blood line. Jesus has opened up the door for us to have unity, love, peace, and happiness with people who are not like us. It's because of his death that we are one. Meaning we should be willing to help those who need our help, so they can become better people. It is not about what's in it for you or the type of help you give because your reward will come later in life. Your love must be real, sincere, and genuine. You know, Maria, the word is a powerful word, and we live in a love-starved world."

"How so; what do you mean?"

"You know that falling in love is only a temporary, romantic, emotional obsession. Love is an attitude that some people view as a behavior. If we want to keep love alive ..."

Maria jokingly interrupted, "Is this like keeping hope alive?" We both chuckled and smiled.

"Actually yes, hope is important, and we must choose to have the attitude of love by looking out for the interest of our children, family, relatives, and friends. In all reality to attract the love you want is to love God first and learn how to embrace your soul. Some people forget that God is love; He should be your first love and the one true love of your life."

Maria exhaled and had a serious look on her face as she said, "Wow, I know I may sound like a tape recorder, but this conversation is so refreshing for me."

"You know most women believe that in order to exhale the way you just did, they need to watch a movie or find that special man in their life, not realizing that a special man already exists in their life and that man is God. He is their husband; they can exhale everyday knowing His love never fails."

Maria looked at Derek as to be amazed by his remarks, "I never looked at it that way. I never looked at love and my relationship with God in that fashion."

"Honestly, Maria, He is the one who keeps us grounded and loves us no matter where we are in our life or what circumstances we may be facing. God is love and His love never fails, but people do fail us."

A few days had passed since I last spoke to Maria. Thinking about the conversation we had and how she was doing, I decided to give her a call. "Hello, Maria, how are you doing?"

"My day is going well. So, what do you have plan for today?"

"I'm going out for ice cream and would like to know if you would be interested in joining me?"

"Sure, Derek, ice cream sounds really good. What time?"

"How about we meet in a couple hours is that enough time?"

"That's plenty of time."

"Great, I will meet you at The Ice Cream Shop in a couple of hours Maria."

"Sounds good. I will see you there." I arrived at The Ice Cream Shop before Maria, but she was not too far behind me. While I was getting out of the car, she was pulling into the parking lot. I waited for her to park so we could go into The Ice Cream Shop together. While looking at the selection of ice cream I heard a voice.

"May I take your order?"

"Maria, go ahead and order."

"I will have a raspberry sorbet."

"Have you decided on what you're going to order, sir?"

"Yes, I am going to have a hot fudge sundae with death by chocolate and butter pecan ice cream."

"Wow, you must like chocolate."

"Oh yeah, chocolate is my weakness." Our ice cream was prepared and placed on the counter, and I paid for them. "Maria, let's go for a walk and eat our ice cream unless you prefer sitting."

"Hey, that sounds good to me. I can eat and walk off these extra calories." While walking and talking, I could see this sparkle in Maria's eyes. She had this lovely smile and an expression of peace and happiness. I took my hand and put it on the small of her back, in a subtle way just to let her know that I'm here. Then gradually and gently put my arm around her waist, pulling her in so she was on the opposite side of me, putting myself between the traffic and Maria. She looked at me with a surprised look on her face and said, "Wow this is different."

"What do you mean this is different?"

"I mean a different type of treatment for me. To be honest I've never been out with anyone that put me on their inside to protect me from the traffic."

"This is how I've been raised as far as being a gentleman towards women, as well as showing respect for women." While we were walking Maria stopped.

"Isn't the sunset beautiful?"

Looking at Maria, "Yes it is,"

"Why are you looking at me that way?"

"You know it is amazing how we as a society and country take so much for granted."

"That's right, go ahead and change the subject; so you were saying, Derek ..."

Derek chuckled, "I was saying: we as a society and country takes so much for granted. We complain about jobs, money, our living accommodations, and our likes and dislikes about food while there are people in other countries that are happy and feel wealthy if they make $200.00 in a month. We live in a selfish country where nothing is done with the intent of compassion, love, kindness, and care. There seems to be an angle or some hidden agenda, and the people who suffer are the ones with little to nothing. Why are you so quiet, Maria?"

"I'm fine; it's just that when you made that comment it just made me think about how selfish and self-centered our country truly can be. This is something that I do think about from time to time. It really bothers me when I hear how our country will spend millions or billions of dollars to build an airplane that we will never get to enjoy or benefit from. Our government comes up with money for things that are important for them. They will put up a fight when it comes to assisting the homeless and our education system that is going to hell."

"Do you remember that evening we were out and talking about love, Maria."

"Yes I do, what about it?"

"Well, this is what I mean: love is about caring for those in need, making a difference in the lives of others that benefit everyone in a special way. To give that kind of love you cannot be self-centered; you have to be Christ centered. When you are able to love in this manner, you are able without any hesitation to think of others first before yourself. Unfortunately, we have parents who put themselves before their children. You know your child needs some basic things, but some people will go and buy new clothes, sneakers, or expensive, name-brand clothing for their child but will not supply their child with school supplies or invest quality time into their child. Children do not need designer clothing. They need to be loved and educated and receive appropriate discipline."

301

"Hey, Derek, like I was saying, our government will invest in what they see as important to them, most likely because certain individuals are benefiting from it somehow."

"Think about it, what doesn't our government benefit from, Maria? They benefit from taxes and the so-called drug war. Our government is so high tech, with the ability to trace so many things and has all this special security and protocols. Why can't we stop drugs from entering this country? I will tell you why, because it's a big business."

"Take it easy, Derek, you sound very angry about that subject."

"I'm sorry; sometimes my emotions can get the best of me."

"I very much know how you feel. This is something I experienced in my family. I witnessed what drugs can do to people." For some apparent reason, there was this brief moment of silence. "I enjoy our conversations, Derek. I mean, I really enjoy talking with you."

Looking at Maria with a smile on my face, "I enjoy talking with you, as well." We continued walking, not talking much but enjoying one another's company.

As I was walking, I heard Maria's voice, "Look at me, Derek." I looked, "Why are you making that funny-looking face? I'm being serious, Derek."

"Well, if you're serious, then who should I be?"

"Would you just give me your undivided attention, please?"

"Okay, Maria, you have my undivided attention. I'm listening."

"You remember the first time we were out at dinner?" "Yes, I remember, what about it?" "When I listened to you, I felt an overwhelming amount of peace, a kind of peace I have not felt from another before. I wanted to tell you this that evening when we were at dinner, but I did not want you to get the wrong idea and avoid me."

"Now how could I avoid you? We get along so well, and I especially enjoy your company."

"Thanks again for inviting me out for ice cream; have a good evening."
"You're welcome, and I will talk to you tomorrow."

Later that evening when I returned home I turned on some music to get in a relaxed mode. I turned on my computer to check my emails before I went to bed and decided to send Maria an email;

Hey you, I enjoyed the evening we spent together. I want you to know that you are a beautiful person who is tenacious with great strength. I hope the rest of your week is pleasant and peaceful. I'm looking forward to spending even more time with you. May you sleep in peace. Good night.

The morning arrived, and it was a beautiful day. I got up and went through my morning routine, giving thanks to God for allowing me to see and breathe another day. Then I was off to the gym for my morning workout. After my workout I returned home, showered, got dressed, and cooked breakfast. After eating my breakfast, I was out the door and off to wo I arrived to my office early. One of the first things I do when I get t office is check my phone messages and emails. Then something t to check my personal email, which I usually don't do at work be honest, I was like a little kid, wondering if Maria replied t If she did, what did she have to say? I started to think ba was a kid, and we would play this game of sending notes b Do you like me; check yes or no? Today we have the a technology, so we don't have to be around to see the othe and feel embarrassed with your friends standing aroun

303

she say?" Anyway, I logged into my email account, and there were four new emails. I went into the inbox and yessssssss ... I received an email from Maria stating:

Your message started my day. You always make me smile. I can't begin to tell you how much it means, but I am afraid, my dear, that you are the beautiful one both inside and out. I listen to you talk about being real and sharing your heart. I want to tell you that I am in love with you and your heart. You make me feel safe, secure, special, and happy. For that, I am grateful to you and to God for sending you to me. Last night... when I told you that you give me peace—you truly give me a peace I have not felt from anyone before. I thank you for this and for you being you. I am so sorry you are experiencing my challenges. I am trying to find the way God wants me to go. I am trying to listen, but I cannot get my head to shut off long enough to hear. Because I trust and feel the way I do about you, you hear my barrage of feelings, questions, doubts, fears, and jubilations. Some days I feel like Sybil. I sometimes wonder if you think I am nuts! However, I guess you walked the walk and understand. I truly recognize how lucky I am to have you in my life. People don't find what we have too easily. Some can't find it at all. The funny thing is that I am still trying to figure myself out. That truly is where my ambivalence lies. It certainly has nothing to do with my feelings for you. I guess I am just trying to

get comfortable in my own skin before I offer myself
to somebody else.

Thank you for your patience, for being so understanding and mostly for your unselfish heart.

I love you beyond words.

I sat at my desk with a smile on my face. My heart was feeling reju-
venated and overwhelmed with joy. As I was sitting, I thought, *Wow*!
I was touched in a way that I have not been touched before. She is so
honest and genuine with her thoughts and feelings. Maria really made
my day; reading her email clearly showed me we are walking on the
same path, having had similar experiences. I decided to call her. "Good
morning, Maria"

"Good morning, Derek; it's nice to hear from you in the morning."

"It's nice to hear your voice. I called to share with you that I received
your email."

"What are your thoughts about it?"

"Well, my first reaction was that I had this huge smile on my heart. I
keep thinking about all you have said in the email."

"I'm sorry. I should not have been so open with so much."

"There was just something about that email you sent me."

"What are you saying, Derek, did it make you feel uncomfortable?"

"No, that's not it at all, Maria. It made me feel more than uncomfortable. It made me feel overwhelmed with happiness and joy."

"You are a jerk. You had me thinking that I scared you off and look
at you, playing games."

"I do like to have fun, too."

"So, you must be a morning person."

"Maria, I can be a morning, afternoon, evening, and night person."

"Okay, just finish before the workday ends."

"Before I was so rudely interrupted I wanted to share with you that what you are going through and experiencing, we have all been there or are there. It is just that some of us do not want to admit to it. Like I tell some of the guys I hang with, there are times you must man up and be true to your heart." I heard this silence as if the phone went dead. I thought I was on one of those cell phone commercials and dropped a call. Maria was there; she was just listening very intently. "People go through life, looking for that special person to spend their life with and hoping to make that beautiful connection. For some people it happens earlier in life, and for others it may occur later, but once you have it, you will know how to appreciate it and enjoy it." I looked at the clock and said, "I have an appointment who will be arriving in thirty minutes, Maria. I need to prepare for it. I also have to finalize my presentation for the conference I'm speaking at in Washington. I would like for us to get together for dinner after work and finish our conversation. It will be nice to spend some time together before I leave for Washington."

"Sure, I'm free."

"I will pick you up about 6:30 p.m."

I returned from Washington, and it felt good to be home. My presentation went well, but I lost my cell phone. Tomorrow I have to go and pick up my new phone. Right now all I want to do is sit back and relax. I did not feel like unpacking, so I dropped my bags at the door. I turned on the television to the sports channel to catch up on what I missed while I was away. I poured a glass of wine and lay back on the sofa, grabbing my laptop to check my emails. I received ten new messages and one from Maria with the subject line saying, Missing You. The email read:

"I don't know if I should call because I left a message last night and you did not respond. I don't want to be a bother to you."

Since I still had a house phone, I decided to call Maria. I did not want her to be concerned or to think I was trying to avoid her. "Hello, Maria."

"Hello, stranger."

"I read your email. I lost my cell phone, so this is why I did not get your call. My flight was delayed, and I was stuck in the airport for four hours. I want to share something with you, Maria."

"You can share anything with me."

"I know you had experienced an unpleasant relationship, and I want you to know that I'm not that type of man. I'm a respectable man. I want to give you time to think about us in a special and different way, time to think about our relationship and if having me as part of your life is something you want."

"You are a respectable man, Derek, in my eyes and so much more. That is never in question, please understand, historically speaking if I did not give 150 percent to a relationship, many times I was punished for it. I am sorry; I don't mean to blame you for another's shortcoming. Sometimes it's just hard to rewire the brain into thinking that partners can be different. You are so very different, and I should know better."

"Maria, I think about the conversations we have had and the many thoughts you continue to share with me about your life. I see something that is very different about you, and maybe I don't understand your unhappiness. I do understand why you are so happy about our relationship, and why you are so open and free with me. There are times I feel you probably lie down at night and think of ways to find our soul a home."

That evening while I was up reading and listening to music, I started to think back to a conversation I had with Maria about faith and the statement she made, in order to have faith, you have to believe. The word *believe*, just stuck in my head. This thought that came to mind was not just a thought for me to keep to myself, but a thought to share with Maria, since it was she who put the thought into my mind from the conversation we had. I sent Maria the following email:

> While I was reading, a thought came to mind about our conversation we were having last night and the word *belief* entered my mind. Yes, to have faith, you have to believe, and belief is about the renewing of our mind and embracing your soul. One of the main causes of emotional, mental, and spiritual problems in life is unpleasant thinking. Thinking wrongfully and untruly, unrealistically, depressingly and irrationally leads to damaged emotions, destructive actions, or behaviors, and a failure to mature in the way we should, losing sight of Christ. For us to experience an abundant life, we must live it out in our daily lives, keeping our soul intact.

Maria replied:

> Although I feel I have a strong belief and spiritual conviction, it's easy to say and often hard to carry out. I admit my thinking at times is unpleasant when it comes to personal issues, but I think it's because I love too much and need to be a little more selfish. I love that you care. I love that you are patient with me. I love that you don't push me but gently nudge me when I need it. I love you for who you are and what you represent to me

One Thursday evening, Maria invited me over to her house for dinner. After dinner we sat listening to music and played backgammon. We played three games and of course, I won two of them. I even assisted Maria throughout the game so she could at least win one game. I looked into her eyes as I grabbed her hands, "I have been through some very challenging and difficult relationships in my life, and I learned about people through my trials and tribulations. I view our relationship as being very different from any other relationship I have been involved in."

"What do you mean, Derek?"

"What I mean, Maria, is that we spent the majority of our relationship as friends for a few years. We have had the opportunity to learn about one another in a working environment as friends. We continued on that course without displaying any signs of interest in one another. What I am saying is that I found you to be an attractive and beautiful woman, but not in the way that I wanted to date or have a relationship with you. Do you know understand what I'm trying to say?"

"Yes, I know exactly what you mean, Derek."

"It was how we grew in getting to know each other that is why we have this wonderful relationship today. We were strangers who became friends and only friends. The two of us spent time together sharing, and what we have now was not either one of our plans. We built this unique pyramid where we started off as colleagues working in the same building as friends and from friends have become soul mates. We care so much about each other that we do not want to hurt each other and do not want to lose what we have built. I have had many relationships, but no serious relationship like ours. Our relationship is very special and unique in its own way."

"I clearly understand what you are saying, Derek, and I too feel the same way. I guess I am afraid and do not want to be hurt. After my last relationship, I told myself that I was not going to get serious with anyone, but look at us. I never felt like this for anyone and never wanted to be with someone as much as I want to be with you."

"The feeling is mutual. I know we are trying so hard to protect each other's heart."

"What do we do and where do we go from here, Derek?"

"How about if we take a week from spending quality time together? I mean we should take the time to truly evaluate ourselves and what directions we truly want this relationship to go. Take a look at how we started out, Maria, and where we are now in our relationship. I know you had a very bad experience in your last relationship, and I do not ask much of you. I want you to be comfortable in your own skin and when we're together. I want you to feel you can be free and happy, and not worrying about being yourself. Keep in mind, Maria, I am not that other person from your past."

"I know this too well. You are far from that person and not even close."

"I'm glad to hear this. Take this week to yourself and make it all about Maria. We don't have to get together, call, text, or email one another."

"We will see each other at work, Derek."

"No we won't."

"Why not?"

"I took the week off from work."

"So, you had this all planned out."

"No, I did not have any of this planned out. I was noticing that you were starting to struggle with us, and I figured you could use some space."

"You are amazing. I guess when you do love someone you have to truly make sacrifices, even if this means taking time away from that person."

"Hey, I'm not just sacrificing time away from you. I'm also giving up some vacation time. This time will also allow me to catch up on some things."

"Well, I can tell you one thing, Derek; it will be very different without having you around for a week, not being able to see you, send a text, or pick up the phone just to hear your voice."

"I'm always there, Maria; all you have to do is just close your eyes, and think of me with my arms around you with your head on my shoulder."

"Is this what you do when I'm not with you?"

"No."

"Then what do you do?"

"I do nothing."

"So, you mean to tell me that you do not miss me when we're not together?"

"I'm only kidding, I miss you when we're not together."

"Is there anything special that you do?"

"Yes, I think of that one special evening we were together watching the sunset, with my arms wrapped around you. I keep the memory of that evening in a secret place, and that place is my heart. So whenever I need to go to that secret place, I close my eyes and enter that place in my heart. I visit for as long as I want, thinking of that special evening. Then I think of other wonderful memories we have created and the ones that we may possibly make."

"Nice, I'm going to use that special evening for my special memory."

"Oh really?"

"Yes I am."

"And what makes you think you could use that for your special memory?"

"It's not just any special memory, it's our special evening and memory."

"Yes, this is true, so I guess you can use it."

"What do you mean you guess? I'm going to use it whether you want me to or not."

I said, "Yes, ma'am," as I gently pulled Maria closer into me to give her a hug.

The week was feeling more like a month. I thought about Maria more than I thought I would. I was very anxious in wanting to talk with her, but I decided that I couldn't give in; I had to be strong. I guess the saying what does not kill you only can make you stronger holds true. This week will not kill me, and it's definitely making me stronger. Besides, I knew the best thing to do was to occupy my time. I continued going to the gym and spending time with the guys. This helped me take my mind off Maria at times, but when I was not thinking about her, somebody would ask me about her. I also thought she might call me. I knew she wanted to, but she was trying to hold out, too. I knew she was saying to herself, *let me be strong, I don't want him to think I'm desperate or insecure.* The week couldn't have gone any slower. Any other time the weeks, months, and years go by in a blink of an eye, but that week was dragging like someone put us in a time machine and pushed the drag button. Then again this was a good thing, because it allowed me to spend some additional time at the bookstore and to work on my manuscript. While sitting I was starting to reflect on life, I evaluated myself and my relationship with Maria. As I looked around the bookstore I noticed the different couples. I noticed the attractive women, but I was not interested in wanting to get to know any of those women. This made me want to be with Maria more. I realized that God wants us to love and respect one another. He has done wonderful and incredible things for us that we do not even do for ourselves. He also gave us life and the gift of love. As I sat there, I realized that God introduced me to Maria, and she is my gift of love. Thank you, God, for adversity, the many challenges I had with relationships, and giving me the strength to be compassionate to others, even in my weakest moments. My spiritual life has assisted me with learning that love has become a mixed-up word with no meaning, and people today are still confused about it, failing to understand that love is an attribute of God. When I learned to have faith and hope working together, cultivating my soul, I was able to understand how God loves.

Okay, only three more days to go before the week comes to an end. I was not too much in a writing mood. I was at the bookstore, and so it was not a total waste of time. I guessed I would catch up with and clean up my emails because I have not checked my emails in over a week. I had twenty unread emails and most of them were junk. *Hey You, Missing You*—Maria sent me this email at 3:00 a.m. What was she doing up at that time of night? What is she doing emailing me? This was not part of the agreement. I smiled and open it to see what she wanted to share with me. Maria's email started off by saying:

This week is dragging. I never thought a week could go by so slowly. The days don't feel like twenty-four-hour days; they feel like forty-eight-hour days. I know I was supposed to take this week to myself; sorry and I hope you are not disappointed in me. Derek, this past week I have tried to keep to myself to figure out the rest of my life. Where do I want to go? Who do I want to spend it with? What do I want? This whole week I was thinking I was crazy to walk completely away from my current life, enter a new relationship after having the unfortunate experience of a horrible one. I began to think "History Trump," right? My heart tells me not. You don't leave me. Something is telling me "it's him"; it's you. So I look back, wondering if I'm doing the right thing. Do you realize I'm leaving everything to do what I said I would not do? It is not easy to do, but impossible not to do. It is 2:40 a.m. I cannot sleep, cannot work, cannot keep a thought, and yes, I cannot smile, but boy when you're not around I sure can cry. I have wasted a valuable part of my life when I look back. Sure I was lonely, even though most of the times I was not even alone. Sadly, I did not even realize it until now. Are you really ready? Do you promise to be kind to me? Do you promise to be gentle to my heart? Do you promise to grab my hand when I reach for yours? Why do I ask? Because I love you too much to let you hurt me. Besides, up to now, I have worked very hard to protect my heart. If I'm not in love with you, then what is this that I'm going through tonight? If my heart is lying, what should I believe in? Why do I go crazy every time I think about you? So I need to keep walking forward. I'm sorry I have stumbled lately, and yes, a little lost. I'm giving a part of me I thought I would never give again to someone I could lose. I give it up to you, praying that you do not ruin me, but renew me.

Wow, Maria and I really needed to talk. This was definitely not email conversation. What time is it—7:00 p.m. Let me give her a call. I grabbed my jacket and checked the pockets, no cell phone. It must be in my bag and it's not in my bag either. Where is my cell phone? I must have left it in the car or at home. I'm definitely not going to get anything done here tonight; this email she sent is on my mind. Let me get out of here so I can call her. I packed up my laptop, grabbed my jacket, and started walking out the bookstore. Maybe I could just stop by her house. As I walked down the stairs in the bookstore, I saw Maria, sitting at a table with her laptop, drinking tea. I looked up and said, "God, you have a sense of humor; who could not love you?" I walked over to Maria and tapped her on her left shoulder, while I was standing on her right. When she realized it was me, she stood up and gave me this big hug and said, "I miss you."

"Looking at her I said, "Ditto."

"So, how did you know I was here?"

"I didn't; God knew."

"What do you mean God knew?"

"Well, I was sitting upstairs. I just read your email you sent to me at 3:00 a.m. last night. I wanted to call. When I went to use my cell phone I could not find it, so I figured I must have left it in my car or at home. I was on my way to my car to check and see if my cell phone was there to call you, but it does not look like I'll have to call you."

"Wow, that is amazing, Derek, because I have been here for about an hour."

"I was here over an hour, so we just missed each other."

"What is it you want to talk to me about? I hope my email did not scare you."

"No, not at all; it touched my heart. Let's take a walk and go to the Café Shop across the street."

"Sounds good, I'm a little hungry. Besides, I could not get anything done anyway."

As Maria and I were about to enter the Café Shop, Maria said, "Someone is calling you."

"Hey, Derek! Derek, over here."

"Do you know that couple sitting at that table?"

"Yes, that is Anthony and Nicole. I met them at a party. They are very good people; let me introduce you to them." Anthony stood up; he and

Derek shook hands and gave each other a brotherly hug. Derek extended himself to Nicole and gave her a hug. "Hey guys, I would like you to meet Maria."

Anthony and Nicole greeted Maria, then Nicole said, "Why don't the two of you join us; we just got here ourselves and we have not even ordered."

"Well, we were going to get a table and discuss some things."

"I don't mind, Derek, we can talk later. Besides, I want to meet some people who know you other than me."

"So, what are you two up to?" asked Anthony.

"Not much," said Derek. "We just came from the bookstore and decided to come here for a cup of tea, and sit and talk."

"We're not taking you guys away from anything personal that you need to talk about, are we?"

Maria replied, "No Anthony, Derek and I always have great stimulating and soothing conversations."

"Yeah, Nicole and I were just having a little discussion about diversity, culture, and race within our country."

"Oh, boy," said Derek.

"What's wrong?"

"When these two get going, Maria, you are in for the ride of your life, but I mean that in good way. You remember at the party the conversation we had about blended families. That was a very deep and meaningful conversation that enlightened me."

Anthony jumps in, "Speaking of blended families. Do you know our nation has grown with diversity, and there is this change in how we socialize with one another, which helps the growth and acceptance of blended families?"

"I do not understand what you mean or where you are going with this," said Maria."

Neither do I," said Derek.

316

"All right, let me tell you what I mean. You remember the presidential candidacy of Barack Obama; he was being known as a son of a black man and a white woman and from a different culture."

Derek replied, "Yes—what about it?"

"This brought about more attention to interracial relationships that leads to people coming together as people. I believe society wanted a president they felt could bring our country together as a whole, not for any special groups, race, religion, culture, or gender, but for all people regardless of their social and economic status."

Nicole interrupts, "Look at the two of you, a black man and white woman. This is becoming more common, and there is nothing wrong with it at all. I'm happy to see people who are capable of embracing happiness regardless of the color of their skin."

"Nicole is right," said Anthony," we have come a long way as a people, and we will always have work to do. Up until the 1960s, interracial marriage was illegal in many states. Unfortunately, today there are still racist emotions and opinions against it today. What I found to be even more disturbing was that it was not until the year 2000 that the United States Census Bureau allowed Americans to say they were of a mixed race. Since then the interracial relationships and families continues to rise."

Nicole grabbed Anthony's hand as he was speaking and then she jumped right in as if they rehearsed this, "The unfortunate thing about this is that some of us still struggle with being able to demonstrate love towards one another or embrace one another even as friends. The only thing that bonds us together as a group is the common ways that we are placed in society. I say this speaking from personal experience. See, my upbringing was based on Native American cultures and traditions. I was lead into a more Asian identity because of my last name, Chung."

Derek interrupts, "This is very interesting to hear from you, Nicole. What I mean to say is that I never heard anyone really explain their experience regarding their culture and race the way you did. You're a person who identifies the different racial mixture in you because when I look at you I must admit I see an Asian woman. I find that it is pretty deep in how you look at the full spectrum of your race and embrace it the way you do. I guess as a black man I always experienced life, growing up with the focus on black people and white people and nothing in between, before, or after—no grey area. I mean even though you know other races and nationalities exist, you would mostly see the black culture as the negative and the white as positive. This is because of the norms our society and culture have developed over the years. There is a handful of whites who are willing to admit we are all one and from the same bloodline. Society does not see it that way, and not all mixed race or interracial relationships have a consistent experience, but the way society continues to respond to mixed race and interracial couples remains to be consistent."

Maria responded, "Even though there is a growing number of interracial couples, mixed races, and blended families, some will say that society's response to them usually has the following elements a mixture of arrogance, disrespect, ignorance, judgment, inconsideration, common sense, and rudeness."

"I like that and I like her," said Nicole.

Anthony looked at Derek as to make eye contact and said, "Yes, she is all right."

"Anthony you started off this conversation talking about the Obama presidential candidacy," said Maria.

"Yes, I did."

"I voted for Obama, and I like the man for various reasons. The main reason I like Obama—and it's not just because he was viewed as a black man running—he was a man I viewed as representing all of America because he was a major supporter and promoter of diversity. I felt this would allow families and people of multicultural backgrounds, interracial couples, and blended families to be able to identify and feel happy to see a man that they could connect to in so many ways, being president of the United States or should I be politically correct Commander and Chief."

"I really like you; you are two for two, said Nicole. You better keep her, Derek."

"Of course I am, because anything else would be uncivilized," respond Derek.

This Is the Day

I was in bed, sound asleep, but I heard this thumping sound. I thought I was dreaming, but when I fully awakened, I remembered Kim was home from school. She was up playing music. As I lay in bed, I took a deep breath, "This is the day the Lord has made; let us rejoice and be glad in it." I lay here reflecting on the adversity and obstacles Kim and I encountered over the years. I closed my eyes and gave thanks:

> Thank you, God, for being there with us and guiding us through it all, through past experiences of life's circumstances, situations, and relationships that did not work out as planned. You were definitely there with me through the adversity and challenges I had encountered; You're more than a friend. You assisted me with understanding that we should not allow our past to become our present or allow our past to become our future. Thank You for life experiences, for blessing me with such a wonderful daughter, introducing me to Maria, and for my supportive and kind-hearted family and friends.

I decided to give Maria a good morning call. "Hello Maria, and good morning."

"Hello and good morning to you; this is a nice surprise and a nice way for me to start my day."

"I was lying in bed, thinking about our relationship. I like to share with you that we have a very special and unique relationship. We have had our good times and challenging times. Through those times we used spiritual wisdom to give us the peace and understanding of any situation we endure."

"It sounds like someone woke up on the caring and sharing side of the bed."

"Yes I did, and I want you to know my feelings and thoughts of you."

"I really appreciate this, Derek, but you have accomplished that in more ways than you could imagine."

"At least let me say this for the official record. We have been together for over three years. You're a caring, understanding, sharing, and giving woman who thinks of me in your decisions."

"That is because I'm respectful of our relationship and have respect for myself."

"Exactly, Maria; you have respect for yourself, a strong, deep, and meaningful spiritual life. You know something else, Maria?"

"What?"

"You support me and assist me with being the man I need to be inside."

"I'm a firm believer that we should encourage each other, Derek, to explore and discover the new areas of our life. If either one of us were entertaining something that could be harmful to our relationship, we should speak up without hesitation. When we're demonstrating this kind of support, I believe this allow us to examine ourselves leading you to discover the plans and calling that God has on your life."

"This is what I find so amazing about you, Maria. May I pray with you?"

"Sure."

"God, thank You for this time; thank You for all that you have done, are doing, and will continue to do. Thank You for bringing us together, allowing my heart to open and creating a special place in my heart for Maria. Well, you know I could lay here and talk with you all day. I do have to get up and go do the great things you ask of me, Amen."

"Amen," replied Maria.

"I have to get up. Kim and I have plans to go out for brunch this morning. She is making a lot of noise; this must be her way in telling me it's time to get up because she is hungry."

"Okay, Derek, enjoy brunch and tell Kim I said hello."

I finally got up and got myself together. "Good morning, Dad."

"Good morning, Kim."

"Why do you look like you have this cheerful glow about you?"

"I do not know what you are talking about, Kim. I feel like my normal self today. Are you ready to go out for brunch?"

"Yes, I am, Dad. I'm starving."

We went to Kim's favorite restaurant. While sitting at the table eating I looked up at her, "So how is school going?"

"School is going well, and I only have one more year to go. Dad, like you always say, one semester at a time."

"I'm looking forward to that day so I can attend your graduation."

"I can't wait, either."

"You know, Kim, you're about to step into the real world."

"Yeah, I know, Dad, but it has to happen sooner or later."

"This is true. Can I share something with you?"

"Sure, Dad, even if I was to say no, you would share it anyway."

"You're right, and you know your dad very well. This is something you would like to hear, but if you are not interested it can wait."

"No, Dad! Go right ahead. I want to know."

"Well, I don't know, you don't seem all that interested."

"Please, stop playing and just tell me."

"Okay, if you insist, I'm planning on asking Maria to marry me." In the middle of the restaurant, Kim let out this high pitch scream.

"I guess that means you approve."

"Of course I approve, Dad, if I didn't I would have said something when you and Maria started dating. I knew you were going to marry Maria. I thought it was going to be sooner. The two of you look and act like you should be married; everybody can tell. Dad, let me be the first to congratulate you and say, I am very happy for you. I want you to be happy because you deserve to be happy. You are a good father, friend, and a good man."

With great enthusiasm, I looked at Kim with a big smile on my face and said, "Thank you, Kim. That means a lot to me, especially coming from you. I want it to be special when I propose, so when I figure it all out, I will let you know."

Kim got up from her seat and walked over to my side of the table and gave me a big hug, and said, "Congratulations, Dad, and I love you."

"I love you, too, and thank you for being such a wonderful daughter."

Maria and I were on our way home from church. I had been thinking all weekend about how I would propose to Maria. I knew I would like it to be a special and memorable day for Maria. Okay, let me think about this for a moment. I know that Maria is an emotional, loving, and caring woman. She is a hopeless romantic and loves surprises even though she tries to pretend she doesn't. All right, I know how this will take shape and form.

Throughout our relationship, Maria and I had many tests to see if we had the connection and strength to maintain our relationship. Maria looked over at me while I was driving, "What's on your heart, Derek?"

"My heart is saying, that you and I should take a day off from work this week, hang out at the park and cookout."

"That would be great; I would love to spend the day with you at the park. I hear the weather is going to be great this week, so what day should we plan for?"

"How about Wednesday? Would that be a good day for you, Maria?"

"Wednesday is perfect; whatever I had planned on Wednesday I will sacrifice to spend a special day with you,"

"Ditto."

Maria and I were at the park having our own private cookout. I was prepping the grill to start the fire. Maria was unpacking the bags setting up the table. Once the table was set, she gradually made her way over to join me at the grill, putting her hand on my back and gently massaging, she said, "Hey Babe, need any help?"

"No Babe, sit back, relax, and enjoy."

"Okay, you know you don't have to tell me twice." I laughed. "So Derek, you never told me what you wanted to talk with me about. Every time we're about to talk, somehow we end up getting interrupted."

"You want to know something, Maria?"

"I know I want you to tell me something."

"As a matter of fact, today would be a great time for us to talk. Let's go and sit down while the coals get hot. You know when God created us; it was not just about man and woman becoming husband and wife, God created us for relationships. Building good and healthy relationships is a very important part of life today. The problem that most of us have with building these relationships is that we don't listen. We don't take the time to hear what others have to say. Listening is important to have a relationship that you feel safe in and know that there is security. It is also important to be supportive, giving reassurance and knowing what it is like to walk in the shoes of other people. When you see life from the perspective of others, you are better able to understand them and demonstrate care and compassion towards them and their situation. Difficult times are sometimes inevitable in a relationship, but this sometimes makes the relationship stronger and more genuine. The unfortunate thing about relationships is that sometimes they do have an ending point and we have to know when to call it quits, if necessary. Sometimes you have to know when to hold, when to fold, and when to walk away."

"Unfortunately, Derek, some people are not able to walk away when they should. There are a lot of hurt people out there with insecurity and trust issues. There are women who stay in abusive relationships because they do not believe in themselves. Some even believe that they cannot do any better. Then those who do leave may develop trust issues. I was once one of those people who had some serious trust issues in people. I felt I would extend myself to some family and friends and did not feel appreciated. I gave to people and they did not respect or appreciate what I did for them. I was starting to feel like I was having the life sucked out of me. I was in a long-term relationship where there was none too little trust or respect. I was feeling like a doormat. At that point, my trust just started to wear very thin. I had my doubts about dating and whether there were any real men out there to have a decent relationship with as a life partner. What about you, Derek? Did you have any doubts about entering a long-term committed relationship?"

"My belief is that relationships are based on trust, and the last time I put my trust out there, it was not appreciated. I experienced a lot of pain and heartache. In my marriage, I dealt with an insecure woman. I was more or less being emotionally and mentally abused. I know I can be stubborn and a little selfish at times. I know the both of us had some unhealthy experiences in relationships that neither one of us wants to revisit. When I think of you, Maria, and when we're together, my heart feels different. Just being with you gives me overwhelming peace and comfort. The relationship I have with you makes me think about marriage at times."

"Wow! I am flattered just knowing you feel that comfortable with me. You are right about us having had unhealthy relationships in the past, and I definitely do not want to revisit those things. What makes me feel good about our relationship is that we are able to sit and talk about our own personal issues and that we are able to discuss those issues, seek God, and make peace with our past and present issues."

"Yes, Maria, I definitely agree; all we can do is confess our part in the failures of the past, be determined in our hearts to do everything we can, and walk in obedience from this point on, strengthening and creating a peaceful soul. I mean that we must make every effort to make our present relationship everything to be at its best."

"I must admit, Derek, throughout the years that we have been dating, we just didn't spend quality time together, but we also invested in quantity of time. I mean, the time we dedicated to spend together was invested quantity time. Just about every time we spent together was quality time, which was never a concern of mine."

"I agree the time spent was special and healthy. It did not matter how much time, as much as what we shared with one another within that time frame. We utilized both quality and quantity effectively in our relationship. So are you comfortable with the amount of quantity time we spend together, Maria?"

"Yes, I'm very comfortable. It's safe to say, that we are good with time management with our relationship. Are you comfortable with the time, Derek?"

"Of course, I just didn't want to assume without asking."

"This is what I love about you."

"What do mean, Maria?"

"You show you care about me, about us, by openly communicating about us spending time together. You take in consideration the little things."

"Well, Maria, they say that the little things mean a lot."

"Yes they do mean a lot, very much no matter how the time is spent. I always feel close to you whether it's sitting on the couch watching television, you calling me keeping me company during my drive home, sending me an email or text in the middle of the day to say, "hi," and I love when we cook together."

"Ditto."

"Throughout the challenges and adversity of my life, I have matured in different areas of my life, realizing that it's these kinds of moments is what drew us close together. Honestly, I can say you are my best friend, Derek. I feel as if I could share anything and everything with you. We keep things honest between us; there is no mind reading and no unspoken expectations. We share with one another our wants, needs, hopes, and dreams." Maria reached over and grabbed my hand, "We developed a lot of trust and respect for one another and not just as a couple dating."

"What do you mean, Maria?"

"This was something we developed before we entertained the dating part of the relationship. The trust and respect was there even when we were just friends. Whether you knew or not, from the beginning you were always a friend. I mean, a man I enjoyed talking with, sharing my worst of times and best of times. You been there for me at my most difficult times, treating me special and you have become my exceptional best friend."

"Interesting Maria, so what is an exceptional best friend? What does that look like?"

327

"It's a rare quality, it's someone you can do and tell just about any-thing. Someone you want to be with as much as possible. When you and this person are in the same room and that person leaves the room for a minute, they are missed. That person respects me as a woman, and I respect him as a man. They respect themselves, take pride in themselves and have class. An exceptional best friend is someone you feel at one with; there's a special bond, Derek, and your souls becomes one."

"That word *need* is strong in itself. Sometimes we confuse our needs with our wants. Over the years society has developed the idea that needing or depending upon another person is a sign of weakness. For example, take a look at those in corporate America in those high-ranking posi-tions. They don't have a life, don't know how to treat people, and fail to realize their world could easily come crashing down, just like anyone else, because they're not in control."

"Do you know why this is a sign of weakness, Derek?"

"No, but I'm sure you are going to share this with me."

"If you do not want to hear what I have to say ..."

Derek chuckled and smile at Maria, "No, Maria, I do want to hear; just having a little fun." Maria stared at me as if she was looking through me. She was quiet for a few seconds, which seemed like an hour before saying anything.

"Well, are you ready?"

"Yes, of course I'm ready, the question is, are you ready to tell me?"

"Okay, I will stop the suspense. As I was saying before you decided to have your moment of being Mr. Funny Man, not being able to need or depend on someone is a sign of weakness means a couple of things, one you are afraid to relinquish power or are afraid of being hurt."

"Wow, I never saw it like that, but I do understand what you mean. I do not feel or see that as a problem between you and me."

With a smile on her face, Maria replied, "Neither do I, Derek; neither do I."

I was having a quiet evening at home, watching one of my favorite classic movies, *West Side Story*. As I sat watching the movie, I started to think about the day Maria and I spent together. The inspiring conversation we had gave me confirmation that it's definitely time to bring us together as one. She is a very special and exceptional woman. She completes and fills my life the right way. It was time to plan this out. I powered up my laptop and got onto the Internet. I emailed family and friends about my plans. Those for whom I did not have email addresses, I called. I was clear to everyone not to let anything slip. I received some comments from family and friends stating things like: and *It's about time*. I guess our relationship was more obvious than I realized. Even our family and friends seem to know that Maria and I were meant to be together.

One evening, Maria and I were window-shopping at the mall. Maria, like most women, enjoyed clothes and shopping. I'm a patient man, so it did bother me to be out at the mall because I like to browse at things for myself. This also gave me the opportunity to see what Maria likes and needs, and it made Christmas shopping easier. We walked through the stores, holding hands laughing and joking with one another. With a serious look on my face I pulled Maria into me. She just stared into my eyes as I looked into her eyes with an intense, nervous, but serious and meaningful look on my face. "Hey, I was wondering something."

"What, Derek?"

"Would you like to go out with me this Saturday for a special dinner?"

"So, what makes this dinner so special?"

"You make it special, because you are an amazing and a special woman."

"Well, that is an invitation I cannot refuse."

Later that evening I called the restaurant I wanted this special moment to take place. "Hello, City View Restaurant. How can I help you?"

"May I speak to the manager?"

"This is the manager. How may I help you, sir?"

"First, I would like to share with you that I've been coming to your restaurant for over three years and that I've enjoyed the ambiance, the pleasantry, and the comfort of the environment you provide for the customers. I'm planning to ask my girlfriend to marry me."

Before I could finish my thought the manager said, "Say no more, we will be honored to assist and to be part of this special occasion for you and your future wife."

"Great! I really appreciate you for assisting me."

"No problem, sir; just tell me what you'd like for us to do."

"I will have friends and family to witness the proposal, so can they sit in the section of the restaurant where they cannot be seen when we first entered the restaurant?"

"Sure, that will be easy, sir. Is there anything else?"

"I'd like a table for two near the window overlooking the city. I would like a bottle of wine and a dozen roses: ten pink, one white, and one red. I will stop by the restaurant a few hours before our reservation time."

"Sir, this sounds great. This must be one special lady."

"Yes, she is a special lady."

"Okay, sir; let me read back your request to make sure I have everything you just shared with me." The manager read back everything I requested verbatim.

"Yes, you have it exactly the way I stated it, thank you again."

"Sir, we look forward to serving you and if anything changes, please give us a call."

"Thank you, and I'm excited."

"Have a good day, sir."

It's show time, and I have a few hours to spare before it's time for me to pick up Maria. This gives me just enough time to stop by the restaurant to check on the arrangements. I arrived at the restaurant and they showed me where our family and friends will be sitting, and it was perfect. Maria would not have a clue that they're here and that something special was about to take place. I asked for the bouquet of flowers and the manager went to get them for me. I pulled out the red and white roses from the bouquet and then took a piece of ribbon and tied the ring to them. I then placed the roses back into the bouquet informing the manager to keep the flowers in a safe place, and place them on the table at exactly 7p.m. I left the restaurant to go pick up Maria.

I arrived at Maria's home, and she looked beautiful as I expected. "Hello, Maria; you look wonderful, but then again you always look wonderful."

"Thank you, and you are not looking too shabby yourself."

"Well, you know, I try because when I am around you I always have to be on top of things."

"So, where are you taking me, Derek?"

"I will take you wherever you want to go."

"Really?"

"Yes ma'am."

"Then let's go to City View Restaurant."

"You sure this is where you want to go?"

"Yes, I've never been to the restaurant and hear it is a very nice place."

"Let me make a call and see if they have any openings."

"Are you serious?"

"Yes, nothing is etched in stone."

"You did not make reservations anywhere else?"

"I had a place in mind, but I like your choice. You know it's nice to be spontaneous at times. I left my cell phone in the car. I will call from your house phone. Where is your cordless phone, Maria?"

"It's in the other room."

"Okay, I'm going to try and make reservations before we go if it's not too late." I went into the living room and grabbed the phone book and looked up the restaurant, City View. I called my cell phone pretending to call the restaurant, because this is where I was taking Maria anyway. After going through the motions of talking with someone, I hung up the phone and said, "Hey babe, we are in luck; they have a table for two. We have to be there within the hour." I just threw that in to spice things up.

"Then let's get going before our table is taken."

We parked the car. As we were walking towards the restaurant there was a florist stand. I stopped and brought Maria a dozen roses to spice things up a little more. "Thank you, I love when you buy me flowers." I winked at Maria.

"I enjoy seeing you smile and sometimes being spontaneous is wonderful. Everything does not requires a special occasion."

"Ahhh, this is what I love about you. You do things just because."

We enter the restaurant, "Hello and welcome to City View. Do you have reservations?"

"Yes we do, and the name is Johnson, Derek Johnson."

"Yes, we have you scheduled for 7:00 p.m. Mr. Johnson; let me check to see if your table is set."

"Sure and thank you."

"Derek, I hope we get a window seat with a view of the city skyline."

"Excuse me, Mr. Johnson, your table is ready. Please follow me." As we followed the hostess, I put my hand on the small of Maria's back to guide her along to let her know I was close behind as we walked to our

332

table. There in the clearing was our table with two chairs and with an elegant-looking white table cloth. On the table were the bouquet of flowers, and some other elegant items. I motioned over behind Maria and pulled her chair out for her. Once she was seated I went to my seat and sat across from her. Maria had this look of amazement on her face and sparkle in her eyes. I gently grabbed Maria's hand as she sat across from me just to let her know everything is fine.

"Hey you, are you okay?"

"Yes, it's that this place is gorgeous and the view of the city is breathtaking."

"I felt like doing something different, and we deserve it; we have a blessed relationship. Besides, life is short and we must learn to enjoy every moment, make each moment special, and not wait for those special moments."

"This is very special moment to me and this place is very, very nice. Thank you, Derek."

"Excuse me, Maria, while I go to the restroom."

"Sure, go right ahead, I'm just going to sit here and enjoy this beautiful view. I'm still taking it all in." I went to the men's room and washed my hands. Before returning to the table, I walked to the other side of the restaurant to see who showed.

"Hello, and from the look of the table, it looks as if everyone is present and accounted for. I'm glad that all of you could make it. I want to give you the details, so when the jazz band start to play the song "The One In My Dream," someone from the restaurant will come over and escort you to us. When you enter our section, Maria's back will be to you, in this way you could observe the proposal and surprise her." As I was talking, the manager came over to get my attention.

"Excuse me sir, I want you to know that the band is going to take a twenty-minute break. They will play your request as their second song."

333

"Sounds great, and everyone, this is the manager of this great establishment. He and his team have been very supportive and cooperative from day one."

"Hello, everyone; as he said I am the manager of City View. We love to assist in people's happiness, especially for special occasions like this. I will be over myself to escort you to their table."

"It sounds like a plan, and thank you again, sir, for all of your assistance."

"It's my pleasure."

"All right guys, let me get back before Maria starts looking for me."

I returned to our table and Maria asked, "Are you all right?"

"Everything is wonderful I was chatting with someone about this restaurant. Hey, did you notice the beauty of the moon?"

"You know I love the moon. I was admiring the moon while you were in the restroom. I still cannot get over how nice this place is; it's like something you would see in a movie. This is definitely a place to take a woman if you want to impress her."

"Yes, I guess you could say that this is that kind of place, but you know, Maria, I believe if a person really wants to impress someone, it is important to be genuine, be yourself, and just be real."

We were still gazing at the moon when Maria said, "How long have we been dating?"

"How long have we been dating, hmmmm. Can I use one of my life lines?"

"Don't give me any hmmm, and you will need a life line if you don't know."

"Yeah, yeah, yeah, I know. I'm only kidding. It's been over three years."

"Yes, that's about right. Are you happy with me?"

"Yes, I am very happy with you and us, Maria. Are you going to ask me to marry you?"

"No, I am not going to ask you to marry me. Derek, I'm glad you decided to take the time in getting to know me so we could have this beautiful relationship." The band was back, and before I knew it they were finish playing the first song.

"This next song is a very special song going out to a very special couple. As the band start to play, I saw the manger start to walk towards the other side of the restaurant to get our family and friends. Keep calm, Derek, this is going to be great, just relax and remember what you need to do, because you love this woman. Before I knew it everyone was standing behind Maria as planned. I reached into my pocket and pulled out a poem I had written. I grabbed Maria's hand to make sure I had her undivided attention and read the poem. I then reached into my other pocket and pulled out a pocket size leather cover Bible and read 1 Corinthians 13: 4–13:

Love is patient, Love is kind. It does not envy, it does not boast, it is not proud. It is not rude, it is not self seeking, it is not easily angered, it keeps no record of wrongs. Love does not delight in evil but rejoice with the truth. It always protects, always trusts, always hopes, always perseveres.

Love never fails. But where there are prophecies, they will cease; where there are tongues, they will be stilled; where there is knowledge, it will pass away. For we know in part and we prophesy in part, but when perfection comes, the imperfect disappears. When I was a child, I talked like a child, I thought like a child, I reasoned like a child. When I became a man, I put childish ways behind me. Now we see but a poor reflection as in

a mirror; then we shall see face to face. Now I know in
part; then I shall know fully, even as I am fully known.
And now these three remain: faith, hope and love.
But the greatest of these is love.

After I finished reading the selected verses I closed the Bible and gave it
to Maria. On the front of the Bible was engraved, Maria Johnson. Maria
began to cry and I focused our attention on the bouquet of flowers. I
looked into Maria's eyes, as the tears slowly rolled down her face. I
reached down on the table and gave her my napkin for her tears. I looked
at Maria and said, "This dozen of roses is for you, just because. These
two roses in this bouquet I specially selected for you, this white rose symbolizes your purity, innocence, new beginnings, and spirituality. This red
rose symbolizes romance, true love, and our love." I pulled the two roses
out of the bouquet and tied to it was the engagement ring. I got down on
one knee. "Maria you are my best friend, you are my breath of fresh air,
you are an exceptional woman with a beautiful spiritual heart and nothing
would please more if you would be my wife. Will you marry me?"

Maria stood up and embraced me with such compassion and said,
"Yes, yes, yes." I gently grabbed Maria by the hand and turned her around
so she could see that our family and friends were part of this special occasion. She was even more surprised to their presence as she continued to
shed tears of joy. I took Maria by the hand and escorted her to the dance
floor where we embraced each other as if we were going to hold each
other all night. "Derek,"

"Yes Maria,"

"This is the happiest day of my life. Before you proposed to me I was
sitting at the table reflecting about what we had been through, throughout
our lives. I thought about what we have been through in a short period of

336

time, how you put forth your whole self into being there for me when I felt so alone. I would think about how you like to see me happy and the little things you do to make me smile. Whenever I think of you, my heart jumps and tears form in my eyes. Derek Johnson, I know I love you with all of my heart. You are the finest man with a beautiful heart."

"Maria, it's all about love; it's all about love."